TEXAS

GETTING STARTED GARDEN GUIDE

Grow the Best Flowers, Shrubs, Trees, Vines & Groundcovers

First published in 2013 by Cool Springs Press, an imprint of the Quayside Publishing Group, 400 First Avenue North, Suite 400, Minneapolis, MN 55401

Library of Congress Cataloging-in-Publication Data

Irish, Mary, 1949-
  Texas getting started garden guide : grow the best flowers, shrubs, trees, vines & groundcovers / Mary Irish.
      p. cm.
  Includes bibliographical references and index.
  ISBN 978-1-59186-552-0 (softcover)
  1. Gardening--Texas. I. Title.

  SB453.2.T4I75 2013
  635.09764--dc23

                        2013013180

Acquisitions Editor: Billie Brownell

Design Manager: Brad Springer

Layout: Pauline Molinari

Printed in China

10 9 8 7 6 5 4 3 2

TEXAS

GETTING STARTED GARDEN GUIDE

Grow the Best Flowers, Shrubs, Trees, Vines & Groundcovers

Mary Irish

COOL SPRINGS PRESS ™
Home and Garden Experts ™

MINNEAPOLIS, MINNESOTA

DEDICATION

To Gary, in recognition of all his hard work and what a great partner he is during our latest adventure.

CONTENTS

WELCOME TO GARDENING

IN TEXAS

There is a certain presumption in offering a book that covers the whole state of Texas. It is, after all, large, nearly 800 miles wide and long, covering four USDA climate zones, with vast differences in rainfall, soils, and temperature. Yet plants are adaptable creatures, and whereas many will thrive only in the moist forest of East Texas, or the windy plains of the Panhandle, or the drier climes of South Texas, a great number are able to thrive throughout the state. In this book, although some regional specialists are happy to live only within their selected zones, most of the plants are suited for a wide range of conditions. The bulk of the plants herein are useful for the greatest number of gardening conditions, and that was the goal.

Naturally, making such choices leaves out a lot. But that is the fun of gardening—experimentation, finding something that grows well for you despite all expectations to the contrary, and looking around for something new, something weird, or just something that pleases you. Gardening is fun, or it should be, and it is my hope that these plants will help all gardeners throughout the state find satisfactory plants for their own special gardens.

Conditions Around the State

Water availability and its partner water use have become increasingly critical in the state. Gardeners have a large part to play in water conservation now and for the future. Using a suite of plants that as they mature grow on natural rainfall, or with only minimal or intermittent supplemental watering, should be the long-term plan for all gardens. Using local natives naturally helps achieve this goal. But numerous other species, for each region, also fill this need.

Outdoor water use, particularly watering a lawn, is usually the largest segment of any homeowner's total water use. Minimizing, or better yet eliminating, as much lawn as possible is a critical step in lowering total water use around the home. Look to the recommendations in each section for plants to satisfy the aesthetic of the garden but reduce its overall water use.

Plants have other roles in conservation. Planting evergreen shrubs or trees along a west or southwestern face of a building cools it dramatically, thus lowering cooling costs. If a tree is large enough to shelter the hot side of the roof, even more energy

Coreopsis tinctoria and *Centaurea cyanus*

savings result. Using deciduous shrubs or trees on a southern wall or, particularly, a window prevents fierce summer sun from heating the house but permits the winter sun to warm it.

As all Texans, and most Americans, know, Texas is a big place. Gardeners in the high dry plains and mesas of the Panhandle have little in common with those in the Lower Rio Grande Valley of extreme South Texas with its nearly tropical shrub lands, gardens, and orchards. East Texas and most of the Gulf Coast is known for its dogwoods, azaleas, and magnolias sharing a gardening heritage with the deep South rather than with Texans in the far West, whose connections are with the southwestern states of New Mexico, Arizona, and Nevada. The Hill Country presents a landscape and plant mix that is uniquely Texan in character.

One of the best ways to ensure a glorious garden without Herculean work is to use plants that are well adapted to the conditions of your particular area. These

Potted kalanchoe & ligustrum in a peaceful garden space.

conditions—soil, rainfall, temperature ranges—are hard to change. It is far better to work with them than fight them, selecting plants that are successful in your garden's conditions. To ensure such success, it helps to understand the conditions a little.

Soils

Despite how it seems, soil is not an inert substance that merely serves to anchor plants in place. It is, in fact, an entire living ecosystem made up of an immense array of bacteria, fungi, insects, and invertebrates living and creating an ever-shifting mix of nutrients and moisture held together on a frame of minerals and organic matter. Plants are an important component of the system, using much of what is available in the form of dissolved nutrients and minerals, as well returning an equally impressive array of nutrients when they transpire, lose leaves, die, and decompose. It is elegant, it is complicated, and it almost all happens invisibly underground.

The nonliving component of soils—minerals mainly—comes from the geologic materials from which they were developed as well the leftovers from decomposition. Soils are described by the size of these particles: tiny particles create clay, whereas the largest are sand. Most soils fall somewhere between these extremes. The other dividing line is their relative acidity (pH of 6.5 or lower) or alkalinity (pH of 7.5 and higher). The size of Texas ensures that there will be a wide array of soil types from saturated and acidic to bone dry and alkaline across the state. Knowing the type of soil in your own area helps you cope not only with the conditions you have, but also informs how to mildly adjust and work your soil.

Container combo of agave, heuchera, thyme, and *Erigeron* 'Sea Drift'

In many cases gardeners try to create a so-called ideal soil by attempting to amend or otherwise change their soil to deal with what they perceive to be soil problems. The best way that I have found to deal with such problems is generally to ignore them. What I mean by that is rather than engage in large-scale soil modifications on your property, it is best to understand your soil and then select plants that will grow well and prosper in your soil type. Rather than fight your local environment, it is best to work within its bounds.

What you can—or at least what you should—do to rearrange soil has practical limits. Trying to amend the moist acidic soils near the coast to grow cenizo, which thrives naturally on dry alkaline soil, is as much a waste of time and money as is amending the dry, highly alkaline soils of El Paso to grow azaleas.

Although attempting radical changes to your soil is a mistake, making small modifications to allow you to grow a wider array of plants is certainly reasonable. In many parts of Texas, soils drain slowly, especially during the rainy spring season. Improving the drainage in such soils is a key to helping many plants prosper or even just survive. For heavy clays, begin by adding copious amounts of coarse sand, gravel, or other sharply draining material. Blending in coarse organic matter helps improve aeration and drainage by increasing the space between soil particles. A relatively new product called expanded shale has shown good results in modifying heavy clay soils this way.

Adding organic matter generously and continuously to rocky or sandy soils has the opposite effect: it shrinks the space between the soil particles with the result that more moisture is retained in the soil.

Creating raised planting areas, either by simply mounding up the soil or by building a container, is a solution for many gardeners. Raised beds allow you to create more ideal soil for selected plants like annuals or vegetables. They also allow modification of a small or localized area to improve drainage. Raised mounds are particularly helpful in high rainfall areas or soils with poor drainage, especially when growing succulents, agaves, or similar plants.

A soil's acidity or alkalinity is almost impossible to modify except in limited and well-defined growing areas. Products that claim to increase or decrease the alkalinity of soil are short term at best. Nothing truly alters the basic chemistry of the soil for long; it is much better to accept it and work with it.

Most plants grow in the middle range of pH from 6.5 to 7.5. A few are only successful in either more highly acidic or highly alkaline soils.

Regional Soils

The Piney Woods of the far eastern part of Texas has light-colored acidic soils that are either somewhat sandy or reddish clay. These soils become dry and hard in late summer, and amendment with organic matter and mulch is helpful.

Toward the low-lying areas along the Gulf Coast soils are often saturated and poorly drained. Here raised beds are particularly useful.

Central and North Central Texas, extending down to the east sides of Austin, Waco, Temple, and San Antonio, is a complicated series of roughly north-south bands of soils. On the eastern edge, soils form essentially a dry woodland with a wide plug of deep prairie soils to their west. The soils of the woodlands are slightly acidic and generally sandy. The prairie soils are typically heavy clay and fertile but dry to a brick-like consistency in the summer or perversely become waterlogged after heavy rains. They are alkaline, sometimes highly so, and although this is congenial for a lot of drought-adapted plants from farther west, the poorer drainage needs to be ameliorated with organic matter, expanded shale, or gravel or by raising the planting area. This region has some of the most complex arrays of soil types in the state, and it is best to check with local sources for more detailed information on your soil type.

The Hill Country is fundamentally an uplifted expanse of limestone. Here soils are thin, really just a coating over the rock. These areas are highly alkaline. Plants generally need to be well adapted to dry, alkaline conditions to grow well in this area, and raised beds are practically required to grow some annuals, some perennials, and shrubs or vegetables.

Soils of South Texas are also highly variable. In the Lower Rio Grande Valley the deep alluvial soils become dry in the summer and wet in the spring. In areas farther from the Rio Grande River many soils are rocky. Most of the region has neutral to alkaline soils, but saline soils also occur.

Soils of the high plains of the Panhandle and south to San Angelo range from clay to sandy loams. In some cases large amounts of lime exists in the subsoil, making them highly alkaline. Where clay predominates, strategies similar to those described for the prairies can be employed.

The soils of far west Texas, including El Paso, depend on the underlying bedrock and topographic position. Some are deep and sandy, especially near the Rio Grande River, whereas others are gravelly. Many are limestone-based. Soils can be thin in the rocky areas with abundant caliche layers. These are generally highly alkaline soils.

Rainfall

Rainfall throughout the state is highly variable, as might be predicted given its size. Averages range from 59 inches at Orange on the eastern edge to 9 inches at El Paso. What can be said is that the widely used term "an average year" rarely occurs in real life.

There is also wide variability in the seasonality of rainfall. The rainiest time of year for most of Texas is spring and fall, when warm, moist air from the Gulf of Mexico slams into the cooler, drier air from the north. The rainiest months for many localities are May and September or October, with most of the state relatively dry during the summer and winter. Long periods without rainfall are common in the plains of northern Texas and throughout the western third of the state. East Texas and most of the Gulf Coast generally enjoy more consistent rainfall. But even there, years can have a vivid overabundance of rain, quickly followed by a drought.

Central and South Texas experience wild swings in rainfall year to year, often with ample rain during the spring or late summer and months with little or no rain in between. Hurricanes deeply affect not only the Gulf Coast but an area up to 150 miles inland when they occur.

Cold and Heat

In this book, I have used the USDA Hardiness Zones. Although these zones are handy and useful, there are caveats to their use in a place like Texas. The hardiness zones roughly fall into parallel bands that run east to west and indicate winter cold air incursions from the north.

The zone's boundaries describe average lows and cannot account for microclimates. Microclimates are reflections of small changes in topography or the position of walls or tall trees that affect growing conditions. The south and west sides of buildings are warmer in winter, but can be blasting hot in summer. A wall holding out cold winds can increase the temperature by as much as 5 degrees Fahrenheit. Evergreen shrubs planted to hold back cold winds and evergreen trees that prevent radiant cooling can have the same effect. The inverse is also true. Areas exposed to the north or to cold winds in winter are cold microclimates.

Another significant localized effect is urbanization. Large cities and their buildings, streets, and parking lots absorb heat during the day and release it slowly at night. This stored heat means that the core of large urban areas is called an urban heat island. In the end, large cities are often as much as 5 degrees Fahrenheit warmer on a winter night than are surrounding rural areas.

Given all this and considering that the zones run in great east-west swaths, the USDA zones are not good indicators of similar gardening conditions overall. For example, Dallas/Fort Worth is well within Zone 8a, as is El Paso. It is hard to imagine a greater difference in soil and rainfall regimes than those of these two cities. And it is much the same for the entire state. My advice is to consider these zones highly practical for cold tolerance, but look to soil type, rainfall, and local microclimate, either in your garden or city, to get a more complete picture of your gardening conditions.

Heat, both its severity and duration, is an important factor in plant selection. Although there is great diversity in winter cold throughout Texas, its southerly latitude and distance from high mountains and cold ocean currents means it is warm to hot throughout the state in the summer. Therefore, all the plants in this book are tolerant of significant summer heat. However, planting in partial shade or on the north or east sides of buildings can be helpful for some. Reflected heat, such as off a west-facing wall or around a pool, requires plants that can take this special condition. Tolerance for such conditions is noted in the plant profiles.

Longleaf pine

Good Gardening Practices
Watering

How and when you water can greatly affect the success of any plant you grow. In general, overhead sprinklers are a poor substitute for more directed water. Drip irrigation is widely used in the southwestern United States because it applies water only where plants take up water—the root zone. It can be used anywhere with great success. Equal success can be had by simply building small berms around trees or large shrubs, or even a bed, and letting a hose run slowly enough to fill it up. As the water percolates into the soil, it goes down deeply enough to provide water for a long time. All plants respond to deep, but less frequent, watering better than shallow, consistent watering. This includes lawns, which rarely need the frequent, shallow watering of lawn sprinklers, but thrive when watered less often but more deeply.

Watering when evaporation is low is also important for growing plants well and saving water. Water when it is dark, ideally just before dawn, for best results. This is the coolest time of the day, and therefore water evaporation is at its lowest.

Planting

It is hard to generalize planting times for all plants. Look to the individual profiles for guidance on timing for specific plants.

When digging a hole for any plant, make it three to five times wider than the rootball, or pot, and just as deep. This is particularly critical for trees and shrubs. If the soil is a heavy clay, rough up the sides of the hole. In areas with caliche or exposed rock, fill the hole with water and leave it overnight. If the water drains out, continue to plant. If not, either choose a plant with a small root system or pick a new location. If water can't drain, roots can't grow.

Agaves, yuccas, cactus, and other desert perennials need a similar-sized hole. With these plants it is critical not to plant them deeply, but set them at the same soil line as they were growing previously. Never let soil collect at the base of the leaves or up the side of the plant.

Mulch

Mulch is one of the easiest tools gardeners can use to lower water use and keep plants healthy. Mulch slows down water evaporation from the soil, making that much more soil moisture available for plants. In addition, organic mulches decompose and slowly improve the soil beneath them.

Fertilization

Details of fertilizer needs and timing are covered in the plant entries. I firmly hold to an organic growing style where plants are fed by growing in a healthy, lively soil. Paying attention to the soil is more important than applying a supplemental fertilizer continuously. Adding generous amounts of compost, maintaining a steady layer of organic mulch, and supplementing this only when needed with the wide array of organic-based fertilizers grows healthy plants without undue stress on our environment.

Making a Garden

Whether you are starting from scratch with a virtually blank slate or modifying an existing garden, getting started can be overwhelming. Asking yourself a few questions and adhering to a few general principles can help.

Cosmos 'Rubenza'

Begin by deciding how you want to use the space. If there are things you must have—a vegetable garden, a place to cook, a patio, or a work area—lay them out. If you are good at drawing, draw it up. If, like me, you can't begin to draw, use old hoses, string, or rope to lay down the outline right where you think it would be ideal.

Once these must-have uses are in place, use the same technique, paper or physical layout, to connect them with paths. Don't neglect to include getting in and out of the garden from the house, the street, or the alley.

Now look around. Do you need more or less shade? How big could a tree be and not get in the way of a view or utility lines? Does something need to be removed to get the space arranged the way you want it? If you have a lawn, do you use it and need it? Could it be reduced without loss of use? Should ramadas, arbors, or trellises be incorporated?

Suddenly you have the beginnings of a design, and the rest becomes filling in. In my experience, the process of filling in is the best part and takes years, and it is usually never-ending. But this will jump start the process and get things moving.

As you begin to plant from your ideas, start with trees and large shrubs, not only because they take longer to mature, but also because they define and secure the space. Move out from the house with your planting and don't neglect to splash your garden generously with natives. Keep an eye out for plants that are favored by birds, butterflies, bees, and others who are your garden helpers as well as some of your most welcome visitors.

I have made gardens in a number of different places. Each one was entirely different, owing so much to where it was made and what I was doing at the time. It should be the same for your garden—it is yours, after all. Making a garden that fits into the area where you live and accommodates your life in it is the best garden of all. It is my hope that this book helps you make that special Texas garden.

- Mary

How to Use *Texas Getting Started Garden Guide*

Each entry in this book provides you with information about a plant's particular characteristics, its habits, and its basic requirements for vigorous growth as well as my personal experience and knowledge of it. I have tried to include the information you need to allow you to realize each plant's potential. You will find such pertinent information as bloom period and seasonal color (if any), mature height and spread, whether it attracts wildlife such as butterflies, bees, or hummingbirds, cold tolerance, and sun preferences. I have also included a pronunciation guide for the botanical name of each plant.

Symbols represent the "added benefits" provided by a plant.

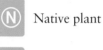 Native plant

 Fall or seasonal color

 Drought resistant

 Attracts beneficial insects such as butterflies and bees

 Attracts hummingbirds

 Edible

Water requirements, fertilizing needs, pruning and care, and pest information are provided for each entry under the sections marked "When, Where, and How to Plant," "Growing Tips," and "Regional Advice and Care."

Sun Preferences

Symbols represent the range of sunlight suitable for each plant. "Full Sun" means a location receiving 6 to 10 hours of sun daily. "Part Sun/Part Shade" means dappled shade, shade in the afternoon, or indirect light all day. "Full Shade" means a location protected from direct sunlight all day. Some plants grow successfully in more than one range of sun exposure, which is indicated by showing more than one sun symbol.

Full Sun   Part Shade   Shade

Companion Planting and Design

In this section I offer tips for combining the plant with others for a particular style or effect. If plants have a special use, it is noted here.

Try These

In this section look for selections, cultivars, or hybrids of the plant discussed. In addition, I have added plants that are closely related that will perform best in areas of the state other than those indicated for the main entry. For some plants I have listed other species that have similar habits or characteristics.

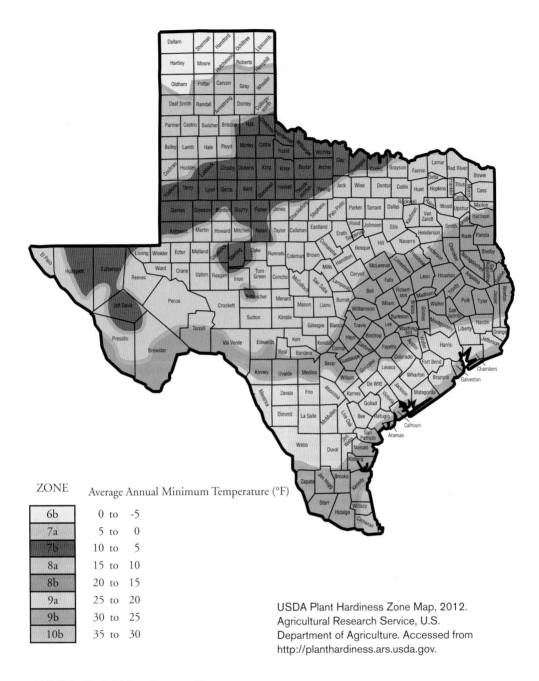

ZONE	Average Annual Minimum Temperature (°F)
6b	0 to -5
7a	5 to 0
7b	10 to 5
8a	15 to 10
8b	20 to 15
9a	25 to 20
9b	30 to 25
10b	35 to 30

USDA Plant Hardiness Zone Map, 2012.
Agricultural Research Service, U.S.
Department of Agriculture. Accessed from
http://planthardiness.ars.usda.gov.

USDA Cold Hardiness Zones

Cold-hardiness zone designations were developed by the United States Department of Agriculture (USDA) to denote the minimum average temperature for each zone. I have designated the zones where each plant can be expected to sustain minimal or no damage during the average low temperature of the zone. These zones are a good guide to cold tolerance, but many factors can work to allow plants to grow well outside the zones designated here. Consider the zone designation a good starting point, but don't be afraid to try something that is not rated for your zone.

ANNUALS

FOR TEXAS

A nnuals are plants that live out their entire life cycles in one season. Whether this cycle is a matter of months or weeks depends on the species and on the growing conditions. Annuals are nature's colonizers. These are the first plants to grow after a fire, a flood, fallen trees, road building, or housing developments have disturbed an area. Many of the plants we designate as weeds are annuals, and some of the ones we revere as wildflowers are annuals; the difference is only in our perception and our uses for these plants.

Annuals Fill Many Needs

The combination of fast growth and quick, reliable bloom makes annuals treasures in a garden. In established gardens, annuals fill in small bare spots, providing quick seasonal color. Annuals are a terrific choice to plant in pots mixed with succulents, grasses, bulbs, or perennials to create a miniature garden in a container. I am especially fond of planting annuals in pots of agaves to contrast with these solid, hard-edge plants.

Annuals are irreplaceable to gardeners with brand-new gardens. Many homeowners find themselves with a lot that has been cleared of all vegetation but for the required tree (or two) and a few shrubs. Annuals are a quick, inexpensive way to get a garden going and relieve the visual rawness of the new place.

Annuals are even more useful to the soil of a new garden. Growing plants in compacted or otherwise compromised soil is the surest way to bring it back to life. Growing plants ensure the return of the abundant microscopic life—fungi, bacteria, invertebrates, and worms—that are the hallmark of a healthy garden. The action of roots and the litter of leaves and flowers left behind transform a lifeless, barren spot into a thriving garden. The abundant use of annuals is a fast way to jump-start this process.

A lovely courtyard garden surrounded by cosmos.

Give Natives a Good Start

The classic wildflower meadow meant to recreate the sensational displays we see on the roadways and pastures is generally more difficult to achieve than it looks. Annuals growing naturally go through up and down years and often do the same in a garden. It is tempting to water native annuals generously to encourage full germination and reliable bloom. But weeds can become a tremendous problem in beds that are generously and continuously watered. Taking a clue from their preferences in nature—good rains at long intervals, often disturbed soil, and whether or not the soil needs to be enriched or left on its own—results in more satisfactory native wildflower beds.

For my money, most annual native wildflowers are much better when treated as a component of a garden, as the colorful reminders of where we live and what is the nature of our surrounding landscape. I think they are sensational as bursts of bloom, as enhancements of the whole garden rather than the focus of a single bed.

Although many native annuals grow with a minimum of preparation, some of

Coreopsis grandiflora 'Early Sunrise'

the other species listed here grow faster and bloom better if given a good start. Prepare the soil by raking the area instead of turning it. Then add a layer of compost or mulch and a light dusting of fertilizer. Broadcast seed as evenly as possible. Mixing seed with sand or mulch helps ensure a more even planting. Annuals generally need good contact with the soil to germinate and grow successfully. Therefore, it is important that the area where you plant annuals is as free of weeds and grass as possible.

Finish by raking in the opposite direction to cover the seed lightly. Keep the area barely moist until the seeds germinate. Watering frequency depends on the weather, but soil should neither dry out completely nor be soaking wet. Once the seeds have germinated, water every other day (less if the weather permits) until they have five true leaves. After that, extend the watering to weekly, less if there is regular rainfall.

Angelonia

Angelonia angustifolia

Other Name Summer snapdragon

Bloom Period and Seasonal Color
Summer, pink, lavender, purple, white

Mature Height x Spread
12 to 18 in. x 8 to 24 in.

Botanical Pronunciation
an-jel-OH-nee-ah an-gus-tih-FOE-lee-ah

Angelonia is an erect plant with thin, deep green leaves that are clustered along the stem. The leaves are fragrant when touched and remind some people of apples. Plants spread to form multiple stems, each of which blooms. The bloom is a dense, showy spike with dozens of flowers. An individual flower has a large, inflated tube and looks somewhat like snapdragon. Angelonia is a prolific bloomer over the entire summer. Perennial in frost-free zones, angelonia is a reliable summer-flowering annual anywhere, but especially in areas with high heat and humidity, it seems to be immune to that combination. Angelonia, particularly the Angelface strain, is a long-lived cut flower. This annual is also a great choice to create a summer floral display in a pot.

When, Where, and How to Plant

Set out transplants in the early spring as soon as the soil is warm enough to work and after all danger of frost is past. Plant angelonia in full sun for the best flowering. In zones with very hot summers, relief from afternoon sun maintains better vigor and longer flowering. Plant in a bed that has been amended with ample amounts of compost or other organic matter and has excellent drainage.

Growing Tips

Fertilize with a well-balanced formulation, or apply a 2- to 3-inch layer of well-composted manure or other organic mulch monthly during the growing season. Keep angelonia evenly watered, never letting it dry out completely or be left in saturated soils or those that hold water.

Regional Advice and Care

It is not necessary to deadhead angelonia. In late summer in zones that have hot, dry summers, plants can decline. Cut back nearly to the soil line, move into more shade, and maintain watering but don't fertilize. Plants will resume growing and flowering when the weather cools. Angelonia can be invaded by aphids in some areas, but vigilance and early control usually makes them only a nuisance.

Companion Planting and Design

Plant angelonia generously to create a colorful border to a bed of larger plants. Angelonia grows well in a pot. Use as many plants as needed to fill the pot completely to create a splashy display on a porch or patio or around a seating area. Blend angelonia with other summer-flowering annuals or perennials.

Try These

Besides the species, there are many strains of angelonia in the trade. 'AngelMist®' spreads and has flowers that are pink, dark rose, blue, white, and purple to lavender striped. 'Angelface®' is an improved hybrid strain with plants up to 18 inches tall that make numerous stems. Stems hold dense, deeply colored flowers that make some of the best cut flowers in the group. Flowers are white, pink, blue, and violet. 'Serena®' is shorter with a mounding habit and flowers in the same color range. This series is rated a Texas Superstar® for its heat and drought tolerance.

Copper Plant

Acalypha wilkesiana

Other Name Copperleaf

Bloom Period and Seasonal Color
Foliage, copper, red, bronze, pink and green

Mature Height x Spread
24 to 36 in. x 18 to 24 in.

Botanical Pronunciation
ack-uh-LYE-fuh wilk-see-AN-uh

Annuals are most often grown for their rapid and prolific flowering. But flowers are not everything, and a plant that offers consistent colorful contrast is a welcome addition to any garden. Copper plant is a showy choice to meet this demand and has delighted gardeners for decades with its spectacular, large leaves, often with deeply indented margins and in a wide array of colors. Because the colorful leaves are the star of the show, copper plant provides a continuous display through the summer and fall. Native to the Pacific islands, copper plant can become a large shrubby perennial, up to 8 feet tall or more, in completely frost-free zones. In most zones it is grown as an annual or even a houseplant.

When, Where, and How to Plant
Set out transplants in the spring after all danger of frost is past and soils have warmed to at least 65 degrees Fahrenheit. Choose a location with at least a half-day of sun; in cold zones provide full sun. Copper plant does not grow well in heavy shade. Amend the soil with ample amounts of good compost or other organic matter. Good drainage is important, and in heavy clay soils amend the soil and raise the bed slightly.

Growing Tips
Apply a slow-release, well-balanced fertilizer monthly during the growing season. Alternately, spread a 2- to 3-inch layer of well-composted manure or compost blend around the root zone monthly. Water regularly, up to twice a week in hot, dry conditions, so that the soil stays evenly moist. Use a 2- to 4-inch layer of mulch to maintain soil moisture and reduce the frequency of watering. Copper plant resents overhead watering, so use a soaker, drip, or other ground-watering technique.

Regional Advice and Care
Pinch the growing tips regularly early in the growing season to encourage branching. Plants grow rapidly, and light pruning creates a tight, regular form. Flowers can be removed anytime. In frost-free areas cut plants back severely in the late winter to reduce the size and reinvigorate the plant. Copper leaf is not susceptible to pests but is susceptible to fungal leaf diseases with overhead watering.

Companion Planting and Design
Use copper plant singly or in large groups within any mixed planting for its exciting leaf colors. It is particularly well suited to gardens that have an abundance of summer-flowering plants where its long season will maintain a colorful display when they are finished. It is excellent in large pots, either singly or in mixed plantings. Use as an informal hedge or boundary planting.

Try These
'Louisiana Red' has glossy, red leaves, 'Marginata' has copper-green leaves with cream and pink edges, 'Macrophylla' has large leaves variegated with bronze, cream, yellow, and red, 'Musaica' has rounded leaves mottled with orange and red, and 'Godseffiana' has green leaves with cream-colored deeply indented margins.

Cosmos

Cosmos sulphureus

Bloom Period and Seasonal Color
Summer, yellow or orange rays, yellow disks

Mature Height x Spread
12 to 18 in. x 18 to 24 in.

Botanical Pronunciation
KOS-mos sul-FEWR-ee-uh

When we moved into our current house, there was a large, fine-leaved plant that stood about 3 feet tall. I wasn't sure what it was until it bloomed. To my delight it was cosmos. But this was a macho version of the short plants I was used to with tall, leafy stems topped by orange flowers high over the foliage. I learned its stature wasn't all that uncommon. A Mexican native, cosmos has been a feature of annual plantings and butterfly gardens for decades. The distinctive, lacy foliage is deep green. The orange or yellow ray flowers are held on long, thin, branched stems. Individual petals are cut, usually into three segments, making it even more elegant. Disk flowers are golden and in a congested column.

When, Where, and How to Plant
Plant from seed in spring after all danger of frost is past and the soil has warmed. Cosmos grows in a wide array of soils from alkaline to slightly acidic, fertile or not. It is not necessary to amend the soil before planting. Turn the soil gently—a rake will do—and broadcast the seed generously. Rake or turn in the opposite direction to cover lightly. A thin layer of mulch helps hold the seed and soil in place until they germinate. Keep moist until the seed germinates, then water sparingly. Transplants can be set out in the spring, but it is best to do it as early as possible. They fail to set well when the weather is too hot.

Growing Tips
Cosmos needs no supplemental fertilization. This is a remarkably drought-tolerant annual. In the warmest areas, watering once every 7 to 10 days is sufficient. Water less frequently where it is cooler or there is ample summer rainfall.

Regional Advice and Care
Remove spent flowers regularly to encourage repeat flowering. Cosmos often quits flowering in the hottest parts of the summer, but resumes once the weather moderates. Cosmos is not susceptible to pests or disease.

Companion Planting and Design
Plant generously to create a stunning and colorful annual show. Mix with other summer-flowering perennials or annuals. Tall varieties work well in the back of the planting bed. Shorter varieties make a fine informal border or edging. Butterflies flock to cosmos; plant it where you can enjoy their daily visits.

Try These
'Crest Red', red rays and golden discs; 'Ladybird Dwarf' in red, gold, orange, and lemon, as well as the Klondyke series, are not as tall. *Cosmos bipinnatus*, also from Mexico, has thread-like leaves and flowers in shades of pink, magenta, and white and is shorter than *C. sulphureus*. 'Gloria', pink; 'Tetra Versailles', red rays, yellow disc; 'Candy Stripe', white with red veins; 'Day Dream', white rays with pink base yellow disc; 'Picotee', white rays with red margin. 'Sensation' series has large flowers in a wide array of colors.

Globe Amaranth

Gomphrena globosa

Bloom Period and Seasonal Color
Summer to fall, purple, red, pink, lavender, white

Mature Height x Spread
18 to 24 in. x 6 to 12 in.

Botanical Pronunciation
gom-FREE-nah glow-BOW-sah

Globe amaranth is the very definition of an old-fashioned cottage garden plant to me. It has been grown for a long time, and you still find it providing its cheerful, colorful bloom all summer throughout Texas. Plants are tidy with a rounded, firm look. The flower stalks rise high over the plant and end in the button-like purple heads. The true flowers are yellowish white and nearly invisible. It is the vivid bracts that create the show. This is the reason the "flowers" last for such a long time and the plant makes such a splendid dried specimen. Our grandmothers revered it for its long flowering and ease of cultivation and as a good cut flower when all others were faded or frozen. And so should we.

When, Where, and How to Plant
Direct seed in spring after all danger of frost is past and the soil is warm. Choose a location in full sun. Globe amaranth will grow in almost any well-drained soil, but a bed improved with well-aged compost or other organic matter makes for more vigorous growth and bloom. Set out transplants in spring as well, as long as there is no danger of frost.

Growing Tips
Globe amaranth does not need supplemental fertilization when grown in fertile or amended soils. Otherwise, fertilize once in spring once growth is underway. Water enough to keep the soil from drying out but avoid ponding or standing water around the plants. Use a soaker hose attachment, drip, or other ground watering techniques rather than overhead watering.

Regional Advice and Care
Pruning is rarely necessary. Light tip pruning in the summer keeps the plant tidy if it becomes overgrown or lanky. Pick flowers anytime. Globe amaranth has no pest problems, although it can get leaf fungal disease when watered overhead.

Companion Planting and Design
Use globe amaranth in a mixed planting of other summer-flowering perennials or annuals. The colors mix well with a wide array of plants. The long flowering period makes it an ideal choice to plant in front of short-season annuals or spring-flowering bulbs to hide their fading leaves. Globe amaranth is also exquisite in a pot either singly or mixed with other summer-flowering species.

Try These
'Buddy' is a purple flowering dwarf form that grows up to 9 inches tall. The Gnome series are even more dwarf, with deep green leaves. These tidy little globe amaranth grow 6 to 10 inches tall and come in red, purple, and white. Texas native *Gomphrena haageana* is best known for its intensely red selection 'Strawberry Fields', but the species flowers in red, pink, and purple. A lilac flowering form is known as 'Lavender Lady'. This species is perennial in warm winter areas, but is grown as an annual throughout Texas. It has a similar habit to globe amaranth and grows to 18 inches tall.

Indian Blanket

Gaillardia pulchella

Other Name Firewheel

Bloom Period and Seasonal Color
Spring to fall, red with yellow tips, red-brown disc

Mature Height x Spread
12 to 24 in. x 10 to 12 in.

Botanical Pronunciation
gah-LAR-dee-yuh pul-KELL-ah

There is a lot to be said for plants that take care of themselves, growing and flowering with minimal effort on our part. I love plants like this; it is like a guilty pleasure—loads of reward for little effort. Indian blanket is one and remains one of my all-time favorite annuals. A true annual, Indian blanket emerges early in the spring with a flat set of deeply lobed, slightly hairy leaves. Once the weather warms it is full of vim and vigor and the nearly constant flowering begins. The prominent flowering heads are composed of brick-red rays that are rimmed with varying amounts of yellow and a reddish brown disk. There is a lot of variation in the amount and location of the coloring.

When, Where, and How to Plant
Direct sow Indian blanket in the late summer or early fall. Try to time the planting for about two months before the last frost date in your area. It is not necessary to amend the soil, but it is important to remove grass and other low-growing plants because the seed must come into contact with bare soil for best results. Scratch the soil, broadcast the seed, and cover lightly by running over the area with a rake. Water in well, but unless it is bone dry for weeks at a time, they rarely need more.

Growing Tips
Indian blanket does not need supplemental fertilization. In fact, too rich a soil is detrimental to the plants, causing them to be floppy and weak and not flower well. Water when the soil is dry, but never more than weekly and often less than that even in the summer.

Regional Advice and Care
Remove spent flowers regularly. This both promotes continuous bloom and lightly prunes the plant. In late summer cut back the stems that flowered to their junction with base of the plant. Water well once. This will promote a flush of growth and good fall flowering.

Companion Planting and Design
Indian blanket is wonderful in areas that receive minimal care but need a little lift. Blend into a bed with other summer-flowering annuals, or mix with perennials that don't require constant watering. Because it prefers growing in drier conditions, Indian blanket mixes well with agaves, cactus, and other succulents.

Try These
Firewheel (*Gaillardia aristata*) is perennial with similar flowers and color range. Firewheel does not have quite as long a flowering period and grows to 3 feet. The hybrid between these two species is *G. x grandiflora*. This hybrid is a long-lived annual or short-lived perennial with the long flowering period of the annual parent. The color range is the same for the species, but the ray flowers are usually lighter orange than either parent. 'Goblin' is the dwarf form of the hybrid, growing up to 12 inches tall with a tight growth habit.

Marigold

Tagetes spp.

Bloom Period and Seasonal Color
Summer to fall, gold, orange, yellow

Mature Height x Spread
6 to 36 in. x 10 to 24 in.

Botanical Pronunciation
tuh-JEE-teez

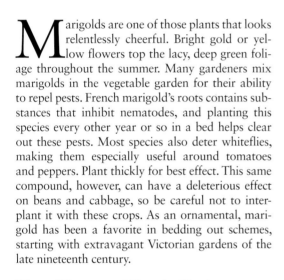

Marigolds are one of those plants that looks relentlessly cheerful. Bright gold or yellow flowers top the lacy, deep green foliage throughout the summer. Many gardeners mix marigolds in the vegetable garden for their ability to repel pests. French marigold's roots contains substances that inhibit nematodes, and planting this species every other year or so in a bed helps clear out these pests. Most species also deter whiteflies, making them especially useful around tomatoes and peppers. Plant thickly for best effect. This same compound, however, can have a deleterious effect on beans and cabbage, so be careful not to interplant it with these crops. As an ornamental, marigold has been a favorite in bedding out schemes, starting with extravagant Victorian gardens of the late nineteenth century.

When, Where, and How to Plant
Direct seed or set out transplants in the spring once all danger of frost is past. Marigold likes it warm, so be sure the soil is well warmed before planting. For seed, it is necessary only to scratch the surface and broadcast the seed. Seed germinates quickly and should be thinned once the plants are 1 inch tall for best results.

Growing Tips
Marigold does not need regular supplemental fertilizer, especially when grown in a well-drained, fertile soil. One application in the spring, particularly for transplants, is usually sufficient. Water to keep the soil from drying out completely but avoid overwatering or keeping the soil continuously wet.

Marigold rots easily under such conditions. It is best to water with a soaker hose, garden hose, or drip irrigation rather than overhead systems.

Regional Advice and Care
Remove spent flowers regularly to maintain continuous bloom. If plants become leggy or ragged, lightly prune in the summer to maintain shape. Marigold is not susceptible to most pests, although it can get a number of fungal diseases when grown in wet conditions or with consistent overhead watering.

Companion Planting and Design
Blend marigold with vegetables for its ability to repel certain insects and to brighten up the summer vegetable bed. Smaller varieties make great small, informal borders. Taller varieties blend with other perennials in a mixed planting. It is also excellent in containers, either singly or with other species.

Try These
African marigold (*Tagetes erecta*) is a large-flowered species from Mexico and Central America that is an important part of the Day of the Dead celebrations. French marigold (*T. patula*) has smaller flowers that are often red. 'Queen Sophia' is short and bushy with abundant orange blooms.

Nasturtium

Tropaeolum majus

Bloom Period and Seasonal Color
Spring to summer, yellow, gold, orange, red, white

Mature Height x Spread
2 to 10 ft. x 2 to 10 ft.

Botanical Pronunciation
troe-pay-OH-lum MAY-jus

Nasturtium is an old-fashioned plant full of nostalgia and pleasant memories carried from generations of gardeners before us. Older forms are loose, rambling vines that crawl away from their trellis to climb over arbors. Flowers are prolific on the plant and open for a long season in a stunning range of colors from red to maroon, butter yellow to orange. Nasturtium blooming begins in late winter in warm winter areas, but by spring all zones have flowering plants. I have grown numerous types over the years in a host of conditions. In one garden my bed faced north and that of my neighbor faced south. Her nasturtium bloomed nearly six weeks earlier than mine, although once they started each bed was glorious.

When, Where, and How to Plant
Direct sow seed in fall in warm winter areas. In cooler areas wait until after all danger of frost is past. Nasturtium grows in full sun or partial shade. Tolerant of almost any soil, including highly alkaline or rocky ones, nasturtium is more vigorous and blooms best in well-drained, fertile soil. Amend the soil with good-quality compost or other organic matter and turn it in well. Cover seed lightly and press the soil gently to prevent seed from washing away.

Growing Tips
Nasturtium needs no supplemental fertilizer; in fact, too much fertilizer results in excessive vegetative growth and poor flower production. Water established plants weekly while blooming, more often if weather turns hot.

Regional Advice and Care
Vining varieties need a trellis or arbor for support. Nasturtium reseeds vigorously, and most varieties come true from seed. It is not susceptible to pests, although in cool, moist conditions, or without enough sun, nasturtium can have problems with leaf fungal disease and aphids.

Companion Planting and Design
Grow vining forms on an arbor or trellis in a mixed planting or in the back of bed. Vining forms make a casual flowering groundcover and are attractive when left to spill over a wall or raised planter. All forms grow well in containers or hanging baskets. New leaves and flowers have a delicate, spicy taste and are excellent in salads.

Try These
'Empress of India' is a striking bushy plant with dark, dusky green leaves and vivid scarlet flowers. This is a variety grown since Victorian times and is still one of the best of the bush type nasturtiums. 'Black Velvet' is a dwarf with nearly black flowers. 'Milkmaid', 'Buttercream', and 'Moonlight' are cream- to yellow-flowered varieties. 'Amazon Jewel' has variegated foliage with multicolored flowers. 'Spitfire' is a trailing form with deep, scarlet flowers. The annual vine canary creeper (*Tropaeolum peregrinum*) has bright yellow flowers with frilly edged petals that look like birds ready to take flight. It grows quickly in the warm spring and flowers prolifically from spring until hot weather forces it out of bloom.

Pansy

Viola x *wittrockiana*

Bloom Period and Seasonal Color
Fall to early spring, red, purple, blue, magenta, orange, yellow, white

Mature Height x Spread
6 to 8 in. x 8 to 12 in.

Botanical Pronunciation
vie-OH-la wit-ROCK-ee-an-ah

Pansies as we know them began with the collections of Mary Elizabeth Bennett, a wealthy Englishwoman, who set about to secure all the forms of *Viola tricolor* she could. She and her gardener began to cross it with other European species, and in 1812 "her" plants were introduced to the world. Around the same time, other enthusiasts began to use a yellow-flowered species for hybridization, seeking a plant with wide, overlapping petals. They not only succeeded, but got the feature we know today as the face, which is the dark splotch at the base of flowers. This multispecies swarm was named for a Swedish botanist, and by 1833 there were some four hundred named varieties. There may be no fewer today of this charming winter-flowering annual.

When, Where, and How to Plant
Set out transplants in fall in most of Texas, early spring in far northern zones. Plant pansies in a location that receives full sun in winter. In warm winter areas, relief from afternoon sun is helpful. Pansies grow best in fertile, well-drained soils that can stay evenly moist and cool. Amend beds with ample amounts of good-quality compost or other organic matter. Set the plants slightly higher than the soil line.

Growing Tips
Fertilize monthly while the plants are actively growing and flowering. Use a well-balanced, granular formulation or a dry organic blend. Water regularly to maintain even soil moisture. Pansies are sensitive to overhead watering, which encourages leaf fungal disease. Water with a soaker hose, garden hose, or drip irrigation to avoid these diseases. Mulch heavily to maintain soil moisture and temperature, but don't let the mulch run up on the plant or touch the stem.

Regional Advice and Care
Remove spent flowers regularly to encourage continuous bloom. Pansies can be susceptible to leaf chewing insects, but in modest numbers this is only a cosmetic problem. Prevent leaf fungal diseases by avoiding overhead or excessive watering and keeping mulch off stems.

Companion Planting and Design
Pansies are dramatic when planted in mass, particularly in one color or one variety, along the edge of a bed. It fills corners or other small spots well. Because it is so short, it works best in the front of a bed or planter. Pansies are a good choice for a large container or raised bed.

Try These
There are an amazing number of cultivars and series of pansy in almost any color or combination of color imaginable. Older cultivars are in clear colors of blue, yellow, or white with a definite dark face. Newer forms reach into dusky rose, lilac, and even black for their colors. Some are tight and tidy; others are long trailing plants best for hanging baskets. Johnny jump up (*Viola tricolor*) has tiny flowers marked with blue, white, and yellow that despite their small size are charming under trees or near a patio.

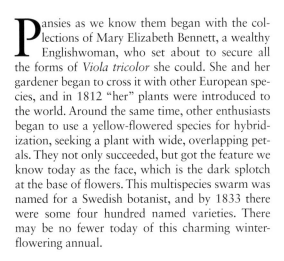

Periwinkle

Catharanthus roseus

Bloom Period and Seasonal Color
Spring to fall, white, pink, dark rose, purple

Mature Height x Spread
6 to 12 in. x 12 to 24 in.

Botanical Pronunciation
ca-tha-RAN-thus ro-SEE-us

Periwinkle is a low, spreading, frost-tender perennial that is used extensively as an annual. This is a plant that has been used medicinally for centuries in countries near its home in Madagascar and has been cultivated for its beautiful flowering for nearly two hundred years. The firm, deep green leaves are held on stiff stems. In frost-free areas plants grow from a short woody base, but as an annual it is a spreading plant. The flat, open flowers bloom throughout the summer and have the happy trait of falling away cleanly when bloom is done. Periwinkle has naturalized in a number of warm areas of the world, including the American South. All parts of the plant are poisonous if eaten or smoked.

When, Where, and How to Plant

Set out transplants after all danger of frost is past and the soils have warmed. Periwinkle flowers best in full sun, as well as filtered shade in hot, dry zones. It thrives in poor, but well-drained, soils. Well amended, highly fertile soils cause it to decline rapidly. Mulch carefully without letting it touch the plant or be more 1 or 2 inches deep.

Growing Tips

Plants in pots benefit from occasional applications of soluble fertilizer, but plants in the ground rarely need fertilization. Water periwinkle on a schedule that permits the soil to become almost dry between waterings. This can be as often as once a week in hot weather or as infrequently as every two to three weeks in mild or cool conditions. Even severely wilted plants recover quickly with a deep soak.

Regional Advice and Care

Periwinkle drops flowers regularly, so deadheading is unnecessary. Lightly prune stems to maintain shape or size. When grown in soils that retain too much moisture or shade or are too fertile. periwinkle is susceptible to an array of root rots (*Phytophora*). Growing it in appropriate locations is the best prevention.

Companion Planting and Design

Periwinkle blends well with other low-growing, summer-flowering perennials, shrubs, or annuals. Plant to line a border, define a planting space, or secure a dry corner. Use it as a potted plant or in large containers with mixed plantings. Hanging baskets are particularly effective.

Try These

'Parasol' and 'Morning Mist' have large white flowers with rose-colored centers and good heat tolerance. 'Tropicana' and 'Pacifica Red' are reliable in high heat and humidity. Many strains of periwinkle have a color range of pink, red, white, and blends. The Carpet series are 3 to 4 inches tall and spread to 2 feet. The Cooler series, including 'Peppermint Cooler' with white flowers marked by a red eye, grows well in cooler conditions. 'Pretty' series are compact plants. 'Cora' is reputed to have good *Phytophora* resistance. 'Victory' is compact with intense clear colors. 'Heat Wave' is the most tolerant of dry, warm conditions.

Plains Coreopsis

Coreopsis tinctoria

Other Name Golden tickseed

Bloom Period and Seasonal Color
Spring to fall, rays yellow, orange, red, bronze,
discs purple to brown

Mature Height x Spread
2 to 4 ft. x 1 to 2 ft.

Botanical Pronunciation
kor-ee-OP-sis tink-TOR-ee-ah

Plains coreopsis has a flower that just forces you to smile. The flat ray flowers are yellow with or without maroon banding. They are held on whisper thin, branched stems high above delicate leaves. This slender appearance belies how rugged this plant is in the face of high heat and drought. A true annual, plains coreopsis blooms after the rush of spring flowering. In nature, it follows bluebonnets and paintbrush with just as extravagant a show. Butterflies are strongly attracted to its nectar, making it an easy addition to a butterfly garden. I am not an especially tidy gardener and leave some to ripen to seed, both to provide next year's crop and to attract seed eating birds, especially goldfinches. Plains coreopsis makes a fine cut flower.

When, Where, and How to Plant
Sow seed in fall. It is not necessary to amend soils before planting. Break the surface of the soil with a rake, broadcast the seed generously, then run the rake over the soil surface to cover the seed lightly. Keep the bed moist, but not saturated, until seed germinates. Set out transplants in the spring as early as the soil can be worked. Plains coreopsis does best in well-drained soils that are not overly rich and are somewhat dry.

Growing Tips
Plains coreopsis needs no supplemental fertilization. Water every one to two weeks while growing and blooming depending on temperature and natural rainfall. It is better to allow the soil to dry out partially between waterings.

Regional Advice and Care
Thin plants early, when they are an inch tall, to prevent overcrowding. To prevent root disturbance, cut the seedlings at ground level rather than pull them out. Plains coreopsis is a tall plant that becomes floppy with too much shade or when grown too close together. Regular removal of dead flower stalks encourages continuous bloom. Plains coreopsis is not susceptible to pest problems.

Companion Planting and Design
Mix plains coreopsis with summer-flowering perennials or annuals. It is particularly effective in the back of a bed where its height can be useful and other plants will cover its sparse foliage. Because it appreciates dry soils plains coreopsis may be mixed with agaves, cactus, or other succulents for late spring color. Sow generously for best effect; the wiry stems make it seem sparse when plants are isolated.

Try These
'Mahogany' has red rays and dark discs. 'Mahogany Midget' is the same but only 10 inches tall. In both, bright yellow pollen contrasts sharply with the dark color of the rays. Tickseed (*Coreopsis grandiflora*) is a popular perennial throughout the eastern United States. 'Sunray' has double flowers, yellow rays, and golden discs. 'Baby Sun' is similar with a mounded growth habit. Lanceleaf coreopsis (*C. lanceolata*) is a perennial with tufts of hairy leaves, bright yellow rays, and discs that forms extensive colonies over time.

Portulaca

Portulaca grandiflora

Other Name Moss rose

Bloom Period and Seasonal Color
Spring to fall, red, pink, yellow, purple, magenta, orange, white

Mature Height x Spread
4 to 12 in. x 8 to 12 in.

Botanical Pronunciation
por-chew-LAH-kah gran-deh-FLOR-ah

Portulaca is a low, trailing plant with narrow, succulent leaves. The leaves look like fattened pine needles and are crowded along the stems. The delicate flowers are either single or double and in almost any color imaginable but blue. Although each flower opens in the morning and will close up later in the day, new ones are formed daily. This habit makes portulaca one of the longest-flowering summer annuals available to Texas gardeners. The species is from the dry high plains of Brazil, Argentina, and Uruguay and has been in cultivation since the middle of the nineteenth century. In warm winter areas, particularly in southern Florida, it has become naturalized, but in most of the country it is a long-season, summer-flowering annual.

When, Where, and How to Plant
Plant transplants in the spring after all danger of frost is past and the soil is warm. Choose a location with full sun in the northern parts of the state and at least half-day (preferably morning) sun in the southern. Portulaca can also be direct-seeded at the same time. Portulaca grows best in soils with excellent drainage, even rocky ones, and those that are not overly fertile. Take care to place it where it will not be consistently wet or where water ponds or stands.

Growing Tips
Apply a well-balanced fertilizer monthly during the growing season. Alternately, apply a thin layer of good-quality compost monthly. Slow-release formulations are especially effective when portulaca is grown in containers. Water sufficiently to keep the soil from drying out completely. Although somewhat drought tolerant, portulaca blooms best when kept evenly moist but not wet.

Regional Advice and Care
Flowers in most selections fall easily when done or can be pruned when they fade. Lightly tip prune through the summer to keep tidy or reduce size. After a long, hot spell plants often look yellowed or thin. Prune back to near the base to rejuvenate and it will begin growing when the weather cools. Portulaca is not susceptible to pests but can get crown rots when it is kept too wet or has regular overhead watering.

Companion Planting and Design
Use portulaca to line a raised bed or fall over walls, rocks, or large stones. Blend with succulents for contrast and color. Portulaca grows well in containers of any size, but is especially attractive in hanging baskets either singly or mixed with other plants.

Try These
There are numerous series and selections of portulaca for both size and style of bloom and colors. 'Sundance' has double flowers that are up to 2 inches across. 'Sundial' series has double flowers and blooms well in cooler and cloudier weather. Purslane (*Portulaca oleracea*) has larger, wider leaves and generally smaller flowers. It is a common garden weed in warm areas, and the leaves are highly valued for salads and seasoning.

Sunflower

Helianthus annuus

Bloom Period and Seasonal Color
Spring to fall, rays yellow, reddish, brown,
orange, discs brown

Mature Height x Spread
2 to 10 ft. x 2 to 4 ft.

Botanical Pronunciation
hee-lee-AN-thus AN-you-us

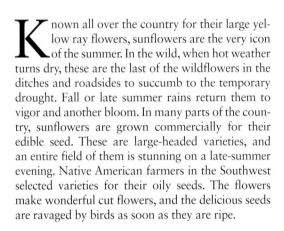

Known all over the country for their large yellow ray flowers, sunflowers are the very icon of the summer. In the wild, when hot weather turns dry, these are the last of the wildflowers in the ditches and roadsides to succumb to the temporary drought. Fall or late summer rains return them to vigor and another bloom. In many parts of the country, sunflowers are grown commercially for their edible seed. These are large-headed varieties, and an entire field of them is stunning on a late-summer evening. Native American farmers in the Southwest selected varieties for their oily seeds. The flowers make wonderful cut flowers, and the delicious seeds are ravaged by birds as soon as they are ripe.

When, Where, and How to Plant
Sow seed in spring once the soil is warm and there is no frost danger. In warm winter areas seed can also be planted in fall. Sunflowers grow best in well-drained fertile soil in unrelieved full sun. Broadcast seed over the bed, mixing them with sand or mulch to help distribute them evenly. Cover lightly by raking the soil, and press the soil gently to prevent seed from washing away.

Growing Tips
Apply a well-balanced fertilizer once in late spring, but further fertilization is rarely necessary. Water regularly, up to twice a week when it's very hot. Do not allow the plants to dry out while blooming.

Regional Advice and Care
Flowers may be cut anytime and regularly removing flower heads promotes continued blooming. Plants are susceptible to mildew on the lower leaves, a condition that is exacerbated by overhead watering.

Companion Planting and Design
Mix with other summer-flowering annuals such as zinnia, coreopsis, and nasturtium. Sunflowers enjoy the same type of soil and watering as vegetables and liven up a vegetable garden during summer. Compact varieties make a charming informal border or edging. Birds are drawn to the seeds and will help spread seed around the garden.

Try These
'Teddy Bear' grows to 2 feet and has large, double, golden-yellow flowers. 'Russian Mammoth', one of the best for home gardeners who want to grow edible seed, has immense heads on tall stalks. 'Tiger Eye' is a mix of "eyed" flowers in bronze, red, red brown and yellow, and 'Moulin Rouge' has deep red-brown rays. There are some 30 sunflower species in Texas, but only this one and two others are routinely sold. The perennial Maximilian sunflower (*Helianthus maximiliani*) grows to 10 feet tall with large yellow-rayed flowers. This species forms large colonies over time. *H. debilis* has brilliant yellow rays on branched stems and does particularly well in wet or coastal zones. Mexican sunflowers (*Tithonia rotundifolia*) have similar growing requirements, but flowers have deep orange rays with yellow disks. The Texas Superstar® sneezeweed (*Helenium amarum*) 'Dakota Gold' has bright yellow, open, spreading rays.

Texas Bluebonnet

Lupinus texensis

Bloom Period and Seasonal Color
Spring, blue, pink, white

Mature Height x Spread
15 to 24 in. x 10 to 12 in.

Botanical Pronunciation
loo-PYE-nus TEX-en-sis

Zones 8 to 10

Every region has its floral signature that identifies where you are, creating a memory of how a place ought to look. In Central Texas it is bluebonnets. I lived outside of the state for nearly 30 years, and it was the wildflower bloom that I missed the most. My first spring back was a year when all the combinations that make a spectacular year fell into place—a year that simply overwhelmed my senses and in which superlatives ceased to mean a thing. Bluebonnets stretched over fields all the way to the horizon, coated urban roadsides, and perked up every walk and trail in or out of town. Up close bluebonnets hold their tightly clustered, pea-shaped blooms on a rigid stalk. Occasionally, there are white or pink ones.

When, Where, and How to Plant
Sow seed or set out transplants in fall. Plants must overwinter to bloom. Germination is enhanced if the seed is treated (scarified) or soaked in warm water overnight. Broadcast seed in a location that receives full sun. Remove all grass when planting; seed must have direct contact with the ground. Bluebonnet needs excellent drainage, and does best in soils that are not overly rich and are slightly to greatly alkaline. Mixing the seed with sand or raking it in helps make a more uniform planting.

Growing Tips
Texas bluebonnet never needs supplemental fertilization. Water regularly in fall until seed germinates. Reduce watering to every two or three weeks over winter. When plentiful, natural rainfall is sufficient.

Regional Advice and Care
Leave flowering heads to form and ripen seed so there is good stand next year. It can take up to three years for an area to fill in completely on its own. Seed is ripe when the pods turn tan to brown and begin to open. Texas bluebonnet is not susceptible pests or disease.

Companion Planting and Design
Texas bluebonnet is breathtaking when planted in mass in gardens that have the right conditions. Mix with other native annuals, particularly if you are making a native meadow or wildflower show. This is an excellent choice to fill in blank areas or places that receive minimal maintenance. Bluebonnets also make good cut flowers.

Try These
There are a number of species in the state, and every one is considered the state flower of Texas. This species is the most widespread through the central part of the state. *Lupinus subcarnosa*, the original state flower, is found mostly in sandy soils of the coastal plains of Texas. The annual Big Bend bluebonnet (*L. havardii*) grows to 4 feet tall with the same intense blue as the others. Big Bend bluebonnet has been the subject of selection and testing for use in the floral trade by Texas A&M researchers. Gardeners can occasionally find the selections 'Texas Sapphire', 'Texas Maroon', and 'Texas Ice' (white) for sale.

Zinnia

Zinnia elegans

Bloom Period and Seasonal Color
Summer to fall, yellow, gold, red, orange, pink, purple, white rays, disc yellow

Mature Height x Spread
6 to 40 in. x 6 to 24 in.

Botanical Pronunciation
ZIN-ee-ah EL-eh-ganz

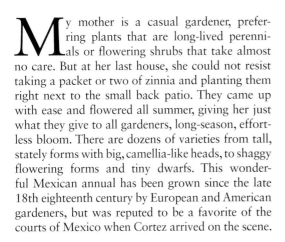

My mother is a casual gardener, preferring plants that are long-lived perennials or flowering shrubs that take almost no care. But at her last house, she could not resist taking a packet or two of zinnia and planting them right next to the small back patio. They came up with ease and flowered all summer, giving her just what they give to all gardeners, long-season, effortless bloom. There are dozens of varieties from tall, stately forms with big, camellia-like heads, to shaggy flowering forms and tiny dwarfs. This wonderful Mexican annual has been grown since the late 18th eighteenth century by European and American gardeners, but was reputed to be a favorite of the courts of Mexico when Cortez arrived on the scene.

When, Where, and How to Plant
Direct seed zinnia in the spring as soon as there is no danger of frost and the soil is warm. In very cold areas this can be as late as May with good results. Set out transplants at the same time. Select a bed that receives at least a half day of sun, preferably full sun is best. Amend the bed to create a well-drained, fertile soil that does not pond or hold standing water.

Growing Tips
Fertilize monthly while flowering with a well-balanced dry formula, a complete organic fertilizer, or by maintaining a 1- to 2-inch layer of good- quality compost. Water regularly, once or twice a week if the weather is hot. Set a schedule that keeps the soil evenly moist, not saturated, but never completely dried out. Avoid overhead watering.

Regional Advice and Care
Remove dead flowering heads regularly to provide for longer bloom. Zinnia are excellent cut flowers, and many have long stems that make that easy. In late summer, prune back by about quarter of their height, maintain watering and fertilization schedule, and it will continue to flower through the fall. Zinnia can be susceptible to a number of leaf fungal diseases with overhead watering. Cutworms visit occasionally but rarely cause more than a cosmetic problem.

Companion Planting and Design
Tall varieties are splendid against a fence, a low wall, or in the back of a mixed planting. Shorter varieties blend well with other small perennials, form an informal, flowering hedge, or fill a corner. Zinnia is irresistible to many species of butterflies, so plant it where these visitors can be enjoyed. All zinnia, but especially the shorter, bushy varieties, work well in containers.

Try These
'Thumbelina' is a dwarf with small flowers in a tight button-like array of rays. 'Cut & Come Again' are tall plants with flowers on long stalks.. 'Dreamland' series has huge 4-inch flowers in many colors. Creeping zinnia (*Zinnia angustifolia*) is a short, compact plant with narrow leaves flowering white, orange, or yellow. 'Crystal White' is a low-growing plant with white rays and gold discs. 'Star' series is available in white, orange, or gold with a bright yellow disc.

BULBS
FOR TEXAS

The term *bulb* is a catchall word for a variable group of plants that may or may not actually be true bulbs. Plants in this chapter may grow from true bulbs, corms, rhizomes, or tubers.

True bulbs have an underground, swollen organ composed of tightly wrapped leaves around a short stem also known as a basal plate. All growth of the plant—leaves, flowers, and roots—arises from this plate. Bulbs may form bulblets around the base, which eventually grow large enough to bloom.

Gladiolus communis ssp. *byzantinus*

Corms are modified stems that are typically flattened with a scaly or fibrous sheath. All the nodes that form leaves are on one surface, and those for roots on the opposite. Corms routinely form numerous smaller corms (cormlets) that increase quickly.

A rhizome is a swollen stem that grows underground and is more or less elongated. Rhizomes never have a hairy sheath. The nodes are arranged along the surfaces, and rhizomes generally grow in one direction as they continue to elongate.

Tubers are enlarged roots that grow underground with ample nodes for the development of leaves and roots all along its surface.

Each of these organs is a storage unit enabling the plant to endure long periods of dormancy with little or no water yet still have sufficient energy to grow and flower. All of next year's energy reservoir is established while the plant is actively growing. Therefore, it is important to provide ample water and a little fertilizer during active growth, but often little to none when it is dormant. It is also important not to interrupt this growth cycle by prematurely removing leaves.

Growing Habits of Bulbs

The growing season for a bulb varies by species. Some send up the leaves first with flowers emerging after weeks or months of growth. These types of plants go dormant quickly after flowering. Others shoot up the flowers first, followed by the leaves, which last for a few weeks or months until the plant goes dormant. Others retain their leaves year-round. Evergreen bulbs grow less vigorously during certain times of the year, often known as a resting period but never lose all their leaves or disappear.

Narcissus tazetta

Relocate bulbs with true dormancy during this time. Evergreen bulbs can be moved anytime, but relocation during their resting period usually has better results. Planting depth varies widely in bulbs; look to descriptions here or other sources for the appropriate depth.

Gardeners in areas with warm or moderate winters find that bulbs that require a chill are often difficult to induce to bloom, whereas gardeners in colder zones find these some of the easiest and most consistent bloomers for their gardens. There are numerous winter-growing, summer-dormant bulbs, like the South African *Freesia*, that are perfectly suited to warm winter gardens. In addition, a long, warm summer makes an ideal area for Mexican summer-flowering species like rain lilies and some of the tropical species of *Crinum* and *Hymenocallis*.

Bulbs Make Good Neighbors

Bulbs blend beautifully into perennial beds, providing vivid, spectacular flowering in season, then obligingly fade away to make way for other flowering plants. Small species add extra drama to the garden as a low border to a perennial bed or when planted in mass. Everywhere there are some species that naturalize and spread freely with minimal effort, creating splendid color displays in their season. Bulbs can also be tucked into tiny spots or fill in small, barren areas of the garden. Many grow extremely well in rocky, alkaline soils and can be used in hot, dry corners of the garden.

Bulbs are outstanding container plants. They can be planted closely together to form an intense display during their blooming period. They also mix well with other bulbs, annuals, or perennials to create miniature gardens in a pot. It is easier to control conditions for plants grown in containers, which permits a wider variety of bulbs than may be possible in the ground.

Amaryllis

Hippeastrum x johnsonii

Bloom Period and Seasonal Color
Spring to early summer red, pink, white, bicolors, and combinations

Mature Height x Spread
1 to 3 ft. x 2 ft.

Botanical Pronunciation
hip-ee-ASS-trum jon-SO-nee-eye

In the late eighteenth century an English watch-maker named Johnson brought forth this hybrid strain. It is still widely available and is the origin of many modern hybrids. This beloved garden ornamental was formed from the union of *Hippeastrum reginae* and *H. vittatum*. Although numerous hybrids and forms have been created as a result of this and other crosses, the species are all native to South America. After World War II, grow-ers in Holland began to form a strain of larger, more robust bulbs from *Hippeastrum leopoldii*. These are the popular large amaryllis sold as potted gift plants. Amaryllis have large, trumpet-shaped flow-ers arranged in a wheel atop sturdy stalks. Amaryllis are effortless repeat bloomers in the garden and also make outstanding and long-lived potted plants.

When, Where, and How to Plant
Set out bulbs as soon as the soil can be worked. Place the bulb so that the neck is as much as halfway above the soil line. Amend the soil by adding gener-ous quantities of good compost, bonemeal, or other organic material high in phosphorus. Amaryllis need well-drained soil; in heavy clays, add sand or raise the planting area. Water well after planting and every ten days to two weeks until leaves emerge.

Growing Tips
For established bulbs, scratch in bonemeal or a bal-anced granular fertilizer once blooming is finished. Fertilize again midway through summer. Plants in containers do best with a slow-release fertil-izer at the beginning of the growing season or a soluble fertilizer, monthly while growing. Maintain

regular watering and fertilization during that time—in warm climates as often as weekly.

Regional Advice and Care
In mid- to late summer, cease fertilization and reduce watering, even for potted plants, to let the plant go dormant. Bulbs can be left in the ground during dormancy and tolerate moderate watering. Apply a 4- to 6-inch layer of mulch to protect them from heavy freezes. Amaryllis are susceptible to slugs and snails, particularly in poorly drained soils. Remove by hand, or if safe use a snail bait. Viruses cause streaking or discoloration of the leaves. If you have, or suspect you have, a virus, remove and destroy the bulb and replant with virus-free ones.

Companion Planting and Design
Plant amaryllis generously for a spectacular show during their short blooming season. Use as an infor-mal border, line a narrow walkway, or mix with other perennials. Amaryllis bloom about the same time as roses and iris and look splendid when inter-planted among them.

Try These
The autumn flowering *Hippeastrum papilio* is breathtaking with its maroon and green flowers. A cross of *H. aulicum* with *H. traubii* known as 'San Antonio Rose' is a vigorous, tough plant with pairs of rosy red flowers. There are countless cultivars but the large 'Appleblossom' is highly reliable, as is the 'Mead' strain and the *H. cybister* cultivars 'Chico', 'Reggae', and 'Rosario' from the breeding efforts of Fred Meyer.

Caladium

Caladium bicolor

Bloom Period and Seasonal Color
Summer, leaves with white, pink, and red markings

Mature Height x Spread
12 to 16 in. x 12 to 24 in.

Botanical Pronunciation
kah-LAY-dee-um BYE-cull-ur

Caladium was first introduced into the United States in the mid-eighteenth century, but has been a garden mainstay for summer color in shady beds since the mid-nineteenth century. Most of those sold are hybrids between this species and *Caladium humboldtii* and are known as *C. xhortulanum*. Growing from contorted, flattened tubers, caladium is a long-lived perennial that is used as an annual bedding plant. It is valued for its large, heart-shaped leaves that are shot through with white, pink, or red. Many forms also have mottling or splashes of color in between the veins. They are an old-fashioned sort of plant that are just as congenial in a more formal garden with crisp lines, true colors, and a long season of beauty.

When, Where, and How to Plant
Plant in mid- to late April in most locations. Tubers rot quickly in cool, wet soils. Caladium grows in a wide variety of soils but thrives in well-amended, fertile soils that are well drained. Set tubers an inch below the surface and cover completely with the eyes facing the top. Water in well, and cover with 2 to 3 inches of mulch.

Growing Tips
Fertilize monthly with a balanced granular fertilizer such as rose food. Alternatively, add a 1- to 2-inch layer of compost monthly. Water sufficiently to keep the soil evenly moist, adding up to 4 inches of mulch to keep the soil cool and evenly moist.

Regional Advice and Care
Remove spent leaves anytime. Occasional greenish flowers can be removed anytime. Caladium is winter deciduous, and leaves begin to fall over and lose color in the fall. Dig up tubers once the leaves are entirely gone, gently shake off the soil, and store in a cool, dry location in dry sand or sphagnum moss. Many gardeners prefer simply to start again each year with fresh tubers. Pests are few; the occasional snail can be removed by hand.

Companion Planting and Design
Caladium are gorgeous when planted in large masses of one or two varieties on the north or east side of a house or a wall. White cultivars in particular make a stunning display beneath large evergreen trees or blended with blue- or white-flowering perennials. All caladium do well in pots. Large pots of one or two complementary varieties make a vivid display on a shady porch or patio.

Try These
There are numerous varieties and selections in an array of colors. Names are confusing, and different names often apply to the same cultivar. The white-leaved varieties are among the most sun tolerant, but all need relief from afternoon sun. The old standard white 'Candidum' is a hybrid with *Caladium humboldtii* that has been around since at least 1868. 'Carolyn Wharton' has a pink center in the leaf, as does the similar 'Pink Beauty', whereas 'Red Flash' has vivid red leaves.

Crinum

Crinum spp.

Bloom Period and Seasonal Color
Spring to summer, white, pink, mauve, reddish

Mature Height x Spread
1 to 5 ft. x 2 to 6 ft.

Botanical Pronunciation
CRY-num

Zones 8 to 10

Crinums are a steady part of old homesteads and gardens throughout the South. This is a largely subtropical genus, with big, funnel-shaped flowers held high over the foliage. Most crinum species and their hybrids are pure white, the hybrids of both *Crinum procerum* and *C. asiaticum* are in shades of pink. The most commonly grown one is *Crinum bulbispermum* and its numerous hybrids and forms. Its tapered, thick, blue-green leaves are distinctive. This South African crinum is also one of the cold hardiest. Crinum bulbs live a long time, increasing with each season until some old bulbs are the size of a football. Most of these exquisite garden bulbs came to Florida by way of Caribbean gardens in the late nineteenth century.

When, Where, and How to Plant
Plant bulbs in the spring or early summer. Although most crinum grow well in bright sun, relief from afternoon sun is best. In West Texas or other hot locations, plants do well in deep shade. Amend the soil with ample compost or composted manure to ensure excellent drainage. I have grown some in rocky, alkaline soils with great success. Plant the bulb so that the entire neck of the bulb is above the surface of the soil. Water well and continue to water weekly for a month to establish.

Growing Tips
Apply a slow-release or dry organic fertilizer each spring. Mulch heavily, up to 2 to 3 inches, to keep the soil from drying out completely. Water every other week in summer and monthly in winter.

Regional Advice and Care
Although most crinums are evergreen, in the early summer plants often lose some leaves and become semi-dormant. Resist removing leaves unless they come away easily in your hand and maintain regular watering. Remove decrepit flowering stalks anytime. Crinums resent disturbance and should not be moved unless necessary. It can take two to three years for plants that are moved to resume blooming. Crinums are bothered by few pests or diseases.

Companion Planting and Design
Crinums are excellent specimen or accent plants. The large deep green, strappy leaves give a lush appearance to a shady bed, perennial planting, or patio garden. Many varieties are sweetly fragrant. Crinums grow well in large containers or planters.

Try These
There is one native species, *Crinum americanum*, with blunt-tipped, green leaves whose white flowers have deeply split petals. Some popular varieties of *C. bulbispermum* include 'Sacramento' with white and pink striped flowers, '12 Apostles' with striking pink and white narrow petals, and 'Gowenii' with curled white petals. Well-known varieties of other crinums are 'Mrs. James Hendry', which is a smaller plant with open white flowers, and the larger 'Ellen Bosanquet', which has big, deep rosy pink flowers. *Crinum moorei* is a shade-loving pink-flowered species. A stunning pink-flowered hybrid between *C. moorei* and *Amaryllis belladonna* is known as x *amarcrinum*.

Daffodil

Narcissus spp.

Other Name Jonquil

Bloom Period and Seasonal Color
Late winter to early spring, yellow, gold, white

Mature Height x Spread
6 to 24 in. x 6 to 12 in.

Botanical Pronunciation
nar-SIS-us

Prized for their early and prolific bloom, daffo-dils do remarkably well in gardens throughout the state. The tubular petals open like wide-mouthed trumpets and are surrounded at the base by a collar of sepals. Most flower in spring among their abundant, linear leaves. In good garden soil these are long-lived bulbs that multiply generously, but are rarely invasive. There are at least five, more according to some sources, groups of this genus. In the southern half of the state, *Narcissus tazetta* and its numerous forms are the best and longest lasting. In all species and groups, there are hundreds of vari-eties almost all in various combinations of white, gold, or yellow. There are selections with ruffled petal tips as well as doubled flowered forms.

When, Where, and How to Plant
Plant in fall in all but the coldest zones. Some vari-eties tolerate the cold well, especially with a mulch or snow cover. Plant in a well-drained soil amended with generous amounts of compost or other organic material with a handful of bonemeal in the hole. Set the bulbs to a depth that is twice their height and cover well. Water weekly until leaves or flowers emerge.

Growing Tips
Apply slow-release or organic fertilizer annually in fall in warm winter area; early spring elsewhere. While daffodils are growing and blooming, water every one to two weeks. Daffodils do not need to remain entirely dry while dormant but will rot in situations of poor drainage or standing water.

Regional Advice and Care
Allow leaves to yellow and dry naturally. Remove them only when they pull away in your hand. Cut flowering stalks anytime. Daffodils are not suscepti-ble to most diseases. Most varieties multiply readily and can be divided every four or five years.

Companion Planting and Design
Daffodils mix well with spring-blooming perennials as well as with other spring-flowering bulbs. Plant generously for a dramatic effect in lawns or large beds or as an informal border along a drive or walk-way. Daffodils make excellent plants for containers or planters. The ones known as paperwhites require no chilling hours to grow and are extremely easy to force into late winter bloom for indoor or holiday use.

Try These
Paperwhite (*Narcissus papyraceus*, also called *N. tazetta*) is often forced for indoor flowering dur-ing Christmas. Paperwhites are reliable garden plants throughout all but the coldest parts of the state. 'Grand Primo' is an extremely vigorous old variety with abundant flowers and persists more or less indefinitely and rarely needs division. 'Golden Dawn' has white and yellow bicolored flowers and is a vigorous choice for Zones 8 to 10, as is the white 'Erlicheer' with its congested head of flow-ers. The diminutive plants known as 'Sweetie' (*N. jonquilla*) are effortless and often naturalize in East Texas.

Daylily

Hemerocallis spp.

Bloom Period and Seasonal Color
Spring to early fall, yellow, orange, red, maroon

Mature Height x Spread
1 to 3 ft. x 2 to 3 ft.

Botanical Pronunciation him-er-oh-KAL-iss

Daylily grows from a tuberous root, and although not strictly a bulb, it grows in a similar style to most bulbs, so it is included here. The long, strap-shaped leaves form a flowing fan. Plants multiply quickly and may form large clumps. The large, showy flowers with flared petals are on branched stems held high above the foliage. They gained their common name because each flower opens for only one day. Breeders have created a phenomenal range of colors from mauve to orange, pink to yellow, and there are evergreen, deciduous, and dwarf selections. Daylilies have been cultivated in their native China and Japan for thousands of years for their beautiful, edible flowers. There are records of their cultivation in Greece as early as 70 A.D.

When, Where, and How to Plant
Plant container-grown plants almost anytime except the coldest part of the winter. Choose a location in full sun or light, filtered shade. In hot areas, morning sun is best. Amend the soil with 2 to 3 inches of compost, combined with composted manure or other organic amendments. Be sure the soil is well drained. In heavy clays, it is advisable to raise the bed or planting area to improve the drainage. Set plants in the hole slightly higher than the soil line, pressing the soil gently around the roots to remove air pockets. Water thoroughly and maintain steady moisture until well established.

Growing Tips
Use a slow-release granular fertilizer in the spring as plants begin to grow and once again in the summer.

Use any organic, dry formulation on the same schedule if you prefer. Mulch generously to keep the roots cool and retain soil moisture, which also has the effect of providing nutrients to the soil.

Regional Advice and Care
Prune flowering stalks anytime after all flowers have finished. Clumps that become crowded can be divided every three to four years in the fall. Daylilies are susceptible to daylily rust. Treat with appropriate fungal formulations and follow label directions carefully. Leaf-chewing insects and snails mar the foliage but cause no permanent harm.

Companion Planting and Design
Plant daylilies as a loose, informal border in front of evergreens or large shrubs. Most daylily varieties mix well with other summer-flowering perennials. Plant generously to line lawn borders or walkways or soften the edges of a patio or pool area. The dwarf forms are particularly well suited for containers either singly or in mixed plantings.

Try These
Hemerocallis fulva is a tawny orange sterile form. The variety 'Kwanso' of this species and the bright yellow-flowering *H. asphodelus* accounted for all the daylilies in cultivation until the 1920s when the difficulties of their propagation and pollination were overcome. The resulting 'Stella d'Oro' and 'Aztec Gold' are still widely grown. Today there are over 36,000 listed cultivars in color combinations and styles for any taste.

Freesia

Freesia spp.

Bloom Period and Seasonal Color
Spring white, yellow, pink, red, lavender, purple

Mature Height x Spread
3 to 6 in. x 3 to 6 in.

Botanical Pronunciation FREE-zha

Zones 8 to 10

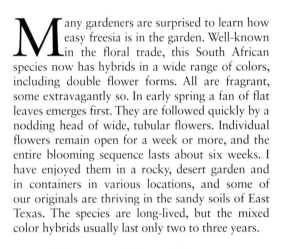

Many gardeners are surprised to learn how easy freesia is in the garden. Well-known in the floral trade, this South African species now has hybrids in a wide range of colors, including double flower forms. All are fragrant, some extravagantly so. In early spring a fan of flat leaves emerges first. They are followed quickly by a nodding head of wide, tubular flowers. Individual flowers remain open for a week or more, and the entire blooming sequence lasts about six weeks. I have enjoyed them in a rocky, desert garden and in containers in various locations, and some of our originals are thriving in the sandy soils of East Texas. The species are long-lived, but the mixed color hybrids usually last only two to three years.

When, Where, and How to Plant
Plant corms in fall. Freesias tolerate any kind of soil from loamy, fertile soils to clay but must have excellent drainage. Plant in raised beds where drainage is poor, amending the soil with compost to increase drainage. Set corms 2 inches deep, making certain that the root bud is facing the bottom of the hole. Cover completely and water thoroughly. Water every two to three weeks until the leaves emerge, and then water every seven to ten days.

Growing Tips
Apply slow-release or organic fertilizer annually in fall. Water weekly when flowering and every seven to ten days while the leaves remain on the plant. Freesia need to be kept entirely dry when dormant. In areas that have regular summer rain, it is best to lift the bulbs and replant in fall.

Regional Advice and Care
Leaves continue to grow for a month or more after blooming. Allow them to dry naturally, and remove them when they come away easily in your hand. Cut flowering stalks anytime. Corms multiply quickly and may be divided every three or four years. Freesia is not susceptible to pests or disease.

Companion Planting and Design
This colorful species is an outstanding addition to any spring flower display. Because freesia grows well in dry conditions, it is a good choice to mix with succulents or fill in barren spots in a newly planted garden. Freesia grows well in containers or planters either individually or mixed with other bulbs, annuals, or perennials. This reliable rebloomer with its dry summer dormancy is a perfect choice for a garden that is left on its own for the summer.

Try These
The small *Freesia alba* has sprays of white flowers with yellow centers. This and the closely related *F. leichtlinii* have a powerful, sweet, spicy aroma. *Freesia laxa* (formerly *Anomatheca laxa*) is a charming, small plant with foot-long sprays of flowers that may be brick red, white with a reddish base, or pale blue. Flowers open in sequence up and down the stalk, prolonging the bloom for up to six weeks.

Gladiolus

Gladiolus spp.

Other Name Sword lily

Bloom Period and Seasonal Color
Spring to early summer, magenta, red, orange, apricot, yellow, white

Mature Height x Spread
18 to 30 in. x 6 to 12 in.

Botanical Pronunciation
glad-ee-OH-lus

Gladiolus is revered for its tall, richly colored spears of flowers in the spring. Tall and stately, they remind me of older gardens where such flowers were left to their own devices and came back year after year. Gladiolus leaves emerge first, forming a fan or shield of leaves. Large, open-petaled flowers arranged along a tall spike follow quickly. Various species and their hybrids are widely grown for both the floral trade and for home cut-flower use. Some of the modern hybrids were created for later blooming, a trait that limits their use where spring turns hot quickly. *Gladiolus byzantinus* is a long-lived plant with deep magenta flowers. It is one of the oldest gladiolus in cultivation and is hardy throughout the state.

When, Where, and How to Plant
Plant gladiolus when soil temperatures reach 60 degrees Fahrenheit. In all but the coldest zones, this may be as early as March. Gladiolus grows best with a long, warm—but not hot—spring; hot weather inhibits bloom and can send them into premature dormancy. In West and South Texas plant as early as possible for good bloom, or use early-flowering forms. *Gladiolus byzantinus* may also be planted in fall. Select a site in full sun or morning sun in hot locales. Good drainage is essential. Add generous amounts of compost, composted manure, or other organic amendments and set the corm in the ground 4 to 6 inches deep.

Growing Tips
Apply slow-release or granular organic fertilizer in spring. Corms are delicate, so scratch in fertilizer carefully to avoid damage. Provide regular, even watering while plants are growing and flowering. It is best if they never completely dry out. A 4-inch layer of mulch keeps the soil cool and retains soil moisture.

Regional Advice and Care
It can be difficult to lift and store gladiolus corms and have them repeat bloom next year. Most gardeners consider them annuals and renew the corms yearly. Cut flowering stalks anytime, but leave the leaves until they come away in your hand.

Companion Planting and Design
Most gladiolus are tall plants, making them suitable in the back of a border or planting. This is also helpful when the flowering is done and the foliage is unsightly.

Try These
Gladiolus communis subsp. *byzantinus*, either the species if you can find it or the variety 'Cruentus', are excellent for most of Texas. *G. dalenii* is used to create many of the modern hybrids and is especially good in areas with poor soils. *G. callianthus* (formerly *Acidanthera bicolor*) flowers at night in summer. This species prefers moist conditions, such as near a pond. It is perennial only along the coast; elsewhere it should be lifted and stored. The small *G. tristi*s has yellow flowers and likes moist conditions.

Iris

Iris spp.

Bloom Period and Seasonal Color
Spring, blue, purple, pink, white, yellow, reddish

Mature Height x Spread
1 to 4 ft. x 1 to 4 ft.

Botanical Pronunciation
EYE-ris

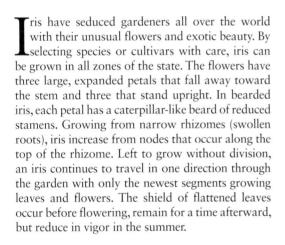

Iris have seduced gardeners all over the world with their unusual flowers and exotic beauty. By selecting species or cultivars with care, iris can be grown in all zones of the state. The flowers have three large, expanded petals that fall away toward the stem and three that stand upright. In bearded iris, each petal has a caterpillar-like beard of reduced stamens. Growing from narrow rhizomes (swollen roots), iris increase from nodes that occur along the top of the rhizome. Left to grow without division, an iris continues to travel in one direction through the garden with only the newest segments growing leaves and flowers. The shield of flattened leaves occur before flowering, remain for a time afterward, but reduce in vigor in the summer.

When, Where, and How to Plant
Plant rhizomes in fall in warm winter areas, spring where it is colder. Dig a shallow trench, mixing in compost, slow-release granular fertilizer, or well-balanced dry organic fertilizer. Be sure the area is well drained. Place the rhizome on the surface of the soil and barely cover it, leaving a small amount of the top visible. Water thoroughly.

Growing Tips
For established iris, apply slow-release granular fertilizer or a well-balanced organic one, or a mix of compost and bonemeal once in the fall and once in the spring prior to bloom. Water carefully in summer, weekly when hot, less often in cooler temperatures or zones.

Regional Advice and Care
Iris leaves grow for months after bloom. Remove dead leaves as they dry, or cut back the entire fan of leaves to 4 inches in fall. Flowers may be cut anytime. Divide every three to four years by removing the entire clump, cutting off all of the rhizome that is damaged or not setting leaves and replanting the remaining (newest) section. Iris are susceptible to snails, slugs, borers, and bacterial soft rot in warm moist conditions. Good drainage, careful watering, and vigilance are the best defenses.

Companion Planting and Design
Mix iris with spring-flowering perennials, shrubs, or bulbs for a grand spring show. Iris and roses are a classic combination because their blooming periods often coincide.

Try These
In most areas of eastern and coastal Texas, spuria iris, *Iris orientalis*, or Louisiana iris, *I.* x *louisiana*, are often better performers than the bearded forms. Both of these tolerate high heat and humidity as well as wetter soils. Spuria prefer rhizomes be covered by up to 3 inches of soil, and Louisiana iris will grow in saturated soil, even in standing water. In hot, arid areas, arilbred irises are exceptional. These hybrids have flowers like bearded iris, but in combinations of maroon, chartreuse, and brown. They require extremely dry conditions during their summer dormancy. An old white form known as *Iris albicans*, introduced long ago from Spain, is extremely reliable in most of the state.

Lady Tulip

Tulipa clusiana

Bloom Period and Seasonal Color
Spring, yellow, white, pink

Mature Height x Spread 6 to 12 in. x 3 to 6 in.

Botanical Pronunciation
TEW-lih-pah CLUE-zee-ah-na

I consider tulips way too much trouble for what you get—a big burst of overdone flowers for a terribly short time. I had entirely given up on the arduous business of lifting and chilling when quite by accident, I started to grow species tulips. There I found treasures—plants that not only were gorgeous during their spring bloom, but would stay in the ground and return year after year. Many were successful, but lady tulip was the clear champion of those trials. One of the last of the spring bulbs to emerge, the leaves come up shortly before the goblet-shaped, upright flowers. The flowers are cream to yellow inside and red to coral on the outside. This is a reliable rebloomer that spreads gently.

When, Where, and How to Plant
Plant bulbs in fall. These bulbs perform well in almost any soil type, including highly alkaline ones. Amend the bed or planting hole with generous amounts of compost. Place bulbs so that the tip of the bulb is 2 inches below the surface, cover completely, and water thoroughly. Water every week or two until the leaves emerge.

Growing Tips
Apply slow-release or organic fertilizer in fall and again in early spring. Keep roots well mulched throughout the year. Water growing and blooming plants weekly, more often if the weather is exceptionally hot or dry. These tulips need a long, dry summer dormancy. Although they do fine left in place to rebloom, be sure that it is not a situation with continuous watering or standing water. Divide in late summer or fall while still dormant.

Regional Advice and Care
Leaves continue to grow for about a month after flowering and should be left to die off naturally. They may be removed when they come away easily in your hand. Flowers may be cut anytime and, if picked early in the bloom cycle, make good cut flowers. Unlike hybrid forms, these species are not susceptible to pests or disease.

Companion Planting and Design
Mix lady tulip with other spring-flowering perennials, bulbs, or annuals. This species is shorter than most of the hybrids and can be used in the front of the border. It spreads to fill in small, barren corners, odd ends of beds, or areas that need a quick burst of spring color. The impact of flowers is enhanced when they are used in groups. It does well in containers or planters either in mass or mixed with other bulbs or perennials.

Try These
'Lady Jane' and 'Cynthia' are well-known hybrids of the species and its variety *chrysantha*. Candida tulip (*Tulipa saxatilis*) has open pink flowers with yellow interiors and does especially well in rocky or dry soils. Wild tulip (*Tulipa sylvestris*) has sweetly scented, lemon yellow to gold flowers and tolerates wetter conditions than the other two do.

Lily

Lilium spp.

Bloom Period and Seasonal Color
Spring and summer, white, orange, pink, yellow

Mature Height x Spread
24 to 48 in. x 6 to 8 in.

Botanical Pronunciation
LIL-ee-um

When I moved into my present house I was astounded to find two big lilies in the back under a pecan. Soon, they bloomed with the typical large, white flowers that smelled sweet on the evening wind. These easy-to-grow bulbs can be left in the ground to multiply and return each year in the central and southern parts of the state. There are a vast number of lily species, and they all send up tall, hefty stalks covered with linear, apple green foliage. The three or six flowers are arranged like a wheel at the tip. Two of the most common are Madonna lily (*Lilium candidum*) with open, trumpet-shaped, white flowers and Easter lily (*L. longiflorum*), which is sold by the millions around Easter.

When, Where, and How to Plant
Lilies grow in any soil with excellent drainage. Madonna lily is especially good in alkaline soils. Although lilies can be planted anytime, late summer and early fall are best. Spring plantings should be as early as possible. Amend a new bed with generous amounts of compost. Set bulbs 3 to 4 inches below the surface and mulch heavily. Water in well.

Growing Tips
Fertilize lilies once in spring before flowers emerge, and again after flowering ceases. Maintain even soil moisture throughout the growing season, up to weekly when the weather is hot.

Regional Advice and Care
Allow the stalk and leaves to dry naturally, which is generally well into summer. Cut at ground level once the plant is entirely dry. In cold areas lift the bulbs in late summer and place in a pot with fast-draining potting soil, moist sand, or sphagnum moss for the winter. The bulbs are composed of layer on layer of small scales, which fall off easily when handled. Each can be individually potted or planted, although it takes up to three years for them to flower. Many lilies are infected with a virus that causes streaking of the leaves and general decline. If you have or suspect a virus, remove and destroy the plant. Replant with a known virus-free individual or one grown from seed.

Companion Planting and Design
Use lilies generously in great swaths at the back of a bed or surrounding a tree with smaller perennials in front to masquerade the fading foliage in the summer. Lilies grow well in containers, which is how gardeners in cold climates best enjoy them.

Try These
Tiger lily (*Lilium lancifolium*) has rolled-back petals in vivid shades of orange. This showy lily prefers acid soils. The so-called Philippine lily (*L. formosanum*), which is from Taiwan, needs afternoon shade. Its pure white flowers arise in late summer. *Lilium regale* is the parent of the 'Olympic' and 'Aurelian' hybrid strains and is the most cold hardy of the lilies. These strains flower white, white with yellow accents, and pink and white.

Oxblood Lily

Rhodophiala bifida

Bloom Period and Seasonal Color
Fall, scarlet

Mature Height x Spread
10 to 12 in. x 24 to 36 in.

Botanical Pronunciation
roe-doe-FEE-ah-luh BIF-ih-duh

Like most gardeners who have this remarkable fall-flowering bulb, I received a bag of bulbs from a friend's garden. At the time, I knew little about their preferences, so I planted them all over the garden, in sun and shade, in improved soils and poorer ones. Every single one of them grew, bloomed, multiplied, and continued to bloom every year. This reliable old standard is from Argentina and was introduced to American gardeners by the Texas nurseryman Peter Heinrich Oberwetter around the turn of the twentieth century. Flowering before the leaves, the brilliant red flowers, in clusters of two or three, are often lined with white on the inner petal. Most of plants passed along are a strain that rarely sets seed but multiplies readily.

When, Where, and How to Plant
Oxblood lily can be planted almost anytime, but spring or early summer planting results in the bloom the first year. This bulb grows in any soil with excellent drainage, even highly alkaline ones. It does, however, grow larger and multiply faster in soils that have been amended with compost, well-composted manure, or other organic material. Set the bulb at least 3 inches deep, cover completely, and water in well.

Growing Tips
Provide a single application of granular slow-release or dry organic fertilizer in the fall. Water every 10 days to two weeks while flowering and growing. Bulbs do not need to be entirely dry when they're dormant, but avoid standing water or daily watering where they are growing.

Regional Advice
The leaves of oxblood lily continue to grow through the fall and winter. Let them die off naturally in the spring and remove them only when they come away easily with a gentle tug. Oxblood lily is not susceptible to pests or disease.

Companion Planting and Design
Because they spread so well, oxblood lily creates a vivid mass of color quickly. Use it to line walkways, or accent an entry. A collection of these bulbs is stunning in front of a large perennial or shrub bed, and their ease of care means they can be spread generously through the garden. Plants do well in containers that are at least 8 inches deep to accommodate the depth the bulbs need during dormancy.

Try These
In nature, this species has a wide color range, from deep red-orange to light pink and white. These forms are offered occasionally in this country. I still prefer the intense red of the strains that arose from the old strains found in Central Texas and through the deep South. 'Hill Country Red' is a name often applied to these bright red, sharp-petaled forms. *Rhodophiala* is a genus of bulbs that are not well-known except by dedicated bulb fanciers. It is closely related to the better-known *Amaryllis*. Find them at specialty growers or through the bulb exchanges in bulb societies.

Rain Lily

Zephyranthes spp.

Bloom Period and Seasonal Color
Summer, pink, white, yellow, apricot

Mature Height x Spread
4 to 12 in. x 6 to 12 in.

Botanical Pronunciation
zef-er-AN-theez

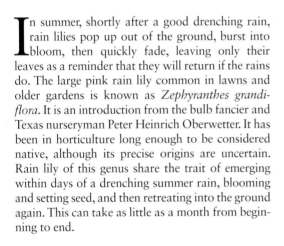

In summer, shortly after a good drenching rain, rain lilies pop up out of the ground, burst into bloom, then quickly fade, leaving only their leaves as a reminder that they will return if the rains do. The large pink rain lily common in lawns and older gardens is known as *Zephyranthes grandiflora*. It is an introduction from the bulb fancier and Texas nurseryman Peter Heinrich Oberwetter. It has been in horticulture long enough to be considered native, although its precise origins are uncertain. Rain lily of this genus share the trait of emerging within days of a drenching summer rain, blooming and setting seed, and then retreating into the ground again. This can take as little as a month from beginning to end.

When, Where, and How to Plant
Plant in spring or fall. Rain lily bulbs do not like to dry out, so plant container-grown plants with the soil or with as much soil as possible if moved from the ground. Amend the bed with ample organic matter and a thin layer of bonemeal or a balanced organic fertilizer. Set the bulbs 1 to 2 inches below the surface and cover completely. Water in well.

Growing Tips
Apply slow-release or organic fertilizer once in fall and spring. Water established plants every two weeks in summer, although the associated watering for those in lawns or perennial beds is sufficient. Plants survive winter dormancy in regularly watered beds with good drainage. Water evergreen species monthly in winter.

Regional Advice and Care
Leaves of rain lily grow for a short time after the blooming and wither quickly. Remove them when they come away easily in your hand. Evergreen species lose a few leaves in summer, and these can be removed by hand. Remove spent flowers anytime. Divide crowded clumps every four or five years in fall. Rain lilies are not susceptible to pests or disease.

Companion Planting and Design
Mix rain lily with summer-flowering perennials or set in large drifts in a lawn. Rain lily grows well in large containers or planters either alone or in mixed plantings. Use evergreen species as an informal border.

Try These
Zephyranthes citrine has clear yellow flowers and does particularly well in areas with poor soils and dry summers. The only widely grown evergreen species is *Z. candida*, with bright white, long-lasting flowers in late summer. The southeastern native, *Z. atamasco*, does not tolerate alkaline soils and is preferred in the eastern half of the state. There are countless hybrids and color forms, of which 'Grandjax' and 'Ajax' are the most widely grown. In Central and South Texas late summer rains cause the eruption of the tall, white flowers of the native rain lily (*Cooperia drummondii*). The closely related *Habranthus robustus* has large, pink flowers that bloom continuously over the summer.

Red Spider Lily

Lycoris radiata

Bloom Period and Seasonal Color
Late summer to fall, red, pink, white

Mature Height x Spread
15 to 20 in. x 6 to 12 in.

Botanical Pronunciation
lie-KOR-iss rad-ee-AY-tah

R ed spider lily begins as slender, slick stems rising from the ground in late summer or fall. The next day you see the vivid red bloom, a sure sign of fall. There are three to six flowers per stalk, and in old stands the effect is of a red blizzard. Spider lilies were brought from their home in Japan to this country with the expedition of Admiral Perry, but were cultivated in England long before that. The common form is sterile and has achieved its astonishing success, and often naturalized status, through vegetative increase. You find it everywhere, in old homesteads throughout the South, in rocky dry gardens in the West, and anywhere that gardeners seek an effortless burst of color and a reliable rebloomer.

When, Where, and How to Plant
Red spider lily grows in any well-drained soil, even those with high alkalinity. Avoid planting it in areas that stay consistently moist or hold water for long periods. Adding compost or other organic matter to the planting bed is recommended and grows bigger bulbs, but bulbs will thrive on benign neglect too. Red spider lily can try a gardener's patience. Bulbs typically wait a year to set bloom after planting, and it can be as long as three years. I had some given to me years ago that took so long to bloom after planting, I forgot I had them and tried for a time to figure out how they simply arrived on their own in my garden.

Growing Tips
Water regularly through fall and winter while the leaves are growing. Bulbs accept some watering while dormant as long as drainage is superb. Fertilize annually in fall with a well-balanced granular fertilizer to enhance growth and encourage successive flowering.

Regional Advice and Care
Leaves fade in early spring or summer and should be allowed to fall off naturally. In some areas the bulbs are susceptible to slugs, snails, cutworms, and various caterpillars. In other areas, particularly those that are drier, they have no pests at all. Use bait strictly according to package directions for slugs or snails and a *Bt* formulation for caterpillars.

Companion Planting and Design
Red spider lily multiplies readily. Use it along narrow walkways or to mark an entry or gate, or use it in combination with other fall flowering bulbs, such as oxblood lily.

Try These
There is a white flowering form 'Alba' (*L. xalbiflora*) and a pink known as 'Carnea'. Naked lady (*Lycoris squamigera*) is a pink, spring-flowering plant that is hardy throughout the state. It, too, rarely sets seed and is considered to be a hybrid of *L. straminea* and *L. incarnata* that came into horticulture in mid-nineteenth century. The yellow-flowered hurricane lily (*L. aurea*, also called *L. africana*) of Florida is not hardy below Zone 9, whereas the yellow-flowering *L. traubii* is hardy through Zone 8.

Spider Lily

Hymenocallis spp.

Bloom Period and Seasonal Color
Midsummer to early fall, white or yellow

Mature Height x Spread
1 to 4 ft. x 1 to 3 ft.

Botanical Pronunciation
hy-men-oh-KAL-lis

Zones 8 to 10

The first spider lily I grew was given to me by a friend who was moving and couldn't take it along. I casually parked the large bulb in an out-of-the-way spot, planning to move it later. Despite rocky soil and benign neglect, it thrived and bloomed every summer with its elegant, dangling white flowers. There is one form, possibly the one I had, known as 'Tropical Giant' that has been grown for a long time, and although ascribed to numerous species, it has uncertain and unknown origins. This common form has large semi-evergreen, deep green strappy leaves. The flowers are a thin saucer from which narrow, draping petals fall. It usually flowers in July, and its huge flowers have a delightful sweet smell.

When, Where, and How to Plant
Set out bulbs in spring or summer once the soil is warm. Spider lily grows well in almost any well-drained soil. However, plants grow larger and bloom more reliably with the addition of generous amounts of compost or other organic matter, either at planting or as mulch during the growing season. Some spider lilies grow naturally in swamps, and these species require moist, fertile soils that are consistently wet. Place the bulb so that two thirds of the bulb and all of the neck are above the soil surface. Water weekly until leaves emerge.

Growing Tips
Most spider lilies grow equally well with or without additional fertilizer. If you choose to fertilize established bulbs, apply slow-release or balanced organic fertilizer once in spring. Keep the roots cool and moist with a 3- to 4-inch layer of mulch and water every seven to ten days while growing.

Regional Advice and Care
Remove finished flower stalks anytime. The attractive leaves of spider lily grow for a long time after flowering. Most species are at least semi-evergreen and a few leaves wilt and die in the late summer. During this resting time, reduce the frequency of watering and do not fertilize. Spider lily bulbs multiply slowly and resent being disturbed. These species are not susceptible to pest or disease.

Companion Planting and Design
The bulbs of the large hybrid varieties increase in size over the years with ever more blooming stalks, making them dramatic specimens or focal plants. Smaller varieties do well in containers or planters, particularly in areas where it is too cold to leave them in the ground year-round.

Try These
Hymenocallis lirosme and its hybrids are commonly grown, reliable, spring-flowering plants that prefer moist soils. *H. latifolia* is a denizen of ponds and even the beach. The native *H. galvestonensis* is a gray-leaved species whose summer flowers emerge on naked stalks before the leaves, a unique feature in this genus. *H. caroliniana* is native in East Texas, growing to 2 feet with heads of six large white flowers.

DESERT PERENNIALS

The term *desert perennials* as used here covers a wide array of plants that don't fit neatly into other categories. Although they are all perennial, in the gardening world the term *perennial* is used mainly for herbaceous plants. Many are succulents, but quite a few are not completely so. Some have tall stems, but none have true wood like trees or shrubs.

This widely disparate group includes aloes, agaves, yuccas, manfreda, sotol, bear grass, and cactus. All of these plants have a legion of adaptations to cope with long periods without rain, almost always in conjunction with high heat. Most have leaves arranged in rosettes, a form where the leaves are arranged around a central axis, like a rose blossom that funnels water to their roots.

Century plant

Low-Water Winners

Knowing some of these adaptations helps gardeners care for them appropriately. These are exquisite long-lived garden plants that provide vivid contrast and superb performance in Texas gardens. They form a dynamic group of plants that should be included generously in any garden that seeks to minimize its water use but stay vibrant and lovely.

Succulents are plants with specialized water-storing tissue found either in their leaves (as in aloes) or stems (as in cacti). Agaves are somewhere in between, with succulent bases to their fibrous leaves. Succulent parts of a plant are hard and firm when healthy and are coated with a waxy cuticle to hold in as much water as possible.

But it is the root system in these plants that is so important to gardeners. The root system fans out from the central axis like a wheel with countless tiny, small feeding roots forming a web-like root system. When the soil reaches a critical level of dry, these small feeding roots die off. When the soil is moist again, they grow back, often in a matter of days. While the roots are alive, they take up moisture without stopping.

This unique root system occurs in all succulents, as well as in agaves. It is why it is important to water them at long intervals, when the soil is almost dry. There is no

Prickly pear cactus fruit

shut-off or feedback system in these roots, as there is in other plants. If there is water, roots continue to take up water often to the point that the plant collapses or splits.

It is also why these plants can be left bare root, without any soil, for long periods of time in the shade between plantings. For all succulents, allowing the roots to dry out when transplanting is an excellent practice to prevent root rot.

Yucca, bear grass, manfreda, and sotol are somewhat different. These plants are semi-succulent, but not entirely so, and although they have a similar root system, they do not have quite the same on-again-off-again strategy. These plants resent being bare rooted for any length of time and need to be transplanted just as one would a shrub or a tree. They do not require excessive amounts of water when in the ground but often accept more than true succulents.

All of these plants require spectacular drainage to thrive regardless of soil type. Look at the individual profiles to understand their sun preference.

All of these plants grow well in containers. This is a way to have more variety in cold climates or in areas that are consistently wet, particularly in the winter. The shallow root system and symmetrical nature of most of these plants makes them attractive in any pot that accentuates their form.

Container Culture

When grown in containers, culture is much the same. Begin with a fast-draining mix. Test to be sure that all the water in the pot is used up before watering. This is a more accurate way to water these plants than establishing a time interval. Check pot moisture with a stick, a pencil, a long screwdriver, a moisture meter, or your finger. Once dry, water thoroughly. The time between waterings will vary with the temperatures, but it is always best to err on the side of dry with these plants.

Aloe

Aloe spp.

Bloom Period and Seasonal Color
Winter to early spring, red, orange, coral, pink, yellow

Mature Height x Spread 1 to 5 ft. x 1 to 5 ft.

Botanical Pronunciation AL-oh

Zones 9 to 10

Aloes are a brilliant succulent choice for gardens with moderate winters. The thick, succulent leaves range from dark green to pale blue-gray. The winter-blooming flowers occur on long stalks in soft shades of coral, pink, and red. Hummingbirds are strongly attracted to the flowers, making them a welcome winter food source. The mainstay of medicinal gardens, *Aloe vera* has long, linear, fleshy leaves with tiny projections along the margins. It has both yellow- or orange-flowering forms and suckers from the base prolifically. Many aloes are too cold tender for use outside, but there is a wide range of cold and sun tolerance in this huge genus of African succulents. Luckily, all aloes do well in containers growing for decades on a patio or a porch.

When, Where, and How to Plant
Plant aloes in the spring after all danger of frost is past and soil temperatures are at least 65 degrees Fahrenheit. In the western and southern parts of Texas, provide relief from afternoon sun. Aloes grow in a wide range of soils from well-drained, fertile soils to rocky or sandy soils. Regardless of soil type, they need sharp drainage. Soil amendments are rarely necessary, but adding compost or gravel to heavy clays will improve the drainage, as will placing the plants in raised mounds or beds. Set in slightly above the soil line. Water immediately following planting.

Growing Tips
Aloes need no supplemental fertilizer. Water established plants carefully, making sure the soil is completely dry between waterings. This could be as long as four to six weeks in the winter and up to monthly in the summer, depending on temperature and natural rainfall.

Regional Advice and Care
Remove dead flowering stalks or leaves anytime. To prune living leaves of *Aloe vera* for medicinal use, cut with a sharp knife at an angle so that water does not collect. In all other species, resist pruning living leaves; it invites infection. Aloes are not susceptible to pests or disease but can develop root rot or sudden stem rotting when overwatered or grown in poorly drained soils.

Companion Planting and Design
Mix aloes with other succulents or among other drought-tolerant plants to provide winter color. Plant generously near seating areas, patios, or pools both for their long cool-season blooms and to attract hummingbirds. Aloes are excellent plants in containers or planters. The flowering stalks make good cut flowers. Aloes are particularly useful in areas of dry shade.

Try These
There are hundreds of species and some hybrids. Cold hardiness is highly variable, so check with a local cactus and succulent society or succulent grower for the best choices for your area. *Aloe saponaria*, a small, clumping aloe with yellow, orange, or coral flowers, thrives outdoors in the southern half of the state. The lightly spotted leaves of this cold-hardy plant (Zone 8) are also attractive.

Beaked Yucca

Yucca rostrata

Bloom Period and Seasonal Color
Spring to summer, white

Mature Height x Spread
6 to 15 ft. x 6 to 10 ft.

Botanical Pronunciation
YUK-ah row-STRAH-tah

Some plants need time to mature into their beauty, others start out gorgeous right away. That is the case with beaked yucca; it is beautiful no matter how young or mature it is. Young plants are rounded balls of thin, narrow, stiff, blue-gray leaves. They end in a rigid, short spine and have a narrow, yellow margin that is seen to best advantage when they are backlit. Mature plants rise on tall, generally straight stems. Flowers are like most yucca, bell-shaped and pure white, and are held in tall, branched stalks high over the rosette of leaves. This is one of the most drought tolerant of all yuccas, at any age, and its cold tolerance permits it to be grown throughout the state.

When, Where, and How to Plant
Plant in spring after soils have warmed. In cold winter areas, it can be planted in early summer with good results. Beaked yucca grows in any soil, including highly alkaline ones and those that are almost pure sand, but drainage is the key to its success. Select a site with excellent, fast drainage, and if there are heavy soils, raise the bed or plant it on a mound. This species will rot quickly in poorly drained areas or where water collects. Full sun is best, but especially when young, this species grows well in filtered shade.

Growing Tips
Beaked yucca needs no supplemental fertilizer. Water at long intervals; providing deep waterings every three to four weeks in summer is ample. In most areas of the state, this species grows on natural rainfall once established.

Regional Advice and Care
Cut dead leaves close to the stem leaving a small piece attached to the stem. Yucca stems are not wood, and these old leaf bases are protection against insects and disease. Never rip or tear off leaves. Borers sometimes invade yuccas; use appropriate borer controls sparingly and only when infestations are evident.

Companion Planting and Design
When young, beaked yucca is an attractive addition to any large perennial or succulent planting. The naturally rounded form and strong leaf color make it a good contrast to leafier, green companions. Mature plants need plenty of vertical space and become outstanding focal or accent plants.

Try These
Thompson's yucca (*Yucca thompsoniana*) was once thought to be a variety of this species. It has shorter leaves and tends to form multiple rosettes on branched 7-foot stems. Blue yucca (*Y. rigida*) is a stunning Mexican species with deep bluish leaves and big heads of creamy white flowers. It routinely makes more than one head, adding a dramatic effect to any garden. Soaptree yucca (*Y. elata*) is the tallest native yucca. It is easily recognized by its narrow, white-lined leaves and crowds of tangled filaments at their base. Flowering stalks of this species tower over the plant rising up to 20 feet.

Century Plant

Agave americana

Bloom Period and Seasonal Color
Summer, occasionally winter, golden yellow

Mature Height x Spread 5 ft. x 7 ft.

Botanical Pronunciation
ah-GAH-vay ah-mare-eh-KAH-nah

Zones 8 to 10

Century plant (also known as blue agave) is grown throughout the world for its sturdy, blue-green leaves that spread slightly and have small teeth along the margin ending with a sharp spine. The surface of the leaf feels glassy and smooth, a trait missing in its countless hybrid forms. The waxy flowers are held in groups (umbels) on huge stalks that are up to ten times the height of the plant. Plants live for a long time but die after flowering. Century plant produces numerous offsets (pups) from the base but rarely sets seed. This species was one of the first agaves brought to Europe by the Spanish explorers. There is evidence that it is not a wild species, but an agricultural selection developed for food and fiber by native peoples.

When, Where, and How to Plant
Plant in fall or spring in warm winter or frost-free areas, elsewhere plant in the spring when soils are warm. Century plant tolerates a wide range of soils as long as they are well drained. Plants succumb to root rots quickly in heavy or poorly drained soils. Dig a hole that is two to three times wider than the container and as deep. Set the plant so that the base is slightly above the soil line. Water immediately following planting.

Growing Tips
Century plant does not need supplemental fertilization when growing in the ground. Fertilize container grown plants with a slow-release fertilizer once in the spring. Water infrequently, no more than every other week in summer, and rely on natural rainfall alone in the winter.

Regional Advice and Care
Dead leaves or flowering stalks may be removed anytime. Resist pruning living leaves; it invites infection. Pups may be removed anytime. Century plant is susceptible to agave snout weevil. If this weevil is a problem in your area, prevent or minimize damage by application of imidacloprid from March to June and follow label directions carefully.

Companion Planting and Design
Century plant is a stunning accent or focal point in any garden. Site it where the large leaves have ample room and pose no danger to passersby. This agave is excellent in large containers.

Try These
There are a number of yellow variegated forms of century plant. A smaller variegate, less than half the normal size, is the white striped 'Mediopicta'. Hybrids with *Agave scabra* are common and are stunning with the recurved leaves and the prominent marginal teeth typical of that species. These hybrids are among the most cold-hardy forms. *A. franzosinni* is closely related with bluish to pure white long leaves. *A. weberi* is large but less aggressively armed agave with wide, gray-green leaves. This species rarely has more than vestigial marginal teeth and a soft terminal spine. It is generally less hardy than century plant. The most cold-hardy large agave is the deep green *A. salmiana*, which is undamaged at 5 degrees Fahrenheit.

Desert Prickly Pear

Opuntia engelmannii

Bloom Period and Seasonal Color
Spring, yellow, gold, orange

Mature Height x Spread 1 to 3 ft. x 4 to 6 ft.

Botanical Pronunciation
oh-PUN-tee-uh ing-el-MAN-ee-eye

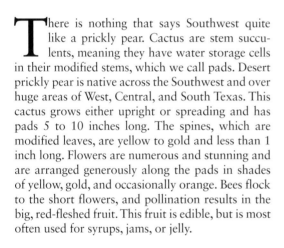

There is nothing that says Southwest quite like a prickly pear. Cactus are stem succulents, meaning they have water storage cells in their modified stems, which we call pads. Desert prickly pear is native across the Southwest and over huge areas of West, Central, and South Texas. This cactus grows either upright or spreading and has pads 5 to 10 inches long. The spines, which are modified leaves, are yellow to gold and less than 1 inch long. Flowers are numerous and stunning and are arranged generously along the pads in shades of yellow, gold, and occasionally orange. Bees flock to the short flowers, and pollination results in the big, red-fleshed fruit. This fruit is edible, but is most often used for syrups, jams, or jelly.

When, Where, and How to Plant
Plant in the late spring once soils are warmed. Planting may continue through the summer. Good drainage is essential, but desert prickly pear grows in a wide range of soils. If the drainage is poor, create a mound or raised bed. Before planting, take the plant out of the pot, shake off most of the soil, and set it in a dry, shady location for a few days before planting. This practice allows the roots to heal from transplanting and prevents root rot.

Growing Tips
Desert prickly pear never need supplemental fertilization. Although capable of withstanding extreme drought, desert prickly pear looks best if watered every three to four weeks in the hottest part of the summer. Rely on natural rainfall in the winter unless there is no rain for over 60 days.

Regional Advice
Pads that are decrepit, diseased, or otherwise unsightly can be pruned anytime it is hot. Cut at the joint, and if the weather is particularly humid, apply powdered sulphur to seal the cut. Prickly pear can be attacked by a variety of sucking and chewing insects. A few insects cause minimal harm, but they multiply quickly. It is best to treat them quickly by either hand removal or contact insecticides to prevent large infestations.

Companion Planting and Design
Desert prickly pear blends with other drought-adapted plants and offers excellent textural and structural contrast. Use as part of boundary planting, to secure a corner, or in a mixed succulent planting. They make a fine hedge that will deter most traffic and are useful in parts of a garden that receive minimal care.

Try These
'Cow Tongue' has elongated, narrowed pads and typically grows tall, often to 10 feet. The similar *Opuntia phaecantha* has light green pads and bright yellow flowers but has dark spines. The erect purple prickly pear (*O. violacea*) has purple-tinged pads, dark spines, and bright yellow flowers. Black-spined prickly pear (*O. macrocentra*) is similar but grows low and has long, jet black spines.

Pale-Leaved Yucca

Yucca pallida

Bloom Period and Seasonal Color
Summer, white

Mature Height x Spread
1 to 2 ft. x 2 to 3 ft.

Botanical Pronunciation
YUK-ah PAL-ih-duh

Texas enjoys a number of native yucca, but I think pale-leaved yucca may be its most beautiful. This attractive yucca occurs in a small range running from the Dallas metroplex west to near Killeen and Waco. In nature, it is often found in grasslands, and this clue indicates that it does well in light shade. The leaves are light blue-gray with prominent ribs running along their length. There are few leaves, and although it produces offsets, they are few as well. Flowers are like most yucca, white hanging bells held on a tall, branched stalk. Moths pollinate yucca, and in most species there is only one species of moth that performs this duty. Because of this, plants in cultivation often have poor seed set.

When, Where, and How to Plant
Plant in fall or spring in warm winter areas but wait until the soil warms in the spring where winters are colder. Pale-leaved yucca tolerates a wide variety of soils, including alkaline ones as long as there is sharp drainage. Plants rot quickly in situations of poor drainage or where water ponds or stands. To help where drainage is poor, in very wet areas, plant slightly higher than the soil line or create mounds or raised beds. No soil amendments are necessary.

Growing Tips
Apply slow-release or organic fertilizer annually in spring. Pale-leaved yucca benefits from a light mulch in the summer. Take care that the mulch does not collect within the base of the leaves. Water established plants every two to three weeks in the summer, depending on rainfall and temperature.

Natural rainfall within its native range is sufficient in winter unless is exceptionally hot or dry or in hot, desert areas.

Regional Advice and Care
Remove any dead leaves when they pull away in your hand. Cut living leaves with care and be sure to leave a small segment attached to the base. Remove spent flowering stalks anytime. Yuccas are occasionally infested with borers but otherwise are not susceptible to pests or disease.

Companion Planting and Design
Blend pale-leaved yucca with low-growing perennials or succulents to take advantage of its lovely coloring and textural contrast. Owing to its small size, this yucca is particularly well suited to patio plantings or to be used in other tight spots. It also grows well in containers.

Try These
Twisted leaf yucca (*Yucca rupicola*) is a slightly larger species and has narrower, light to deep green leaves with a visible twist at mid-leaf. Its natural range extends far enough north for the two species to intergrade, and these blended forms can be extremely attractive. One such intergrade is sold as *Y. pallida*, but it has large, wide leaves with a decided twist that is absent in pure species. Buckley's yucca (*Y. constricta*) is somewhat larger with narrow, stiff, gray-green leaves, and it usually grows on a short prominent stem.

Plains Yucca

Yucca glauca

Bloom Period and Seasonal Color
Summer, white

Mature Height x Spread 1 to 3 ft. x 2 to 4 ft.

Botanical Pronunciation
YUK-ah GLOK-ah

Zones 7 to 9

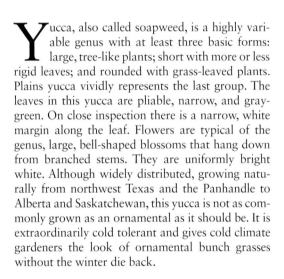

Yucca, also called soapweed, is a highly variable genus with at least three basic forms: large, tree-like plants; short with more or less rigid leaves; and rounded with grass-leaved plants. Plains yucca vividly represents the last group. The leaves in this yucca are pliable, narrow, and gray-green. On close inspection there is a narrow, white margin along the leaf. Flowers are typical of the genus, large, bell-shaped blossoms that hang down from branched stems. They are uniformly bright white. Although widely distributed, growing naturally from northwest Texas and the Panhandle to Alberta and Saskatchewan, this yucca is not as commonly grown as an ornamental as it should be. It is extraordinarily cold tolerant and gives cold climate gardeners the look of ornamental bunch grasses without the winter die back.

When, Where, and How to Plant
Plant plains yucca in any season except the coldest part of the winter, although spring planting gives the plant the longest time to establish a healthy root system. Plains yucca grows in a wide variety of soils, but deep, fertile, well-drained ones suit it best. If there is poor drainage or places where rainfall is abundant, situate the plant on a mound or raised area of the garden. When planting arrange the plant with its base slightly above the soil line and be sure there is no opportunity for water to pond around it.

Growing Tips
Plains yucca need no supplemental fertilization. Water established plants every two to three weeks in summer, although plains yucca grows satisfactorily on natural rainfall within its native range. Natural rainfall in the winter is sufficient in all zones unless there has been no precipitation for over sixty days.

Regional Advice and Care
Remove dead leaves any time during warm weather. Prune living leaves only when absolutely required. Cut as close to the stem as possible, leaving a tiny piece of the leaf attached. Never shear or cut across the plant, as you would with a grass. Yucca leaves do not regenerate from this type of pruning. Plains yucca is rarely bothered by insects or disease.

Companion Planting and Design
Plains yucca blends well with small evergreens or seasonal perennial plantings. Because of its cold hardiness it offers a solid anchor for a winter garden. Use it generously to form a border or fill in a space that is hard to maintain.

Try These
Throughout the West there are grass-leaved yuccas that resemble this species and can be used similarly. These include the most western, *Yucca harrimaniae* and *Y. angustifolia*. In the more humid South, *Yucca filamentosa* has wider leaves but is also remarkably cold hardy. *Y. gloriosa* var. *recurvifolia* grows to 3 feet tall with stiff, deep green, ribbed leaves. This widely grown yucca has excellent heat tolerance coupled with cold hardiness to Zone 7 and lower. There is a yellow variegated form of this species that is equally hardy.

Red Hesperaloe

Hesperaloe parviflora

Other Name Red yucca

Bloom Period and Seasonal Color
Spring through summer, coral, pink, yellow

Mature Height x Spread 3 to 4 ft. x 3 to 6 ft.

Botanical Pronunciation
hes-per-AL-o par-vi-FLOOR-uh

Red hesperaloe is one of the most reliable and widely used of all desert perennials, except perhaps century plant. The narrow, gray-green leaves roll inward and are crowded into a tight rosette. Plants spread quickly from root suckers and form dense clumps that can be difficult to separate. The flowering stalks tower over the foliage. The stalk is usually a spike, but other forms have branched or arching stalks. The narrow, tubular flowers are bright pink to coral, often with a creamy center. Flowers open in sequence, and the entire bloom can last for months. Hummingbirds are steady visitors to these flowers. Many gardeners leave the dead stalk for years because they are used by these birds and ladder-back woodpeckers as perches.

When, Where, and How to Plant
Plant in spring after the soil is warm; in cold winter areas, planting can continue into early summer. Red hesperaloe tolerates almost any type of soil, including highly alkaline ones as long as they are extremely well drained. If your soil is heavy or the drainage is poor, add generous amounts of expanded shale, gravel, or compost and create a mound. Dig a wide hole and position the plant slightly higher than the soil line. Soil amendments are not necessary. Water immediately.

Growing Tips
Red hesperaloe does not need supplemental fertilizer. Water newly planted plants every two to four weeks in summer, depending on natural rainfall and temperature. In most of the state, established plants rarely need more than intermittent supplemental watering and usually grow well on natural rainfall. It is best to provide long, deep soaks at long intervals rather than brief, shallow watering.

Regional Advice and Care
Remove finished blooming stalks anytime. Remove dead leaves only if they will pull away in your hand, or cut them as close to the base as possible. Never shear or cut leaves straight across. Leaves grow only from the base, and such pruning ruins the form of the plant. Red hesperaloe is not susceptible to pests or disease.

Companion Planting and Design
Red hesperaloe mixes well with perennials and other succulents, providing striking textural contrast. It is immune to heat, making it excellent around pools or against hot walls or other areas where reflected heat is intense. Use red hesperaloe to form an informal border, fill in barren spots, or to line drives, walkways or large beds.

Try These
Giant hesperaloe (*Hesperaloe funifera*) has large, broad, stiff leaves and a massive, branched flowering stalk with night-opening, white flowers. Beautiful hybrids between the two abound with the big, open flowers of the larger plant and the coral colors of the smaller. Bell-flowered hesperaloe (*H. campanulata*) has finer leaves and flared pink flowers. *H. nocturna* has grass-like leaves and branched flowering stalks with flared, white flowers that open at night. All are hardy to at least Zone 8.

Sotol

Dasylirion texanum

Bloom Period and Seasonal Color
Summer, inconspicuous creamy white

Mature Height x Spread 3 to 4 ft. x 4 to 5 ft.

Botanical Pronunciation
DAZ-ih-leer-ee-on tex-AN-um

Sotol grows hundreds of thin, shiny dark green leaves along a short trunk. The effect is of a fountain of leaves. These rugged plants from the Hill Country and west easily replace bunch grasses with considerably less water and care. Sotol is at home in dry gardens throughout the state. Flowers are tiny and insignificant by themselves, but they occur by the thousands in an 8-foot stalk that resembles a plume. Hillsides of this plant are striking when the plants are in bloom. In some species, particularly in Mexico, the new leaves are used for the weaving of fine ornaments, mats, baskets, and bags. The fiber is strong and highly resistant to moisture but as soft and pliable as silk.

When, Where, and How to Plant
Plant in fall or early spring. Established plants are difficult to move, and often resent transplant, so choose a site where the plant can live undisturbed. Sotol grows best in fast-draining soil that is somewhat alkaline, although more fertile soils are fine as long as the drainage is excellent. Dig a hole that is two to three times wider than the container and as deep, but there is not need for soil amendments. Situate the plant so that it is slightly higher than the soil line. Water immediately.

Growing Tips
Sotol does not require regular supplemental fertilizer when grown in ground. Water established plants every two to four weeks in summer, depending on natural rainfall and temperatures. This species rarely needs water in the winter unless there has been no rain for over sixty days.

Regional Advice and Care
The oldest leaves of sotol naturally die off as they age. These leaves can be removed once they will come off with a gentle tug, otherwise leave them to protect the trunk. Leaves grow from the base of the plant only, so shearing or otherwise cutting off leaves ruins the natural form of the plant. Remove spent blooming stalks anytime. Sotol is not susceptible to pests or disease but will rot in heavy or poorly drained soils.

Companion Planting and Design
Mix sotol with other drought-adapted shrubs or perennials to provide contrast to a mixed planting. Plant generously to create borders or for areas where care is minimal. The symmetrical form makes it a striking specimen or focal plant, particularly in a small garden. It grows well in large containers.

Try These
Dasylirion leiophyllum is a larger plant with wider leaves and lacks the frayed tips that are common in this genus. *D. acrotriche* has deep green leaves that end in frayed tips that when viewed from above, making a stunning swirl. Desert spoon (*D. wheeleri*) is larger with longer, blue-gray leaves. *D. longissimum* is even larger, rising up on a stem to 8 feet tall and 6 feet wide with long, stiff, narrow leaves.

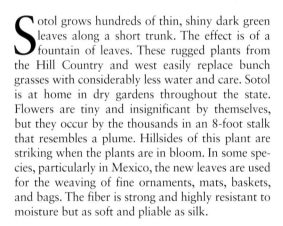

Spanish Dagger

Yucca treculeana

Bloom Period and Seasonal Color
Spring, white

Mature Height x Spread
5 to 25 ft. x 5 to 12 ft.

Botanical Pronunciation
YUK-ah tray-COOL-ee-an-uh

Zones 8 to 10

Spanish dagger is one of easiest of the tree-like yuccas to incorporate into a garden. Although it can become quite tall, it is more common to see it growing less than 10 feet tall. The plant tends to form multiple trunks of roughly the same size. The leaves are smooth and rigid, range from dark green to blue-green, and are lined with a fine brown margin. The flowering stalks are huge, fat plumes of bright white flowers. They do not rise far over the leaves, so that in shorter plants the flowers are easily seen up close. Occurring mainly in Mexico in the states adjacent to Texas, it occurs in Texas in a rough line from the Gulf Coast through Austin to the Pecos River.

When, Where, and How to Plant
Plant in spring or early summer when soils are warm. Plant in full sun or light, filtered shade where there is ample vertical room for the plant. Tolerant of a wide range of soils, even alkaline and sandy ones, Spanish dagger does require excellent drainage. In areas with heavier soils, or where drainage is poor, plant on a raised mound or in large raised beds. Set the plant so that it is slightly higher than the soil line and be sure that water does not pond or stand around the plant.

Growing Tips
Spanish dagger does not need supplemental fertilizer. Water at least monthly, particularly in dry summer areas. In most of its range, established plants grow well on natural rainfall. Rely entirely on natural rainfall in the winter when the plant is more vulnerable to rot from cold, wet soils.

Regional Advice and Care
Spanish dagger has a demonstrated cold tolerance to 10 degrees Fahrenheit, but during extended or extreme cold it may be severely damaged. Wait to clear out any cold-damaged stems until there is no danger of frost and the weather is very warm. Make clean cuts and dust with powdered sulphur to prevent infection. Prune dead leaves to near the stem, leaving a short piece attached. This species is not susceptible to most pests and disease.

Companion Planting and Design
Spanish dagger is a fine choice to accent a corner or serve as a focal plant. Particularly within its native range, it is useful for areas of the garden that do not receive regular watering or care but where the exquisite blooms can be fully enjoyed. Like most yuccas, it does well in a container as long as it is large enough.

Try These
Eastern Spanish dagger (*Y. aloifolia*) tolerates wetter and more acidic conditions better than most other tree-like yuccas. This variety has short, flat, rigid, spine-tipped leaves. Individuals form numerous stems of various heights, and some run along the ground, whereas others are upright. Some forms of this Spanish dagger have a purple caste to their leaves in winter.

Spice Lily

Manfreda maculosa

Bloom Period and Seasonal Color
Summer, chartreuse, maroon, red-brown, cream to pink

Mature Height x Spread 4 to 6 in. x 4 to 6 in.

Botanical Pronunciation
man-FRED-ah mack-YOU-low-suh

I am fond of manfredas with their spotted, soft but brittle leaves and almost clownish blooms. Spice lily is a native manfreda from southern Texas that forms a low rosette of few, narrow leaves that are heavily spotted with maroon. Related to agaves, manfredas likewise send up tall flowering stalks, up to ten times the height of the plant, in the spring. In this genus, however, plants do not die after they bloom. The flowers of spice lily begin white and are delightfully fragrant. They fade to a dusky rose or pink as they age. In all manfredas, the floral parts are thrust out far from the petals, in some species up to 6 inches or more. Opening at night, the flowers attract moths to pollinate them.

When, Where, and How to Plant
Plant spice lily anytime but in the coldest part of the winter. This species is evergreen and continues to grow throughout the year. Provide relief from afternoon sun and do not put where there is strong reflected heat. Spice lily grows in any well-drained soil and should be set on a mound or raised bed when soils are heavy or poorly drained.

Growing Tips
Spice lily requires no supplemental fertilizer. Water established plants every other week in the summer and no more than monthly in the winter. Often natural rainfall is sufficient to grow it well.

Regional Advice and Care
Remove spent flowering stalks as soon as they dry out. Lift and divide in the early summer. Spice lily is not susceptible to pests or disease.

Companion Planting and Design
Mix spice lily with other small succulents such as aloes, gasterias, dudleyas, or sansevieras. Plant generously to form a low, succulent border along a dry walkway. The striking foliage and small size makes spice lily especially useful in large containers or planters.

Try These
Rattlesnake master (*Manfreda virginica*) is native to eastern Texas and is the most cold hardy of all manfredas. Plants are deciduous and bloom in early summer with green to yellow-green extremely fragrant flowers that are typically held in pairs on the stem. The native Siler's tuberose (*M. sileri*) is a short, well-marked plant with bright yellow flowers in the summer. A vigorous form with long, folded, light green, evergreen leaves variously marked with purple and bright chartreuse flowers is a sterile garden hybrid commonly sold as *M. variegata*. It is a vigorous and reliable groundcover for dry locations and tolerates full sun everywhere but West Texas. Manfredas hybridize readily with many agaves. One is 'Macho Mocha', a hybrid with *Agave celsii*, growing 4 to 6 feet across. This striking garden plant has large, wide leaves densely marked with purple splashes and is hardy through Zone 7b. A number of recent selections have emerged, most differentiated by the amount and style of spotting. 'Chocolate Chip' is highly spotted with wavy, almost ruffled, edges.

Texas Bear Grass

Nolina texana

Other Name Sacahuista

Bloom Period and Seasonal Color
Summer, cream, yellow

Mature Height x spread 3 to 6 ft. x 3 to 5 ft.

Botanical Pronunciation
no-LINE-ah tex-AN-ah

*N*olina is a small genus of plants with grassy leaves that thrive in hot, dry conditions. This bear grass is one of the smallest and most refined looking. The light green leaves are thin but wiry, and plants are rarely more than 3 feet tall. It is the most cold hardy as well, able to withstand temperatures to well below zero. I find this species to one of the best substitutes for ornamental grass providing much the same look and feel in the garden, but with little of the care and considerably less water. The flowers are innocuous but are held on stalks that barely rise above the foliage in this species. The dried flowering stalk is attractive as part of a cut or dried arrangement.

When, Where, and How to Plant
Plant in spring as soils begin to warm. This species will grow in full sun to shade. Plants grown in continuous shade need much less water and are subject to rotting if watered too frequently. All nolinas need well-drained soils but will tolerate highly alkaline ones as well as more acidic soils. They do not tolerate heavy or poorly drained soils and in these situations need to be grown on a mound or a raised bed. Dig a hole that is two to three times wider than the container and as deep. Soil amendments are unnecessary, but setting the plant slightly higher than the soil line is helpful.

Growing Tips
Bear grass needs no supplemental fertilizer when grown in the ground. Water established plants every two to three weeks in the summer in the hottest zones, much less often when temperatures are

milder. Rely on natural rainfall in all zones through the winter.

Regional Advice and Care
Remove spent flowering stalks anytime. If dead leaves become prominent, remove by cutting back to the base but do not shear or cut as you would a grass. Bear grass is not susceptible to pests or disease, although root and crown rots may occur in heavy or poorly drained soils.

Companion Planting and Design
Bear grass adds a soft contrast to plantings of agaves, cactus, or other succulents. Plant in mass as you would ornamental grasses to create an informal border or in areas of the garden that receive minimal care. Most species of *Nolina* grow well in containers or planters. The softer leaves of this species makes it leaves make them useful along walkways or around pools.

Try These
Nolina matapensis has broad, dark green leaves. These leaves are long and as the plant grows often hang to the ground as the trunk grows. *N. nelson* has stiff, blue-gray leaves and is especially striking in a large container or as a focal point. Both of these species eventually rise on 4-foot trunks. The rarely offered *N. erumpens* from West Texas has erect but pliable 2- to 6-foot leaves.

Thorn-Crested Agave

Agave lophantha

Bloom Period and Seasonal Color
Summer, occasionally winter, yellow flowers

Mature Height x Spread
20 to 40 in. x 12 to 24 in.

Botanical Pronunciation
ah-GAH-vay LOW-fan-thuh

   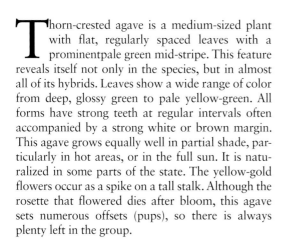

Thorn-crested agave is a medium-sized plant with flat, regularly spaced leaves with a prominentpale green mid-stripe. This feature reveals itself not only in the species, but in almost all of its hybrids. Leaves show a wide range of color from deep, glossy green to pale yellow-green. All forms have strong teeth at regular intervals often accompanied by a strong white or brown margin. This agave grows equally well in partial shade, particularly in hot areas, or in the full sun. It is naturalized in some parts of the state. The yellow-gold flowers occur as a spike on a tall stalk. Although the rosette that flowered dies after bloom, this agave sets numerous offsets (pups), so there is always plenty left in the group.

When, Where, and How to Plant
Plant in spring once the soil has warmed. Planting may continue through the early summer in cooler zones. Thorn-crested agave is tolerant of a wide range of soils, from well-drained, fertile soils to rocky, alkaline ones. Agaves, including this one, succumb to rot and quick decline in heavy or poorly drained soils. Dig a hole two to three times wider and amendments are not necessary. Set the plant in the hole so that the base is slightly above the soil line. Water immediately following planting.

Growing Tips
Thorn-crested agave does not need supplemental fertilization unless it is grown in a container. Fertilize container-grown plants once in the spring, or apply a slow-release fertilizer in the spring. Water established plants every two to four weeks in summer depending on the temperature. Rely on natural rainfall in the winter in all zones.

Regional Advice and Care
Remove completely dead leaves or spent flowering stalks anytime. Try not to prune living leaves unless absolutely necessary. It invites infection. If plants crowd a path or walkway, prune just the tip of the terminal spine for greater safety. Pups may be removed anytime.

Companion Planting and Design
Thorn-crested agave is such a prolific plant it makes a fine groundcover in areas that are out of the way. It blends well with smaller perennials and other succulents as well. It is excellent in containers or raised beds where its stunning leaves can be appreciated. This species is especially useful in areas of the garden that receive minimal care.

Try These
'Quadricolor' is a striking variegate with pale green mid-stripe, lined with deep green, then surrounded by yellow and cream stripes. Shindagger (*Agave lechuguilla*), a hardy native, has narrow, upright deep green to blue-gray leaves that are spotted on the reverse. Thorn-crested agave has been hybridized with shindagger both purposefully and by close association for decades. Some of these hybrids are stunning but are rarely named. Other midsize agaves include the blue-gray, wider-leaved *A. parryi*, *A. havardiana*, and *A. neomexicana*, all of which are hardy in all zones.

GRASSES

Grasses are tied closely with human needs and endeavors. The grains that dominate the human diet—rice, corn, wheat, and barley—are grasses. Livestock, both domesticated and wild, graze extensively on grass, which allows them in turn to provide us with food and other products.

Two Categories of Grasses

As garden plants, grasses break into two categories: turf grasses, which are low growing, annual, or perennial and spread by rhizomes (underground stems) or stolons (flat, elongated stems), and ornamental grasses, which are taller and perennial and grow in congested bunches with dozens of stems.

Ornamental grasses are a beautiful addition to any garden. They add softness, texture, and elegant form. Many are extremely drought tolerant or have showy flowering stalks. Ornamental grasses make a solid wall to frame perennial plants. Planted in mass, ornamental grasses add drama to a difficult spot or line a drive. Grasses hold soil tenaciously and can help stabilize a steep slope.

Choose ornamental grasses that are well-adapted or locally native grasses. Not, but, like all well-suited plants, resist disease and pests better and demand minimal care.

Local natives also do not tend to run amok and become regional pests. And that is the caution about the use of all ornamental grasses, particularly those from analogous but distant locales. Many are fierce competitors without the controls at work in their native land. It is harder to remove aggressive invaders than to be careful about planting them in the first place. Look for grasses that are sterile hybrids or have a demonstrated history of remaining where they are planted.

Lawns Are Demanding, but Popular

I do not care for lawns in a home garden. They are, first of all, too thirsty. Over the entire life of the lawn it will use more water than anything you plant. Lawns also demand enormous amounts of care; feeding and mowing are just the beginning. A lawn never achieves the independence that well-adapted trees and shrubs or many ornamental grasses do. It demands constant care. A bermudagrass lawn, even though winter dormant, requires the equivalent up to *42 inches* of rain a year to stay green.

Together with their heavy water use, it is how they look—blank, boring, and so irrevocably green—that fails to inspire me. The longer I garden, the more I find that the old maxim "Garden where you live" resonates for me. Swards of green do not blend well in my eye with the rich textures of the trees, shrubs, or perennials, especially those that are native or drought-adapted. Succulents are not enhanced by a backdrop of deep, evenly colored green. The rocks, hills, forests, and stunning backdrops found throughout the state are not enhanced for me by ribbons of mowed lawn.

Despite this, lawns continue to be popular, and many gardeners feel they cannot do without a lawn. The best news in lawns is that there is a lot of recent research devoted to developing grasses that are considerably more water conservative than older varieties. Buffalograss leads the way with blends, such as Habiturf™ from the Lady Bird Johnson Wildflower Center, newly available.

Most grasses are healthier when watered with long, deep soaks at weekly or biweekly intervals that soak the entire root zone. Light, daily sprinklings are invitations to shallow rooting, fungal disease, and other lawn problems.

Choose Wisely

To maintain a lawn without breaking the bank on the water bill, consider

Muhlenbergia rigens

these strategies: 1) choose a well-adapted grass for your area; 2) plant only what you use, such as a playground; 3) water correctly, delivering the right amount of water and no more; 4) water early in the morning; and 5) set sprinklers low to the ground to reduce evaporation.

Never be afraid to consider how lovely your garden might be without an expansive lawn. Just think how much time you will have left over without the mowing and constant care to enjoy your Texas garden.

Bermudagrass

Cynodon dactylon

Mature Height x Spread
1.5 to 2 in. x 24 to 48 in.

Botanical Pronunciation
SIN-oh-don DAC-ti-lon

Bermudagrass and about nine related species are native to Africa and Asia and were brought to the Caribbean by the Spanish and ultimately the United States as early as the seventeenth century. Common or pasture bermuda is a coarse plant with widely spaced blades and tall blooming stalks. Improved and hybrid bermudagrass varieties are shorter and denser and spread wider. The modern hybrid forms are sterile as well. These are the commonly grown lawn and pasture grasses today. Bermudagrass is a warm-season grass that is winter dormant in most of the state. It spreads by seed, which it sets prolifically, or long trailing stems (stolons). It is drought tolerant as well as tolerant of extreme heat.

When, Where, and How to Plant
Plant by seed, plugs, or sod in spring after all danger of frost is past and the soil is warm. Turn the soil, working in a generous layer of compost, mulch, and/or lawn fertilizer. Water and let it dry for three days. Water lightly just before planting. Broadcast seed at a rate of 2 pounds per 1,000 square feet. Set out plugs at spacing from 4 to 8 inches. Use 10 to 15 bushels of stolons for most of the sterile hybrids. After planting, by any of these methods, water two to four times a day for the first two weeks and then once a day for the next two weeks or until seed germinates or plugs or sod are established.

Growing Tips
Apply lawn or organic fertilizer two weeks after seedlings emerge or plugs or sod were installed. Fertilize weekly until the lawn is entirely filled in.

Fertilize established lawns beginning four to six weeks after last frost and then every ten weeks while actively growing. Water established lawns to apply 1 inch of water per week, reducing that to every other week when temperatures are below 90 degrees Fahrenheit and then once a month in winter.

Regional Advice and Care
Mow regularly, taking no more than one-third of the blade each time. Bermudagrass lawns are susceptible to pearl scale and fungal disease when the soil is compacted or drainage is poor. Prevent these problems with regular aeration and dethatching.

Companion Planting and Design
Lawns form a frame or background for colorful perennial flower beds. Bermudagrass lawns form play areas for children and pets.

Try These
There is an astounding number of bermudagrass choices. Bermudagrass is invasive and runs away from cultivation quickly. Using sterile forms helps, but even they spread easily by stolons. Check with local authorities or county agents for the best varieties for your area. Many of the fine textured Tif-type hybrids are most useful on golf courses but can have maintenance issues in home gardens.

Blue Fescue

Festuca glauca

Mature Height x Spread
4 to 12 in. x 6 to 12 in.

Botanical Pronunciation
fess-TOO-cuh GLOK-ah

Zones 7 to 8

Blue fescue is a perennial grass with numerous thin leaves that are a remarkable, powdery blue. Plants are tidy looking, like a globe of blue. In some selections the color is so brilliant the plants look painted. Blue fescue is native to southern France and grows best in areas that are neither severely cold nor exceptionally hot. This grass is a cool-season grower, and hot, humid conditions reduce its vigor and appearance. Blue fescue spreads gently and is rarely invasive in the garden. The flowering stalks emerge in late spring or summer. These attractive spikes are tall and thin, rising high above the foliage, and are numerous in well-established plants. They begin as blue as the foliage but fade to a light tan.

When, Where, and How to Plant
Set out transplants in early spring as soon as soil can be worked. Blue fescue is very shade tolerant but also does well in full sun. Choose a well-drained, fertile soil and amend it with compost or other organic matter to improve drainage if needed. Dig a hole that is two or more times the width of the container and as deep. Set the plant in slightly higher than the soil line, backfill, and water in thoroughly.

Growing Tips
Apply slow-release or organic fertilizer annually in spring. Use a thin layer of mulch to keep soil evenly moist. Established plants are significantly drought tolerant and in cool-summer climates grow well on natural rainfall. If the weather is exceptionally hot or dry, water twice monthly in summer.

Regional Advice
Plants often die out in the center after a few years, particularly if stressed by high heat or too much water in the winter. Cut back severely in fall to tidy it up and prolong the life of the grass. Shear or remove flowering stalks in summer once they are done blooming. Blue fescue is not susceptible to pests or disease.

Companion Planting and Design
The stunning blue to silvery leaves make blue fescue an excellent choice to mix with smaller perennials or annuals. It is often used generously as a groundcover or to fill a space that is hard to maintain regularly. Because of its smaller size, blue fescue grows well in containers, either singly or in a mixed planting. It also makes a tidy edging for a large bed, or along a drive or walkway.

Try These
'Elijah Blue', with deep silver-blue leaves, is a durable and long-lived selection. 'Blaufink' grows to 6 inches tall with silver-blue foliage. 'Blauglut' ('Blue Glow') has intense blue-gray foliage. 'Blue Silver' ('Blaussilber') is one of the best of the silver-leaved forms. 'Siskiyou Blue' has bright, shimmering blue foliage. Seeigel ('Sea Urchin') has thin, hairlike leaves. 'Daeumling' ('Tom Thumb') grows to 4 inches tall. 'Harz' has dark olive green leaves tinted with purple. 'Caesia' has intense vivid blue foliage.

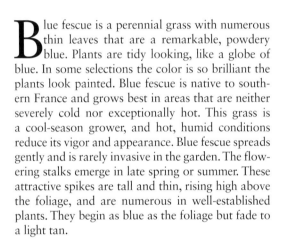

Buffalograss

Bouteloua dactyloides

Mature Height x Spread
2 to 6 in. x 2 to 6 in.

Botanical Pronunciation
boot-ah-LOO-ah dak-till-LOY-deez

Zones 7 to 9

Buffalograss is a native grass that is gaining in popularity as a turf grass in Texas. Plants form colonies from their underground stems (rhizomes) and over time form the closed cover that most gardeners prefer in a lawn. Blades are thin and usually have a blue-green color. In winter and during extended drought, buffalograss is dormant. Many older selections were slow to cover all the ground, allowing the penetration of weeds, but newer selections are denser and fill in better. Buffalograss grows naturally throughout the state except for the Trans-Pecos and eastern piney woods. Within its natural range, it is an outstanding choice for a lawn or as erosion control without the need for intensive watering, feeding, and mowing that all other lawn grasses require.

When, Where, and How to Plant
Plant buffalograss in the full sun; it declines dramatically in shade. Sow seed or set out transplants in spring as soon as the soil can be worked. Prepare the area by lightly raking or turning the soil, removing any large obstructions and breaking up any clods. Rake to smooth, apply a thin layer of good-quality compost, well-composted manure, or other organic matter solely or mixed. Broadcast at a rate of a half to 5 pounds per 1,000 square feet, depending on the type of seed. Water in thoroughly.

Growing Tips
Buffalograss does not need fertilization but responds to a light application of nitrogen once in the spring. Water established buffalograss with infrequent, deep soaks, down to 6 inches or more, rather than with overhead sprinklers. One inch of water per week is adequate to maintain buffalograss as turf. Use a soaker hose, garden hose, or even drip irrigation to water to avoid overhead sprays.

Regional Advice and Care
Mow to a height of no less than 2 inches, or leave to grow to its natural height. Buffalograss grows more slowly than other lawn grasses, so mowing is often at two- to three-week intervals. Buffalograss is not susceptible to pests or disease.

Companion Planting and Design
Buffalograss is best used in areas that do not receive steady, heavy foot traffic. This makes it a good choice for meadow or naturalistic wildflower planting as well as areas that are the edge of the garden. It is also a good choice near the reflected heat of exposed walls or pools.

Try These
'Prairie' and '609' produce dense, uniform turf from sod or plugs. 'Stampede' grows to only 4 inches tall. 'Cody' has good winter hardiness and deep color and establishes rapidly. 'Sharp's Improved' is a seeded variety. 'Tech Turf' was developed for its drought tolerance and is reported to stay on a mere 2 inches of water a month. 'Habiturf™' is a blend of buffalograss, blue gramma (*Bouteloua gracilis*), and curly mesquite (*Hilaria belangeri*) offered by the LBJ Wildflower Center for Texas.

Gulf Muhly

Muhlenbergia capillaris

Other Name Sweet grass

Bloom Period and Seasonal Color Fall, pink

Mature Height x Spread
3 to 4 ft. x 1 to 3 ft.

Botanical Pronunciation
muh-len-BERG-ee-ah kap-ill-AIR-iss

Zones 8 to 10

If you walk around in the old town of Charleston, South Carolina, you find artists selling baskets from what they call sweet grass. The baskets are lovely and tight and in tones of tan and brown. They are made from the dried blades of Gulf muhly and are just one of the countless charms of this species. As an ornamental, Gulf muhly is a modest-sized, clumping perennial grass with thin, wiry stems. It is in the fall when Gulf muhly's tall plumes of flowers arise that its great glory for a gardener emerges. The plumes range from light to dark pink and are brilliant when grown in mass or backlit. Tough, durable, and immune to heat, it is one of the most easily grown ornamental grass.

When, Where, and How to Plant

Plant in spring after all danger of frost is past and the soil is warm. Plants grow and flower best in full sun but tolerate partial shade in hot areas. Avoid deep shade. Gulf muhly grows in almost any soil from dry, rocky ones to sandy, moist soils. Any average soil is fine, and only light amendment is needed. Set out transplants so that the crown is slightly above the soil line.

Growing Tips

Fertilize Gulf muhly once a year in spring as the new growth emerges. In hot, humid climates with reliable summer rain, Gulf muhly grows well on natural rainfall. Where summer rainfall is less certain, water established plants every two to three weeks in the summer. Use a soaker hose, garden hose, or drip irrigation and be sure to water deeply, up to 6 inches.

Regional Advice and Care

Cut back the plant in the spring before growth begins to within 6 inches of the soil line. This will reinvigorate the plant and provide access to any dead or decrepit stems, which can be removed. Gulf muhly has no pests or disease problems.

Companion Planting and Design

The exquisite flowering is best enjoyed by planting generously to fill a corner or section of the garden that does not receive regular maintenance. Placing the plants so that they are backlit in the fall creates a dramatic effect. Gulf muhly also blends well with other perennials or even succulents in a large bed.

Try These

'Regal Mist™' has dark pink plumes. *Muhlenbergia* is a large genus that has over fifty species such as big muhly (*Muhlenbergia lindheimeri*), which has silvery plumes in the fall that are 4 to 6 feet tall. Seep muhly (*M. reverchonii*) has short pink to cream plumes in autumn. Deer grass (*M. rigens*) is widely used in hot, dry, arid regions and is known by its stiff, dark green leaves and thin, tan flowering stalks. Bamboo muhly (*M. dumosa*) has jointed, bamboo-like stems and long, dissected blades that give it a feathery look. It is particularly attractive in large containers.

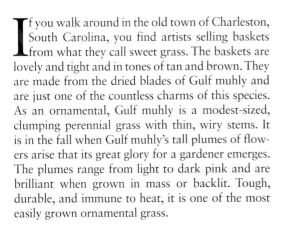

Inland Sea Oats

Chasmanthium latifolium

Bloom Period and Seasonal Color
Summer to fall

Mature Height x Spread
2 to 4 ft. x 2 to 6 ft.

Botanical Pronunciation
kaz-MAN-thee-um lah-teh-FOLE-ee-um

Zones 8 to 10

It isn't often that you find a good-looking ornamental grass that will grow in the shade, yet inland sea oats does just that. This short grass has long, wide blades that nod and fall over the stems. The flowering heads are made up of flattened spikelets that strongly resemble the beach-dwelling sea oat's flowering head. The striking heads rise up and then arch over the leaves, making a graceful accent to the foliage. Heads are first a light green and then turn red or bronze in the autumn, finally fading to tan. They are persistent for months and make excellent dried flowers. Inland sea oats is native from Texas east through most of the southeast and is found in wooded slopes and moist areas and alongside creeks.

When, Where, and How to Plant
Plant by transplant in fall. Broadcast seed in the late summer or early fall. Inland sea oats grows best in filtered or even deep shade. In cold areas it will tolerate full sun but needs more watering to thrive in that condition. It is not necessary to amend the soil, but it does help to remove other plants, especially grasses, and rake the soil lightly. Seed germinates best when there is good contact with the ground. Inland sea oats grows well in poorly drained soils and those that stay moist more or less continuously. Even heavy clay is congenial to this species. If using seed to cover a large area, broadcast at 2 pounds per 1,000 square feet for best results.

Growing Tips
Fertilize inland sea oats once in the spring as new growth emerges. Water to maintain even, continuous moisture around the roots. Heavy mulch, up to 4 inches deep, throughout the summer helps maintain the moisture it needs without excessive watering.

Regional Advice and Care
Cut inland sea oats back severely in the early spring to within 4 inches of the soil line. If plants grow too quickly or get too large, cut again in May or June by about half its height. Inland sea oats is not susceptible to pests or disease.

Companion Planting and Design
Inland sea oats is outstanding in moist, shady conditions, such as around the north side of a house or patio. Plants reseed and spread easily, making it a good choice to fill a poorly drained corner or other spot that is hard to maintain. Its twin needs for moisture and shade make it ideal in woodland or creekside planting.

Try These
Sea oats (*Uniola paniculata*) grows along the dunes and beachheads of the Gulf coast of Texas and up the Atlantic coast through Virginia. This is a much larger species, with tall, elegant flowering heads. If you live near the beach, then treasure it; in most areas it is a protected species and diminishing in number. Sea oats is hardy to Zone 8.

Maidengrass

Miscanthus sinensis

Bloom Period and Seasonal Color
Summer to fall, tan

Mature Height x Spread 2 to 10 ft. x 6 to 8 ft.

Botanical Pronunciation
mis-KAN-thus sigh-nin-sis

Zones 7 to 9

Maidengrass is clump-forming, perennial grass native to Japan, China, and Korea. Many forms are huge and need adequate space in the garden, whereas others are selected for variegated leaves or their fall foliage color. All maidengrass flowers in late summer to fall with tall plumes of tan flowers. The heads are delicate and create a pleasing wave of color in a gentle breeze. In some regions of the country, maidengrass has become an invasive plant, particularly along waterways or in moist areas. In other regions, it is benign. Although there are no records of its invasive character in Texas, choose where it is planted carefully, especially in the eastern half of the state, and select an alternative if you are adjacent to a natural area.

When, Where, and How to Plant
Plant in spring after all danger of frost is past. Site in full sun or where it receives at least half-day sun. Maidengrass fails quickly in dense shade. Maidengrass is variable in its growing requirements depending on the variety. Check with local sources or grass authorities to determine which conditions suit your choice the best. Most prefer well-amended, fertile, well-drained soils, although a number of varieties do best in poorly drained sites or in pond-like conditions.

Growing Tips
Although maidengrass grows well without any supplemental fertilization, particularly in a fertile soil, it can be fertilized once in the spring as new growth begins. Water all varieties to maintain even soil moisture, and do not let the soil dry out completely.

Apply a 4- to 6-inch layer of mulch to maintain soil moisture through the summer.

Regional Advice and Care
Cut plants back in early spring to within 6 inches of the soil. Time the pruning early before the plant has resumed growth. Pull out any dead stems at this time. Maidengrass is not susceptible to pests or disease.

Companion Planting and Design
Maidengrass is large enough to anchor the boundaries or edges of a garden. The tall plumes wave beautifully in a breeze, and a full, generous planting emphasizes this effect. Maidengrass blends with other ornamental grasses or accents in back of a large perennial bed.

Try These
The widely grown 'Zebrinus' has wide bands of yellow on the leaves with a lax, recurved habit. One of the oldest selections is 'Gracillimus', which has a delicate, silver mid-rib. It blooms late in the season, and flowering persists long into winter. Both varieties require long, hot summers to flower well. 'Strictus' has yellow-banded foliage but grows more upright with narrow leaves. It is often known as porcupine grass for this habit. 'Yaku Jima' grows to 3 to 4 feet and is considered a dwarf form. It has reddish fall foliage. The more than one hundred named varieties of maidengrass make it one of the most widely used of all ornamental grasses.

Ruby Grass

Melinis nerviglumis

Other Name Pink crystals

Bloom Period and Seasonal Color
Summer, pink

Mature Height x Spread 1 to 2 ft. x 1 to 2 ft.

Botanical Pronunciation
mel-EYE-nus ner-vee-GLUE-miss

Zones 8 to 10

Ruby grass is a diminutive perennial grass growing as tidy, compact clumps of blue-green foliage. The wispy flowering heads emerge in the late summer and range in color from light, hazy pink to deep, rich rosy pink. They are feather-like and flow like a wave in the slightest breeze. Do not be fooled by this beautiful plant's delicate beauty; it is extremely heat and drought tolerant. Native to a wide swath of sub-Saharan Africa and Madagascar, this charming plant is often grown as an annual because it will germinate, grow up, and flower quickly. Seed shatters readily and seedlings erupt in the spring and can be removed as they arise. Although not reported as invasive, be cautious about planting it near parks or natural areas.

When, Where, and How to Plant
Plant from either seed or transplant in spring once all danger of frost is past. Prepare the area for seed by gently raking the soil and removing all weeds and grass. Broadcast seed, mixing it with mulch or sand to help distribute it evenly. Ruby grass grows best in full sun, even where there is strong reflected heat. Ruby grass is tolerant of almost any soil type, but good drainage is important. In areas of poor drainage create a slight mound or raised bed for the plants. Although ruby grass tolerates fertile or moist soils, it does best in those that are on the dry side.

Growing Tips
Providing supplemental fertilizer for this grass is not necessary. Water only often enough to keep the soil slightly moist. Use a soaker hose, garden hose, or drip irrigation to provide deep soaks at long intervals. Avoid overhead watering, which provides too little water and too frequent an interval for this species.

Regional Advice and Care
In the zones listed here, ruby grass is perennial and should be sheared to within 6 inches of the soil line in early spring. Remove the flowering heads before the seed sets or ripens to reduce the number of seedlings. Where ruby grass is grown as an annual, allow the seed to ripen and collect it to replant the following spring. Ruby grass germinates readily from fresh seed. Ruby grass is not susceptible to pests or disease.

Companion Planting and Design
Ruby grass is small enough to blend with a summer-flowering perennials or annuals. The late-season bloom and the long period when the heads are attractive provide good color through fall. Ruby grass's preference for dry soils and full sun make it a wonderful contrast to the rigid forms of succulents, like smaller agaves and yuccas. Use this grass generously to maximize the drama of its intensely pink flowering heads.

Try These
Ruby grass is often sold as 'Pink Crystals', which has light pink, full flowering heads. 'Savannah' is similar, but its flowering heads are darker pink.

St. Augustine Grass

Stenotaphrum secundatum

Mature Height x Spread
2 to 3 in. x 2 to 4 in.

Botanical Pronunciation
sten-no-TAY-frum seh-coon-DAH-tum

Zones 8 to 10

St. Augustine grass is the go-to lawn grass throughout much of the state for its ability to withstand a great deal of shade. The blades are wide and deep green and held closely along the short stems. It forms a thick patch quickly. However, St. Augustine grass does not tolerate heavy or repeated traffic well and is best used as a visual ground rather for playgrounds or other well-used areas. Often considered native along the Gulf Coast, it is most likely an introduction from Africa extremely early in the settlement of the Caribbean. It originally served as forage for cattle and found a congenial home along the Gulf and Caribbean coast. It has been used ornamentally and as forage since the eighteenth century in this country.

When, Where, and How to Plant
Set out plugs or sod in spring once the soils are warm and all danger of frost is past. Although a good choice for shade, St. Augustine does best when it receives at least four hours of sun daily. Prepare the bed by turning and raking to smooth the soil. Add a generous amount of well-composted manure, compost blends, or other organic matter and a well-balanced fertilizer. Water well before setting out the grass and keep it evenly watered until it is established.

Growing Tips
Fertilize with a well-balanced, granular formulation in spring when growth resumes. Continue to apply at about 10-week intervals, but do not fertilize through winter. Water to keep evenly moist, and do not let the soil dry out completely. St. Augustine grass wilts dramatically when water-stressed, and recovery can be erratic. Deep soaks that penetrate 3 to 6 inches at a time with longer intervals between waterings is better than frequent, shallow waterings.

Regional Advice and Care
Mow to a height of 1 to 2 inches. Typically, St. Augustine needs to be mowed about every other week. More frequent mowing indicates it is probably receiving too much water or fertilizer. St. Augustine is susceptible to a number of insects and fungal leaf diseases. Keep the plants healthy, do not let water pond on the lawn, and periodically aerate the soil to prevent these problems.

Companion Planting and Design
St. Augustine is one of the few grasses, or even plants, that can outcompete bermudagrass. Where they come together, St. Augustine will prevail. It is easy to keep out of flower beds by cutting the long runners with a sharp spade or pulling them out back to the main growing point.

Try These
'Seville' is a short variety with deep green leaves. 'Delmar' is dark green with good shade tolerance. 'Raleigh' a good choice for areas with heavy clay and cooler temperatures. Two other species include centipede grass (*Eremochloa ophiurioides*), which forms a thick mat and does well in sandy, acid soils, and zoysia (*Zoysia japonica*), a fine-bladed, drought-tolerant perennial.

PERENNIALS

Early in the nineteenth century, gardening traditions were much different than we know today. Important public gardens and large private gardens relied heavily on evergreen trees, long vistas with meadows, clipped hedges, and trimmed shrubs nearer the house, and if there were flowers, roses, or vegetables grown for the house, they were securely tucked into various corners and harvested when they were needed.

People of more modest means, if they lived in the country, just let things grow up all around the house, willy-nilly, finding their own way, with random, often gaudy color combinations. Later, as England gained wealth from its worldwide trade, public and formal gardens began to use huge expanses of bedding plants, laid out in astounding numbers, changed seasonally, with all the perfection a nearly limitless labor force could provide.

Gaura 'Siskiyou Pink'

The Switch to a Less Formal Garden Style

A revolution was ready to happen, and it did. Through the writings and efforts of two famous English gardeners, William Robinson and Gertrude Jekyll, a less formal style began to take shape, one that owed much to the informal plantings of flowers, roses, and shrubs in country gardens. This new style relied heavily on the planting of flowering perennials that came back every year without undue fuss. The effect was big and showy, and it could be done on any scale and with any budget. Gardeners have never looked back.

Perennials are still great favorites, and their advantages resonate today as they did more than 150 years ago. Well-chosen perennials live a long time, repeat the show annually, and do not demand excessive work on our part.

It is important to remember that a perennial garden is a style and does not require stringent duplication of the plant lists offered in the countless books on perennial gardens. There are a wealth of plants that tolerate local conditions, regardless of where you live, and a glorious perennial garden is possible anywhere.

How Perennials Are Used in the Garden

In botany the term *perennial* refers to plants that live and bloom over more than one season. But in horticulture and to gardeners, it means any herbaceous plant that is generally less than 4 feet tall and has colorful flowers. The gardener's definition does not include woody plants like shrubs and trees, grasses, bulbs, or succulents, even though they are perennial within the botanical meaning of the term.

Pine leaf milkweed

Perennials are often planted in large beds or along the edges of a lawn in a border. Such arrangements are known as perennial borders. Some borders are elaborately laid out to move through the color spectrum or create vivid color combinations. Others are set out to bloom for a long time with one area gently blending into another as they bloom. This lovely style came to us from England and works particularly well for a large area or garden, and it would be just as successful with native and low-water-use perennials.

Some perennials are referred to as groundcovers, but this term describes a function more than a specific type of plant. A wide array of species, including some we think of as vines, may serve as groundcovers. Perennial groundcovers grow long, trailing stems instead of sturdy, branching, or upright stems. In addition, when trailing stems touch the ground they often take root, securing the plant firmly to the ground. Plants like this are superb at holding back a bank or mitigating soil erosion. Perennials may be used as a groundcover by planting them closely together and allowing their stems to barely touch. Closely set plants of one or multiple species form a continuous cover over the soil that both shades and cools the soil. Plantings like this form a living mulch, holding down water loss from the soil, ironically reducing rather than enhancing water use.

Many perennials attract a vast and varied number of butterflies and birds. Choosing plants that flower over a long season and with a variety of flowering styles provides food for these flying visitors most of the year.

Asian Jasmine

Trachelospermum asiaticum

Bloom Period and Seasonal Color
Spring, white

Mature Height x Spread
12 to 16 in. x 6 to 10 ft.

Botanical Pronunciation
track-el-oh-SPER-mum ah-see-AT-ti-cum

Zones 8 to 10

During a recent move, we lived for a time in an apartment to get our bearings and find a permanent home. Asian jasmine was planted throughout, under oaks, along walkways, and in the six months we lived there I only saw it watered twice. The deep green, glossy leaves grow quickly, creating a dense mat on the ground. Asian jasmine received its common name undoubtedly because the wheel-shaped, white flowers with a yellow center have a delicate fragrance reminiscent of true jasmines. This is not a jasmine, but in the same family as oleander and periwinkle. Like those species, the stems exude a milky sap, which can be irritating to some people and should never be allowed into your eyes, nose, or other tender spots.

When, Where, and How to Plant
Set out transplants in spring when all danger of frost is past and the soil is warmed. If planting as a groundcover, space plants 6 to 8 inches apart. Asian jasmine grows best in light, filtered shade but will tolerate full sun if given ample water. Choose a site out of the path of cold winds. Asian jasmine needs a well-drained, moist soil, although it can be quite drought tolerant when established. Amend the soil or planting hole with plenty of compost, composted manure, or other organic material before planting.

Growing Tips
Apply a well-balanced fertilizer once in the spring when growth resumes and again about two months later. Provide regular deep watering, weekly at least, to get plants established and to fill in an area. Once established, reduce water to as little as twice a month, depending on temperatures and summer rainfall regimen. Plants do poorly in soggy conditions, so reduce watering schedules when rain is abundant. Rely on natural rainfall in the winter. Use a light, 2-inch layer of mulch to maintain soil moisture and reduce watering frequency.

Regional Advice and Care
Cut back in the spring just as growth resumes to remove any winter damaged stems or to control its spread. Lightly tip prune in the early summer to keep plants tidy or within bounds. Asian jasmine has few pest or disease problems.

Companion Planting and Design
Use as a groundcover beneath the canopy of oaks or evergreen trees. Asian jasmine fills in difficult corners or areas that do not need routine maintenance. The bright white flowers are charming, but do not occur in profusion. When in flower it makes a nice contrast to the deep green of associated evergreen shrubs or trees.

Try These
'Asia Minor' is a dwarf spreading to 4 feet. There are numerous variegated forms with cream, red, or bronze leaf colors. Confederate jasmine (*Trachelospermum jasminoides*) is a slightly less hardy relative that is a fast-growing vine whose larger and highly fragrant flowers are white but lack the yellow throat. This species tolerates more sun but otherwise requires similar culture.

Autumn Sage

Salvia greggii

Bloom Period and Seasonal Color
Spring to fall, red, pink, purple, magenta, white

Mature Height x Spread
1 to 3 ft. x 2 to 3 ft.

Botanical Pronunciation
SAL-vee-uh GREG-ee-eye

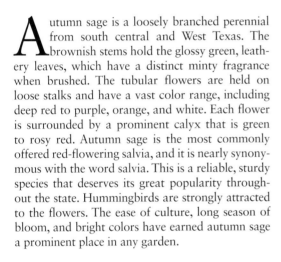

Autumn sage is a loosely branched perennial from south central and West Texas. The brownish stems hold the glossy green, leathery leaves, which have a distinct minty fragrance when brushed. The tubular flowers are held on loose stalks and have a vast color range, including deep red to purple, orange, and white. Each flower is surrounded by a prominent calyx that is green to rosy red. Autumn sage is the most commonly offered red-flowering salvia, and it is nearly synonymous with the word salvia. This is a reliable, sturdy species that deserves its great popularity throughout the state. Hummingbirds are strongly attracted to the flowers. The ease of culture, long season of bloom, and bright colors have earned autumn sage a prominent place in any garden.

When, Where, and How to Plant
Plant in the fall or early spring in warm winter zones and in the spring after all danger of frost is past in colder zones. Choose a location with a half-day sun (preferably morning) with the roots in a shaded, well-drained fertile soil, particularly in the warmest parts of the state. In mild areas, autumn sage grows well in full sun.

Growing Tips
Apply slow-release or organic fertilizer annually in spring. Watering frequency depends on the temperatures and the exposure. In mild summer areas with regular rainfall, natural rainfall is sufficient. In hotter areas, or during extended hot spells, water every seven to 10 days. Rely on natural rainfall in the winter in all zones. Mulch heavily through the summer to maintain even soil moisture, lengthen watering frequency, and keep the roots cool.

Regional Advice and Care
Prune in early spring to remove winter-damaged stems and reinvigorate the plant. Light tip pruning through the summer plus removal of spent flowering stalks, keeps the plant tidy and encourages repeat flowering. Autumn sage is not susceptible to pests or disease.

Companion Planting and Design
Mix autumn sage with other summer-flowering perennials for a long season of color. Plant densely to form an informal hedge or border along a drive or walkway or to surround a patio, pool, or seating area. Locate plants where the hummingbirds that are constant visitors can be enjoyed.

Try These
'Furman's Red' is a deep, rich red; 'Purple Pastel' and 'Purple Haze' are purple, 'Desert Red' is velvety red, 'Big Pink' is pink, and 'Wild Thing' has pink flowers with a wine-colored calyx. 'Hot Lips' is a scarlet red and white bicolor that may be one of the many hybrids with the cherry sage (*Salvia microphylla*). Other hybrids include 'Cerro Potosi', magenta flowers, and 'San Carlos Festival' rosy-red flowers. Scarlet sage (*S. coccinea*), a perennial only in zones 9 and 10, has intensely red flowers on hairy, branched stalks. Selections include 'Coral Nymph' a bicolored pale salmon and pink and 'Snow Nymph' white. Mountain sage (*S. regla*) has deep red flowers and a persistent orange-red calyx.

Blackfoot Daisy

Melampodium leucanthum

Bloom Period and Seasonal Color
Spring to fall, white

Mature Height x Spread
6 to 12 in. x 12 to 18 in.

Botanical Pronunciation
mel-am-POH-dee-um loo-kan-thum

Blackfoot daisy is a low, spreading mound of a plant. The flowers have pure white rays and yellow disks and appear to coat the plant. Often cantankerous about its growing conditions, many gardeners treat it as a long-season, summer annual. But when the conditions of good sun, minimal water, and sharp drainage are met, this is a delightful addition to any garden. I grew blackfoot daisy for several years in Arizona, where they were happy and content, until a large rain event flooded them out. Learn from me; be sure they are only lightly acquainted with standing or ponding water and this native of the western half of the state will reward you grandly. Butterflies of many species crowd the plants for its abundant nectar.

When, Where, and How to Plant
Plant in spring once the soils are warm and all danger of frost is past. Planting may continue through early summer. Place blackfoot daisy in full sun even in areas of reflected heat. Good drainage is essential, so be sure that the area is extremely well drained, adding gravel or raising the planting area if necessary or in heavy or tight soils. Keep blackfoot daisy away from areas where water drains or collects, even intermittently. Other than drainage, it is not particular about soils and grows well even in highly alkaline ones.

Growing Tips
Blackfoot daisy does not need supplemental fertilization. Water carefully. In the hottest areas, water in the summer every ten days to two weeks unless the weather is especially hot or dry. In milder areas, water as infrequently as once monthly in summer depending on rainfall. Rely on natural rainfall in all areas through the cool months.

Regional Advice and Care
Deadhead the plants regularly through summer to promote continued flowering. In the early spring, cut the plant back by half to reinvigorate it. Light tip pruning in the summer maintains its natural, rounded form. Although blackfoot daisy has no pest or disease problems, overwatering or standing water causes plants to rot quickly. Prevention is best. Plants typically live four to five years but reseed in congenial circumstances.

Companion Planting and Design
Butterflies are strongly drawn to this species, making it a splendid addition to a butterfly garden. Use blackfoot daisy to soften a succulent or cactus garden or in areas of the garden that may not receive routine maintenance. It blends well with other low-growing perennials, as long as its cultural conditions are met. This is a perfect foundation plant for a rock garden or a dry area.

Try These
The South Texas native hoary blackfoot (*Melampodium cinereum*) looks similar but is not common and may not be hardy beyond San Antonio. White zinnia (*Zinnia acerosa*) looks similar on first glance, but this species has half as many ray flowers and the flower is backed by numerous overlapping scales.

Butterfly Milkweed

Asclepias tuberosa

Other Name Butterfly weed

Bloom Period and Seasonal Color
Spring to fall, orange

Mature Height x Spread 18 to 24 in. x 24 in.

Botanical Pronunciation
az-KLEP-ee-as too-ber-OH-suh

Zones 7 to 9

Butterfly milkweed is a bushy plant with thin, deep green leaves. As they age, plants spread and fill out. Bright orange flowers are held on the top of the foliage in a flattened top. The flowers, as in the entire family, are complex. In most plants, the lowest ring of sepals (calyx) is below the colorful petals (corolla). But in this genus, there is yet another colorful ring known as a corona. Plants grow from a large swollen root (tuber) and live for a very long time in congenial conditions. The best part—and why I like all milkweeds so much—is their strong appeal to butterflies. Many species prefer these plants for larval food, and monarch and queen butterflies are especially drawn to this species.

When, Where, and How to Plant
Plant butterfly weed from seed in early spring. Cuttings are easily made from established plants by removing the plant in fall and cutting the taproot into sections. Plant each section and keep it evenly moist. Seed can take three to four years to grow into a full plant and often takes almost that long to flower. Plant in full sun for best flowering in well-drained, sandy, or loamy soil. Set plants where you want them; they are difficult to move successfully once growing in the ground.

Growing Tips
Butterfly milkweed needs no supplemental fertilizer. Water carefully; plants that are overwatered or have poor drainage rot quickly. The older the plant the larger the taproot and therefore the more drought tolerant it is.

Regional Advice and Care
Pruning is not required, although old flowering heads can be removed anytime. The milky sap is poisonous if ingested by people or animals, and in sensitive individuals it can irritate or burn the skin. Use gloves to be safe. Aphids are common. Use a strong jet of water or insecticidal soap to keep them under control. Left untreated aphid's exudate (honeydew) attracts the leaf fungus sooty mold. Damage is rarely more than cosmetic.

Companion Planting and Design
Butterfly weed offers rich color in a mixed perennial planting. It is drought tolerant enough to be successful in areas of the garden that do receive routine or regular care. Blend with other natives, including wildflowers or other annuals, to continue a long seasonal display.

Try These
The brilliantly flowered bloodflower (*Asclepias curassavica*) is a tropical species that has become naturalized throughout the warm winter areas of the country. Often weedy, bloodflower grows 4 feet tall with small orange, yellow, or scarlet flowers with a yellow corona. Antelope horns (*A. asperula*), one of the numerous native species of milkweed, has large, rounded, cream-colored flowering heads. Swamp milkweed (*A. incarnata*) has pink to creamy flowers and prefers to grow in moist conditions. Pine-leaf milkweed (*A. linaria*) is a wispy plant with pure white flowers for areas with winter temperatures above 25 degrees Fahrenheit.

Chocolate Flower

Berlandiera lyrata

Bloom Period and Seasonal Color
Spring to summer, yellow rays, dark brown disks

Mature Height x Spread 1 to 2 ft. x 1 to 2 ft.

Botanical Pronunciation
ber-lan-dee-AIR-ah lye-RAH-tah

Zones 7 to 9

When I first encountered chocolate flower, I was skeptical, believing it unlikely that a flower could replicate the sweet, seductive smell of real chocolate. I was wrong; this small perennial reeks of the real thing, and it is a must for serious chocolate lovers. Chocolate flower is also a lovely garden plant with deeply lobed, softly hairy leaves. The flowers are held high above the foliage on thin stalks. The ray flowers are deep and yellow, and the disk flowers are dark brown and flat. After the bloom is finished the petals fall off, revealing the light green receptacle formed by multiple rows of green bracts. This feature is as ornamental as the flowers both in the garden and when dried for use in floral arrangements.

When, Where, and How to Plant
Plant in fall or early spring. Choose a location in full sun. In very hot areas, like western Texas, plant chocolate flower where it receives morning sun only or filtered shade. Chocolate flower grows in moderately fertile, well-drained soils, including those with high alkalinity. Amend the bed with a thin layer of compost or mulch before planting.

Growing Tips
Apply slow-release or organic fertilizer annually in spring. Water established plants every week in summer, more often if it's exceptionally hot or dry. In areas with reliable summer rainfall, chocolate flowers grow well on natural rainfall. Mulch roots well to keep the soil from drying out completely. Monthly watering or reliance on natural rainfall is sufficient in winter.

Regional Advice and Care
Prune flowers regularly to encourage repeat blooming. Plants can be severely pruned, even mowed, in early summer after the first round of flowering if they become unsightly or floppy. Chocolate flower is not susceptible to pests or disease, although it can be short-lived in desert areas. Plants reseed freely in most gardens. Leave the seedlings to grow where they germinate or move them to other locations in the late fall and winter.

Companion Planting and Design
Mix chocolate flower with other small perennials for a colorful, long-season display. This plant has a tidy, rounded form that nicely complements sprawling or spreading perennials. Plant generously to form an informal border at the edge of the bed or to fill a tight corner. Use chocolate flower near a seating area, patio, or pool to enjoy the aroma of chocolate in the evening and early morning when its aroma will fill the garden. Chocolate flower is a good container plant either planted alone or in a mixed planting.

Try These
Another Texas native, green eyes *(Berlandieri betonicifolia* syn. *texana)* is equally attractive. This species grows taller than chocolate flower with larger leaves. The yellow rays surround the few dark brown disk flowers, and both are underlain by a bright green receptacle. It blends well into a mixed planting of ornamental grasses and taller perennials.

Evening Primrose

Oenothera speciosa

Other Name Mexican evening primrose

Bloom Period and Seasonal Color
Spring to summer, pink, white

Mature Height x Spread
8 to 24 in. x 12 to 48 in.

Botanical Pronunciation
ee-noh-THEER-ah spee-see-OH-sah

Evening primrose is a spreading, low-growing perennial with thin, weak stems. The leaves are widely spaced on the plant and are deeply lobed. They are often tinged with red on either the margins or the underside. Flowers are delicate cups of pink from a pale shell tone to deep, rosy pink. There are rare white forms and some with dark veins throughout the petals. Despite how fragile it looks, this is one tough plant. It grows as well in desert conditions as it does in high rainfall areas. However, it can spread aggressively in areas with regular or consistent water, so it is advisable to grow it as dry as possible. The flowers open for one night only and are lightly fragrant.

When, Where, and How to Plant
Plant in early fall or spring in warm zones. In the coldest zones, plant in spring, as early as the soil can be worked. Plants grown in mild winter areas are evergreen, whereas those in cooler climates are usually summer dormant. Evening primrose grows well in full sun or light shade but does poorly in deep shade. Soil amendments are rarely necessary, but plants grow more thickly in well-drained, fertile soils.

Growing Tips
Fertilize once in early spring, although plants do well without annual supplemental fertilizer. Water infrequently, particularly when it is actively growing. In all but the driest areas, or during extended dry spells, rely on natural rainfall.

Regional Advice and Care
Cut back or mow in fall and/or early spring to control the spread or remove winter damage. Plants can be lightly pruned in the late spring to control growth. Evening primrose is strongly attractive to flea beetles, which cause cosmetic damage to the leaves. In areas near the coast, these insects can reduce flowering.

Companion Planting and Design
Evening primrose is an excellent groundcover for dry areas or can be used to fill in corners in areas that receive minimal maintenance. Use it for erosion control on dry, steep slopes. The intense spring flowering makes this species a good filler for large perennial beds or within a meadow style planting. Evening primrose forms a dense enough mat to be a lawn substitute in areas with minimal foot traffic. Used this way, maintain regular watering to keep the plants actively growing.

Try These
'Pink Petticoats' has a pleasant fragrance, 'Woodside White' is whiter than average, and 'Siskiyou' has large pink flowers. Yellow evening primrose (*Oenothera macrocarpa* syn. *O. missouriensis*) is a prairie native with bright yellow flowers. Beach evening primrose (*O. drummondii*) has pale yellow flowers and is a good choice for coastal gardens. Tufted evening primrose (*O. caespitosa*) has a profusion of large, white flowers smothering a tight, 12-inch mounded plant. In the eastern parts of Texas, the biennial giant evening primrose (*O. hookeri*) is an upright plant with showy clusters of yellow flowers.

Ferns

Mature Height x Spread
1 to 2 ft. x 2 to 5 ft.

Ferns are soothing plants, perhaps because they are so old; here for at least 300 million years, they calmly fit into the garden the way old houses fit into their region. There are some 12,000 species, and although they are usually grown in shady, moist gardens, some species grow in dry, hot, or rocky locales. Ferns are in-between two vast classes of plants. Like mosses, they do not make flowers or seed but have vascular systems, stems, and leaves as do flowering plants. Ferns increase either from rhizomes or by spores. Unlike seeds, which form a tiny plant when fertilized, spores germinate and form a structure that then divides into male and female forms whose cross results in fertilization, and a new fern is made.

When, Where, and How to Plant
Plant from transplants or divisions in early spring. Choose a location suitable for the type of fern, some prefer deep shade, others light shade, and a few accept full sun, especially in cold areas. Amend the soil with abundant amounts of organic matter before planting.

Growing Tips
Fertilization depends on the species. Most ferns do best in rich soils with ample leaf litter on the soil surface. That will be sufficient to maintain soil fertility. Water most ferns to keep the soil evenly moist. Deep layers of mulch renewed at least annually help maintain consistent soil moisture.

Regional Advice and Care
Most ferns are winter deciduous. Fronds can be removed when they fade if they are messy or untidy or can be cut away in the early spring. Old fronds from the lower part of an evergreen plant can be removed anytime. Ferns have few pest or disease problems, although snails can sometimes feed aggressively on young fronds.

Companion Planting and Design
Ferns blend well with low-growing perennials in a shady garden. Large ferns create a backdrop for other plantings, particularly in shady gardens. These are excellent plants to cover the ground beneath large trees, or groves, where shade makes more colorful choices difficult.

Try These
The easily recognized maidenhair (*Adiantum capillus-veneris*), with its parsley-like leaves and jet black petioles, requires a wet wall or stones, either natural or man-made, but is otherwise easily grown. Holly fern (*Cyrtomium falcatum*) has glossy green, deeply cut, evergreen fronds and is hardy to Zone 7 with protection in severe winters. It grows to 3 feet tall and as wide. Bracken fern (*Pteridium aquilinum*) is equally large and spreads aggressively to fill in a dry shade situation. Christmas fern (*Polystichum acrostichoides*) is an evergreen with clusters of leathery fronds and prefers cool, moist shade. Wood fern (*Thelypteris kunthii*) has lime to medium green fronds growing in all directions from clusters of stalks along the rhizomes and prefers a pond or water garden. Shield fern (*T. ovate* var. *lindheimeri*) is found along many streams in the Hill Country and is moderately drought tolerant in shady areas.

Flame Anisacanthus

Anisacanthus quadrifidus var. *wrightii*

Bloom Period and Seasonal Color
Late spring to frost, orange, red-orange

Mature Height x Spread 2 to 4 ft. x 2 to 4 ft.

Botanical Pronunciation
ah-nee-sah-KAN-thus RITE-ee-eye

I find orange a difficult color to use well in a garden. It is garish and demanding and often blends poorly with other colors. But I would never want to be without the bright orange flowers of flame anisacanthus. This 3-foot-tall deciduous perennial to small shrub has light green, lance-shaped leaves that are some of the last to arrive in the spring. As the heat intensifies, the plant comes ablaze with brilliant orange tubular flowers whose tips flare at the end like a star. The color of the flowers seems to shift over the season, beginning a bright, clear orange and softening to a deep russet in the fall. Hummingbirds love it for its nectar; I love it for its toughness and long, brilliant bloom.

When, Where, and How to Plant
Set out plants in spring after all danger of frost is past and the soil is warm. Choose a location in full sun. Flame anisacanthus also grows well in partial sun in the southern and western regions of the state. This perennial grows in almost any well-drained soil including dry, rocky ones.

Growing Tips
Flame anisacanthus needs no supplemental fertilizer. Water established plants two or three times a month in summer in the hottest areas, much less often where it is cooler. Flame anisacanthus grows well on natural rainfall in most areas with supplemental watering only during times of extended drought. Rely on natural rainfall in winter in all areas. Mulch the roots to keep the soil from drying out too quickly in the summer and to protect the roots in winter.

Regional Advice and Care
Prune in spring just as leaves emerge to remove dead or damaged stems. Plants bloom on new wood, so prune early to avoid loss of flowering. Every two or three years cut to a foot tall to reinvigorate the plant. Flame anisacanthus is not susceptible to pests or disease.

Companion Planting and Design
Use flame anisacanthus in mixed perennial plantings with other summer flowering perennials. Plant generously near patios, pools, or seating areas. Locate where you can enjoy the continuous visits by hummingbirds. The brilliant flowers are particularly attractive when backlit.

Try These
'Selected Red' has a deeper color than the type, and 'Pumpkin' is light orange. Pink anisacanthus (*Anisacanthus puberulus*) is a deciduous shrub found in the Big Bend country of Texas and adjacent Mexico. This loosely branched shrub has light pink flowers in early spring and typically flowers before the leaves emerge. Narrow-leaf anisacanthus (*A. linearis*), also from the Big Bend country, is a deciduous shrub, with orange, tubular flowers and narrow, dark green leaves. There have been hybrids between this species and flame anisacanthus offered from time to time. Desert honeysuckle (*A. thurberi*) is an upright 8-foot shrub with deep red flowers from far western Texas and the deserts of the western United States.

Four O'Clock

Mirabilis jalapa

Bloom Period and Seasonal Color
Summer to fall, purple, yellow, red, magenta, white

Mature Height x Spread
3 to 4 ft. x 1 to 2 ft.

Botanical Pronunciation
MERE-ah-bill-is ha-LAH-pah

I am immensely fond of four o'clock and have carried seed of a particular strain to each garden I have owned. That strain is a highly prized pure white form from a neighbor's garden in New Orleans. Many gardeners in zones too cold for four o'clock to be perennial grow it as an annual because plants germinate quickly and flower through the entire summer. Four o'clock is sustained by a huge, black, tuberous root from which sturdy, pale green stems arise. The flat, button-shaped flowers open every evening and have a sweet, delicate fragrance. Native to tropical South America, the Spanish found this species growing in Aztec gardens and quickly sent plants back home. By the mid-sixteenth century it was being grown in English gardens.

When, Where, and How to Plant
Sow seed or set out transplants in spring after all danger of frost is past and the soil is warm. Seed germinates quickly and will bloom that season. In hot areas, four o'clock does best in filtered or light shade. In more moderate climates, plant in full sun. Four o'clock grows in any well-drained, moderately fertile soil. Amendments are not strictly necessary, although plants grow faster with some additional compost or other organic additions in the soil.

Growing Tips
Four o'clock does not require supplemental fertilizer. A light mulch around the roots keeps the soil from drying out and protects the tuberous root in winter. Water established plants every seven to ten days if growing in full sun, less frequently in shade. Rely on natural rainfall while they are dormant in the winter.

Regional Advice and Care
Plants are winter deciduous, and stalks can be cut down anytime they begin to decline in the fall. Seedlings can be relocated easily in early spring. In cold zones, the large root may be dug and stored in dry peat or sphagnum moss. Four o'clock is not susceptible to pests.

Companion Planting and Design
Plant in mass for dramatic effect and to brighten a shady bed. Use four o'clock generously near seating areas, porches, patios, or pools where the evening flowering and delicate scent can be readily enjoyed. Four o'clock attracts a wide array of night-flying moths.

Try These
'Jingles' is a seed strain that produces somewhat smaller plants with flowers that bloom in a wide array of colors, often on the same plant. 'Broken Colors' also flowers in a wide array of colors, but each flower is splashed erratically with magenta. There are mixed-color packs available wherever seed are sold. To create a single-colored strain, remove all that aren't your preferred color. By consistently removing the "wrong" colors, in a couple of years you will have the one you want permanently. Showy four o'clock (*Mirabilis multiflora*) is a low-growing, attractive native perennial species with brightly colored bracts in rose, pink, or magenta and is hardy to 0 degrees Fahrenheit.

Four-Nerve Daisy

Tetraneuris scaposa

Bloom Period and Seasonal Color
Spring to fall, yellow

Mature Height x Spread
6 to 12 in. x 10 to 12 in.

Botanical Pronunciation
THE-trah-noor-is skay-PO-sah

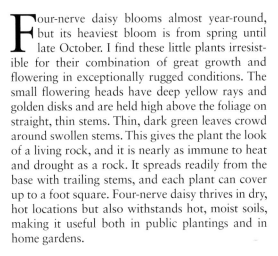

Four-nerve daisy blooms almost year-round, but its heaviest bloom is from spring until late October. I find these little plants irresistible for their combination of great growth and flowering in exceptionally rugged conditions. The small flowering heads have deep yellow rays and golden disks and are held high above the foliage on straight, thin stems. Thin, dark green leaves crowd around swollen stems. This gives the plant the look of a living rock, and it is nearly as immune to heat and drought as a rock. It spreads readily from the base with trailing stems, and each plant can cover up to a foot square. Four-nerve daisy thrives in dry, hot locations but also withstands hot, moist soils, making it useful both in public plantings and in home gardens.

When, Where, and How to Plant
Set out transplants in the late summer or early fall in warm winter areas. Plant in early spring in cooler zones after all danger of frost is past and the soil has warmed. In these zones, planting may continue through early summer. Choose a location in full sun in all zones. Plants fail quickly with too much shade. Four-nerve daisy tolerates almost any type of soil as long as the drainage is excellent.

Growing Tips
Four-nerve daisy does not need supplemental fertilizer. Water established plants every week or two in summer, depending on the temperatures and rainfall. This is an exceptionally drought-tolerant species, and it will often grow well on even less frequent watering. Water only monthly in winter, or rely on natural rainfall. Avoid overhead watering; it encourages dieback in the center of the plant.

Regional Advice and Care
Remove dead flowering stalks anytime. Prune plants back in early spring to remove old flowers and damaged stems or to rejuvenate the plant. Four-nerve daisy is not susceptible to pests or disease but suffers root rots when grown with too much shade, overhead water, or in soils with poor drainage.

Companion Planting and Design
Plant four-nerve daisy close together to form a groundcover or a low front border for a large bed. Its tight, rounded form makes it a natural for a rock garden or interplanted with similarly sized succulents. It mixes well with winter flowering, summer dormant bulbs, and Mediterranean perennials such as rosemary and lavender. Use against a hot wall or building, as a border around a pool, or in other locations where reflected heat is intense.

Try These
The similar Angelita daisy (*Tetraneuris acaulis*) has a stem that resembles a swollen ball at the base of the plant with the leaves rising out of it. The flowers are nearly identical, but the leaves have dense hairs, which are lacking in four-nerve daisy. However, these are fine differences, and there is a lot of individual variation in both species on this characteristic. As a result, plants are often offered under either name.

Garden Phlox

Phlox paniculata

Bloom Period and Seasonal Color
Summer, pink, red, white, lavender, purple, bicolors

Mature Height x Spread
3 to 5 ft. x 1 to 3 ft.

Botanical Pronunciation
FLOCKS pah-NICK-you-lah-tuh

arden phlox reminds me of the casual blowsy summer gardens that one of my grandmothers maintained. It was a garden where the plants were free to set the design, and big, bold plants like fragrant shrubby roses, huge hollyhocks, and garden phlox dominated. Today I find them just as delightful, although now there are many newer varieties and colors within this group. Garden phlox grows from a basal set of dark green leaves. The tall, congested flowering stalks are resplendent with the fragrant blooms throughout the summer. Some of the old varieties, like those in my grandmother's garden, can be found only in old gardens to be passed along from gardener to gardener. Garden phlox is long-lived, particularly in the northern half of the state.

When, Where, and How to Plant
Plant in spring as soon as soil is warm enough to work. Although garden phlox grows easily from seed, colors are not consistent in seed-grown plants. Plant in full sun or partial shade in well-drained, fertile soil. Garden phlox prefers to grow in soils rich with organic matter that never fully dry out.

Growing Tips
Apply slow-release fertilizer or organic fertilizer annually in spring. Water established plants weekly in summer and intermittently in winter. Mulch roots heavily to extend watering frequency and prevent the soil from drying out. Resist overhead watering, which encourages mildew infestations.

Regional Advice and Care
Remove dead stems and dead blooming stalks in fall to keep plants tidy. Mulch the roots to protect them in the winter in the coldest zones. Plants spread by underground stems (rhizomes) as well as reseed freely. Maintain spacing and good air circulation, thinning out the clumps every couple of years to prevent mildew.

Companion Planting and Design
Use garden phlox with other tall perennials. It looks especially at home blended with roses. Plant garden phlox and let it spread generously to form a background for small perennials or annual wildflower beds. Dwarf varieties are well suited for use as a low border or to line a walkway or seating area.

Try These
'Mt. Fuji' and 'David' have tall, congested flowering stalks with pure white blooms. 'John Fanick' was introduced by Texas horticulturist Greg Grant in the late 1990s. This is a vigorous plant that is somewhat shorter than typical with a regular form and excellent vigor and mildew resistance. The profusion of flowers are pale pink with dark centers. 'Victoria' has a more open habit than those above with deep magenta pink flowers. The native downy phlox (*Phlox pilosa*) grows to only 2 feet tall in a tidy mound. The more open flowers are in clusters of pale pink to lavender. This species grows well in rocky, dry soils. Louisiana phlox (*P. divaricate*) is a trailing plant with loose heads of pink or blue flowers and is well suited for East Texas gardens.

Gaura

Gaura lindheimeri

Bloom Period and Seasonal Color
Summer to fall, pink, white

Mature Height x Spread
2 to 4 ft. x 2 to 3 ft.

Botanical Pronunciation
GAR-ah lind-HI-mer-eye

Gaura starts out as a low set of deep green, basal leaves. The leaves are tinged with maroon or reddish hues. In the late spring, long, branched blooming stalks rise high over the plant, transforming this modest little plant. Small, star-like white flowers emerge from pink buds and continue to open in staggered sequences through the summer. The flowering stalks are so thin and the flowers so delicate the effect is of a cloud floating over the garden. To complete the illusion, as the flowers fade they turn a pale, ethereal pink. Over the last decade or so, gardeners and breeders have favored tighter, more compact plants with shorter flowering stalks. But I still prefer the spreading older forms with their tall, delicate flowering stalks.

When, Where, and How to Plant

Set out transplants in early fall in southern parts of the state and early spring in more northern regions. Gaura grows well in full sun or partial shade in most of the state, particularly in the hottest parts of West Texas. Gaura is not particular about the soil as long as it is well drained and moderately fertile. Amend the soil with compost or a blend of composted manure and other organic material, particularly in areas with dry soils. The plant has a long taproot that makes transplanting difficult and often unsuccessful.

Growing Tips

Gaura needs minimal supplemental fertilizer; once a year in the spring is sufficient. Too much fertilizer shortens the life of the plant. Water weekly in summer when weather is extremely hot, but established plants can generally do well on natural rainfall except during intense drought. Apply 2 to 3 inches of mulch in summer to keep soil evenly moist and reduce watering frequency. Rely on natural rainfall in winter in all zones.

Regional Advice and Care

Prune gaura back to within 6 inches of the ground in the spring just as the plant resumes growth. This hard prune removes dead stalks, old flowering stalks, and any winter damage and reinvigorates the plant. Remove bloomed-out flowering stalks anytime. Gaura is not susceptible to pests or disease, although it can be short-lived if grown in soils that are too rich.

Companion Planting and Design

Plant in groups for best effect; solitary plants often fail to show up in mixed plantings. Use gaura to form a low border, line walkways or drives, or utilize as a filler for barren spots in a newly planted garden.

Try These

'Siskiyou Pink' is one of the oldest selections, with dark pink buds and flowers that open white but fade to pink. The foliage is strongly marked with red. In 'Whirling Butterflies' flowers are consistently white. 'Crimson Butterflies' is compact with dark rose-red flowers and dark red foliage and stems. 'Blushing Butterflies' has soft pink flowers and dark green leaves. 'Passionate Pink' features dark pink flowers above reddish green foliage.

Golden Columbine

Aquilegia chrysantha

Bloom Period and Seasonal Color
Spring or fall, yellow

Mature Height x Spread
24 to 36 in. x 12 to 18 in.

Botanical Pronunciation
ak-will-EE-ji-uh kris-AN-thah

Columbines have long been favored for their spectacular displays of graceful spurred flowers and reliable blooming over a long season. Golden columbine is one of the few columbines that will grow well in warmer areas. This Texas native forms a spherical base of dusky green, lobed, three-part leaves that arise from a central crown. Tall branched flowering stalks hold the pure golden yellow flowers. The flowers open over the six-week period, early spring in southern Texas, late summer in northern Texas. As is typical of the genus, the flowers are large, up to 4 inches long, and the spur that forms behind it is nearly that long. In some areas these perennials are short-lived, but golden columbine reseeds freely, thereby maintaining a continuous stand.

When, Where, and How to Plant
In warm winter zones, plant in fall. In colder zones, plant in early spring as soon as soil can be worked. Golden columbine grows in full sun in all zones in well-drained, but well-amended, rich soils. Add ample amounts of compost, composted manure, and other organic matter to the bed or planting hole before planting. Good drainage is important, so if the area holds water consistently raise the planting area slightly. Mulch the root zone heavily after planting.

Growing Tips
Golden columbine needs no supplemental fertilizer. Water established plants weekly when blooming, monthly or less when out of bloom. Maintain a 4- to 6-inch layer of mulch on the root zone. Golden columbine tolerates a great deal of heat and sun on the leaves and flowering stalk, but the roots must be kept cool and moist.

Regional Advice and Care
Cut the blooming stalk after the seed has set. Either collect the seed to plant elsewhere, or let it fall in place to increase the number of plants next year. Free seedlings can be relocated in fall or early spring. It is not susceptible to pests or disease.

Companion Planting and Design
Mix golden columbine with other spring-flowering annuals or spring-flowering bulbs. This species is especially useful in areas of dry shade either singly or mixed with other shade-loving perennials. It is suitable for containers or planters either in mass or in mixed plantings.

Try These
The var. *hinckleyana* is endemic to the Big Bend area and is a favored choice for Texas gardens. It is somewhat smaller and with fewer divided leaves than the species has. The Texas Superstar 'Texas Gold' is from this variety. Red columbine (*Aquilegia canadensis*) is a woodland species with red flowers tipped with yellow. Suitable for moist areas, it freely hybridizes with golden columbine when they are grown together. One of these hybrids, 'Blazing Star', has excellent heat tolerance, good size, and flowers that are bicolored red and orange. 'Flora Pleno' is a double-flowered form with red-orange petals tipped in yellow while 'Silver Queen' has white flowers with yellow stamens.

Liriope

Liriope muscari

Other Name Lily turf

Bloom Period and Seasonal Color
Summer, lilac, purple, white

Mature Height x Spread
9 to 15 in. x 6 to 10 in.

Botanical Pronunciation
li-RYE-oh-pee mus-KAR-ee

In many gardens, finding a plant that is interesting, much less blooms in deep shade, can be challenging. Liriope has, however, come to rescue for decades for gardeners throughout the state. Native to the forest of China, Taiwan, and Japan, it thrives in the deep shade of oaks or pines. The wide, strappy leaves of this member of the lily family arise from the base and form a small fountain of foliage. Leaves are usually deep green, but many selections are available with alternate leaf colors or variegation. The purple flowers are held in dense spikes that rise above the foliage. Liriope forms a dense root mass over time, making it an excellent choice for steep, shady slopes as well as holding down weed growth.

When, Where, and How to Plant
In cold zones, plant in spring once the soil is warmed. In warm winter zones, plant either in fall or early spring. Choose a location in partial, filtered light, although this species does well in dense shade or full sun. Liriope grows best in fertile, well-drained soil. Amend the planting area with ample amounts of compost mixed with composted manure and other organic material. In heavy soils or those with poor drainage, plant with the crown raised slightly above the soil line.

Growing Tips
Fertilize in spring as growth resumes or just after the last frost. Fertilize every other month through the growing season, stopping a month before the expected first frost date. Water weekly and mulch thoroughly to maintain even soil moisture.

Regional Advice and Care
Prune hard, or even mow, in early spring to refresh and remove dead or winter-damaged leaves. Prune flowering stalks by hand anytime. Removing flowering stalks before they set seed prevents unwanted reseeding. Bothered occasionally by snails, liriope is otherwise pest and disease free.

Companion Planting and Design
Plant as a border or base for woodland beds, or to line a perennial bed in a shady location. Use as an overall groundcover in shady areas, or any location that does not receive foot traffic or regular care. The variegated- and paler-leaved forms are good choices to light up a dark corner of the garden.

Try These
'Okina' has white leaves in the spring that speckle with green as the weather warms and then turn entirely green by autumn. 'Royal Purple' is larger with deep purple flowers. 'Peedee Ingot' has bright golden foliage that fades to chartreuse in the shade, but stays gold in the sun. Other good selections include the low growing 'Lilac Beauty', 'Silver Midget', and the variegated 'Silver Sunproof'. Taller selections include 'Evergreen Giant', 'Majestic', and 'Big Blue', all of which are over 15 inches tall with dark blue flowers. Monkey grass (*Ophiopogon japonica*) has similar thin leaves and flowers held within the foliage. Black monkey grass (*O. planiscapus* 'Nigrescens') has purple-black leaves and pink flowers.

Mealy Blue Sage

Salvia farinacea

Bloom Period and Seasonal Color
Spring to frost, blue, violet, white

Mature Height x Spread 2 to 3 ft. x 2 to 3 ft.

Botanical Pronunciation
SAL-vee-uh fare-eh-NAY-see-ah

Zones 8 to 10

It is easy to get inundated by the vast array of salvias available. For Texas gardeners, they are irresistible, and there is a color, form, and style for gardens in any location. Of the blue-flowering salvias, mealy blue sage is among the best for gardens in the southern two-thirds of the state. The plant grows numerous, normally erect, stems from the base. Linear leaves are light gray-green but are not densely arranged. The deep blue to dark violet tubular flowers are crowded into a terminal cluster. Each bloom is half covered by the calyx (sepals). The calyx is coated with fine, whitish hairs, which in some individuals are vivid and prominent, creating the look that is the source of the common name.

When, Where, and How to Plant
Plant in fall or spring in warm winter areas; plant in spring in colder areas after all danger of frost is past. The ideal situation for mealy blue sage is half day of full sun but shaded roots. In desert zones, plant in filtered shade or with morning sun.

Growing Tips
Apply slow-release or organic fertilizer annually in spring. Water every seven to ten days in summer in the hottest parts of the state. Where there is regular summer rainfall, rely on natural rainfall. Mulch the roots heavily during the summer to retain soil moisture and provide the cool root zone favored by this species. Natural rainfall is sufficient in winter.

Regional Advice and Care
Prune severely in early spring to remove winter-damaged stems and reinvigorate the plants. After a flowering cycle, stems can be cut back to the new basal growth. Mealy blue sage is not susceptible to pests or disease.

Companion Planting and Design
Plant generously to form an informal hedge or border along a drive or walkway or to surround a patio, pool, or seating area. Locate plants where the hummingbirds that are constantly in attendance can be viewed and enjoyed. Use mealy blue sage to fill in a small dry corner or relieve the boredom often associated with too many green leafy plants.

Try These
'Henry Duelberg' is a vigorous blue selection, and 'Augusta Duelberg' is white. 'Victoria Blue' and 'Victoria White' are small selections used as annuals. The striking 'Indigo Spires' has deep purple flowers and is reported to be a hybrid with *Salvia longispicata*. Shrubby blue sage (*S. ballotiflora*) is a shrub with aromatic foliage and small blue flowers. Pitcher sage (*S. azurea*) has sky blue flowers and is one of hardiest of the blue-flowering salvias. Blue Chihuahuan sage (*S. chamaedryoides*) has deep blue flowers and tiny, gray-green leaves. Mexican bush sage (*S. leucantha*) is a purple-flowering salvia up to 6 feet tall. Its selection 'Midnight' has a purple calyx and deep purple flowers, whereas 'Santa Barbara' has rose-lavender flowers with a purple calyx.

Mexican Hat

Ratibida columnifera

Bloom Period and Seasonal Color
Spring to summer, yellow, red-orange, brownish red rays, dark brown disks

Mature Height x Spread 2 to 3 ft. x 2 to 3 ft.

Botanical Pronunciation
RAH-tib-eh-dah kal-um-NIF-err-ah

This willowy Texas native enhances both annual wildflower and traditional perennial plantings. Plants begin as a basal set of finely lobed, apple green leaves that grow to nearly a foot tall. In the late spring Mexican hat sends up a sturdy, branched flowering stalk. The compound flowers are fanciful, and their unusual shape accounts for the common name. The dark brown disk flowers are jammed into a finger-like receptacle, and the wide ray flowers ring the base draped like a flashy skirt in combinations of yellow, maroon, and brown. The entire flower looks like a thimble with a skirt. Mexican hat reseeds freely, so keep the ones you want and pull out the rest. I find that the seedlings often have unusual flower forms and color combinations.

When, Where, and How to Plant
Plant from seed or transplants in fall in warm winter areas. Wait until early spring when soil can be worked in regions with cold winters. Grow Mexican hat in full sun in all zones, although it tolerates filtered shade in extremely hot, dry zones. Mexican hat grows best in well-drained, moderately fertile soil. When planting from seed, work in a thin layer of slow-release or organic fertilizer to the bed. Broadcast seed evenly and rake to cover lightly.

Growing Tips
Apply slow-release or organic fertilizer annually in the spring just as growth resumes. Water regularly; weekly is usually sufficient even in summer unless it is unusually hot or dry. In areas with regular summer rainfall, it grows on natural rainfall. Rely on natural rainfall in winter. Mulch the roots to maintain even soil moisture, provide slightly increased fertility, and extend the watering frequency.

Regional Advice and Care
Cut flowering stalks down to the basal leaves once bloom is finished. Plants are semi-dormant in winter. Although root hardy to 0 degrees Fahrenheit, it helps to cover the roots with a 4- to 6-inch layer of mulch in cold winter areas. Mexican hat is a vigorous reseeder. Seedlings can be relocated in late fall or winter in warm winter zones or early spring in colder ones. Mexican hat is not susceptible to pests or disease.

Companion Planting and Design
Mexican hat is delightful mixed with other spring or summer flowering perennials. It is also a colorful addition to wildflower or meadow plantings, extending the flowering season through the summer. Use Mexican hat generously to fill in barren spots in newly planted beds or hide winter dormant plants. Mexican hat blooms later than most spring annuals in warm areas, making it particularly useful to extend the season around seating areas, patios, or pools.

Try These
Prairie coneflower (*Ratibida tagetes*) has numerous wiry stems, each of which is tipped by a similar style of flower to Mexican hat. The rays are generally yellow, whereas the disk is reddish brown with a looser appearance than that of Mexican hat.

Mexican Oregano

Poliomintha maderensis

Bloom Period and Seasonal Color
Spring to fall, purple fading to white

Mature Height x Spread 2 to 4 ft. x 3 to 4 ft.

Botanical Pronunciation
PO-lee-oh-men-thuh MAH-der-in-sis

Zones 8 to 10

We tend to value plants mostly for their visual appeal. But one touch of the leaves of Mexican oregano releasing its spicy, tantalizing smell reminiscent of a Mexican kitchen makes it apparent that plants can delight all our senses. Numerous plants are called oregano in Mexico, and this is just one of them. It's also called rosemary mint. The flavor of this species is more delicate than the other culinary oreganos, but it is most valued as an ornamental rather than a kitchen herb. Deep green leaves are crowded on arching stems with the tubular flowers tightly congested along the ends. Flowers begin purple, fade to lavender, and then turn white, so the plant appears to have three colors at once while in flower. Hummingbirds feast on the nectar of its flowers.

When, Where, and How to Plant
Plant in the fall in areas with no expectation of frost. Otherwise, plant in spring after all danger of frost is past. Mexican oregano grows in any well-drained, moderately fertile soil. It handles soils with high alkalinity but rots quickly in heavy clays or consistently wet soils. In areas where these soils dominate, raise the bed slightly or add copious amounts of gravel or other rock to the bed.

Growing Tips
Mexican oregano does not need supplemental fertilizer. Water established plants every seven to ten days in summer, less often if there is ample summer rainfall. Water once a month in winter depending on the temperatures. Mulch the roots through the summer to keep the soil from drying out completely.

Regional Advice and Care
Prune plants carefully and resist annual shearing or other aggressive pruning. Prune lightly in fall after flowering is complete or in early spring when growth resumes to tidy up the plant or removed damaged stems. Cut the oldest stems to the ground every two or three years to reinvigorate the plant and encourage new stem growth. Mexican oregano is not susceptible to pests or disease.

Companion Planting and Design
Mexican oregano is an excellent perennial near a patio, pool, or walkway where the spicy fragrance of the leaves can be enjoyed. It mixes well with other warm-season perennials. Its small size and tidy growth habit make it a good choice for an informal border or boundary marker or to back up a bed of small, flowering perennials. Hummingbirds are strongly attracted to this species, so place it where these enchanting visitors can be viewed and admired.

Try These
Hoary rosemary mint (*Poliomontha incana*) is native to western Texas. This is an upright, shrubby plant with gray-green leaves with a silver to white blush. Small sky blue flowers are abundant, and the leaves have a pungent but crisp aroma. Hoary rosemary mint grows best in extremely well-drained, even sandy soils on a lean watering schedule.

Mexican Petunia

Ruellia brittoniana

Bloom Period and Seasonal Color
Spring to summer, purple, pink, white

Mature Height x Spread
1 to 3 ft. x 2 to 4 ft.

Botanical Pronunciation
roo-EL-lee-a brit-tone-ee-AN-ah

Zones 8 to 10

Mexican petunia is a deceptive-looking plant. The narrow, dark green leaves that are densely arrayed along its numerous thin stems look tender and ready to wilt. But the fact is this is one of the most drought- and heat-tolerant perennials available to gardeners in the state. Mexican petunia spreads rapidly from underground stems, making it a nuisance in gardens with too much water, but the parade of paper-thin purple flowers make it a splendid choice for summer color in drier locations. I have had this plant in gardens in New Orleans, Arizona, and South Texas, and it has thrived in each of them. Even left on its own, it may lose lots of leaves but recovers almost immediately with a good soaking rain.

When, Where, and How to Plant
Plant in the spring once all danger of frost is past and the soil is warm. Mexican petunia grows well in any amount of sun and will bloom beautifully in deep shade. Mexican petunia tolerates and even thrives in well-drained soil either slightly acidic or alkaline. In a moderately fertile soil the plant is virtually carefree.

Growing Tips
Mexican petunia needs no supplemental fertilizer. In fact, when grown with too much fertilizer or too much water, it becomes a rapidly spreading thug. Water sparingly in summer just often enough to keep it from severe wilt. In most areas of the state it grows well on natural rainfall except during extended periods of heat or drought. Rely on natural rainfall in winter when it is semi-dormant.

Regional Advice and Care
Prune selected stems to the ground in spring to remove damaged or decrepit stems. Badly overgrown clumps can be pruned to within inches of the ground in the spring to rejuvenate the plant. Divide crowded clumps or relocate seedlings in late winter. Mexican petunia is not susceptible to pests or disease.

Companion Planting and Design
Mexican petunia makes an excellent—and low-maintenance—informal border or hedge to line a driveway, walkway, or patio. Use Mexican petunia generously near a pool, against a hot wall, or in other areas where reflected heat is intense. Plant dwarf forms along walkways or paths as edging or place in front of larger perennials or shrubs. Mexican petunia makes a good container plant, and this is a good way to control its spread in a small garden.

Try These
'Chi Chi' has pink flowers, and there is an unnamed white-flowered form. 'Katie' is a dwarf, growing to 12 inches tall with dark purple flowers. A pink-flowered dwarf is sometimes sold as 'Colobe Pink' as well as a lovely white dwarf called 'Katie White'. Softseed wild petunia (*Ruellia malacosperma*) has wider, deep green leaves without the purple tinge and the same range of flower color. It is somewhat hardier than Mexican petunia. The white-flowering form is most common in the trade.

Mistflower

Conoclinium greggii

Bloom Period and Seasonal Color
Spring to fall, blue

Mature Height x Spread
12 to 18 in. x 18 to 24 in.

Botanical Pronunciation
con-no-CLIN-nee-um GREG-ee-eye

Zones 8 to 10

There is a section of Kerrville State Park that is planted as an enclosed butterfly garden full of wonderful local flowering plants. The first time I visited was in September, and the mistflower was in full bloom. The plants were so smothered with Queen butterflies feeding on its nectar that it appeared to bloom butterflies. Mistflower, or Gregg's mistflower, is a multistemmed perennial with numerous, weak stems that rise from a semi-woody base. The palmate leaves are then further divided, giving them the appearance of ferns. The flowering heads are crowded onto the end of the branches and consist of pale lavender to blue disk flowers and no ray flowers. This gives the flower the misty appearance of its common name. Plants are all or at least partially winter dormant.

When, Where, and How to Plant
Plant in spring once the soil is warmed or can be worked. Select a site with full sun or light, partial shade. Amend the soil with ample amounts of compost, composted manure, or a blend of these and other organic material. Work it in fully and be sure that the bed is well drained. In areas with poor drainage or heavy soils, raise the bed slightly before planting.

Growing Tips
Mistflower does need supplemental fertilization. Renewal of a thick layer, up to 6 inches, of mulch annually is sufficient to maintain soil fertility for this species. Water as often as weekly during its first summer depending on temperatures. Once established, mistflower can usually rely on natural rainfall, watering it only when the weather is particularly hot or rainfall is especially scarce. This species is tolerant of high heat coupled with high humidity, making it a great choice for gardens near the coast.

Regional Advice and Care
Prune out dead or damaged stems in early spring just before growth resumes. Plants can be cut almost to the ground if necessary. Light pruning through summer helps maintain its shape and vigor and promotes continued flowering. The most intense flowering is in late summer, so don't wait to prune too late.

Companion Planting and Design
Queen butterflies in particular find this species irresistible, making it a good foundation for a butterfly garden. The delicate flowers that seem to float over the top of the plant provide textural contrast when mixed with harder-edged or firmer-leaved perennials. Mistflower increases by underground stems (rhizomes) and will fill a space quickly, which helps maximize the effect of the filigreed leaves and gossamer flowers. Use it to fill in areas of the garden that do not receive regular watering or maintenance.

Try These
Blue mistflower (*Conoclinium coelestinum*) has large, entire leaves but sparser flowers and prefers moist, sandy, or loam soils. Blue mist (*Ageratum corymbosum*) has darker blue flowers and is equally attractive to a wide array of butterflies. Use blue mist in locations with high heat but low humidity.

Narrow-Leaf Coneflower

Echinacea angustifolia

Bloom Period and Seasonal Color
Spring to fall, purple, rose, white

Mature Height x Spread
1 to 3 ft. x 2 to 4 ft.

Botanical Pronunciation
eh-kuh-NAY-see- an-gus-tih-FOE-lee-ah

Zones 8 to 10

The name *Echinacea* is synonymous with the various compounds from this genus with a reputation for protection from colds and other ailments. But it is the flowers that ought to share equally in that reputation and recognition. Standing like sentinels, narrow-leaf coneflower blooms rise in solitary heads on tall stems. Narrow-leaf coneflower blooms repeatedly over a long flowering season with long, light purple rays that fall away from the brownish disks like a skirt. Like many of its relatives, this is an excellent cut flower. When cutting for use in an arrangement, look for flowers where the disk flowers are barely open. Plants form a significant taproot that increases in size, and therefore storage ability, over its life and helps explain its great drought tolerance.

When, Where, and How to Plant
Plant from either seed or transplants in early spring, as soon as soil can be worked. Choose a site in full sun for best flowering. Plants grow in a wide range of soils, including highly alkaline ones, but are better in moderately amended soils. Add up to 3 inches of good-quality compost to the bed before planting. Good drainage is essential; consider raising the bed slightly if the soil is heavy or drainage is poor.

Growing Tips
Fertilize once in spring with a balanced formulation such as is used for roses. Water carefully, providing enough water to keep the soil from drying out completely, but not allowing the plants to remain wet consistently. Natural rainfall is often sufficient except during the hottest or driest weather.

Regional Advice and Care
Narrow-leaf coneflower reblooms well even without deadheading. However, plants look tidier and reseed less vigorously if old flowering stalks are routinely removed. Every three or four years, divide the clumps in spring if they become overcrowded. Narrow-leaf coneflower will self-seed if some of the flowers are left to allow the seed to mature.

Companion Planting and Design
Narrow-leaf coneflower, and indeed all coneflowers, looks especially fine blended with ornamental grasses to create garden meadows or prairies. Their great drought tolerance makes them good filler plants for areas of the garden that do not receive intensive cultivation. Use at the back of borders to give lift and interest to a planting of low-growing perennials. Goldfinches are attracted to the seeds, so consider leaving a few heads to go to seed so you can enjoy these stunning birds.

Try These
Purple coneflower (*Echinacea purpurea*) grows to 5 feet tall with large, dark purple rays surrounding a domed cluster of reddish brown disks. 'White Swan' is white. Pale coneflower (*E. pallida*) has thin, drooping rays that are light lavender to pink. It grows in a wide range of soils from acid to alkaline, moist to dry, but it prefers those that are fairly rich. The unusual flowers look best in mass or blended with grasses.

Plains Zinnia

Zinnia grandiflora

Other Name Yellow zinnia

Bloom Period and Seasonal Color
Spring to fall, yellow rays, yellow to gold or brown disks

Mature Height x Spread
8 to 12 in. x 8 to 10 in.

Botanical Pronunciation
ZEN-ee-uh GRAND-ih-flor-uh

We have all grown the charming and durable annual zinnia, but there are outstanding perennials in this genus as well, and plains zinnia is among the best of the clan. This is a low, spreading plant that sprawls quickly by underground stems (rhizomes) and over time forms dense mounds or mats. The flowering heads in plains zinnia have four to six bright yellow rays and upright orange to brown disks. The flowers are so prolific they often cover the foliage entirely. I like the combination of deep green, narrow foliage and the bright, yellow flowers. Plains zinnia has the added bonus of flowering over a long season. Butterflies are strongly attracted to plains zinnia, often covering the plant as much as the flowers do.

When, Where, and How to Plant
Plant from transplants or sow seed in fall or early spring. In cold zones, spring planting is preferred. Choose a location in full sun for best flowering and form. Plains zinnia is more tolerant of heavy soils than are most perennial zinnias but does need excellent drainage. Amend the soil with ample amounts of compost, composted manure, other organic material, or a combination of these prior to planting.

Growing Tips
Plains zinnia does not require regular supplemental fertilization. In most areas, plants grow well on natural rainfall except during unusually hot or dry spells. During those times, water once a week until the weather moderates. In hot zones, water established plants weekly in the hottest part of the summer.

Regional Advice and Care
If rainfall is scarce, plants may go dormant. Growth resumes when moisture, either by rain or watering, is restored. Tip prune in summer only to keep plants in bounds or to tidy up unruly stems. Plants are short-lived in hot zones and may need to be replanted every three or four years. Plains zinnia is not susceptible to pests or disease.

Companion Planting and Design
The trailing stems of plains zinnia are lovely when planted where they can fall over low walls or as a low border along a paved walkway. Use the casual form of plains zinnia to give a hint of randomness in an otherwise tidy perennial planting. Plains zinnia is a good choice for erosion control or to fill in a spot in the garden that does need regular maintenance.

Try These
White zinnia (*Zinnia acerosa*) is also a low, sprawling plant. Less hardy than plains zinnia, white zinnia's green stems are covered with fine hairs, giving them a white blush. The silvery to gray leaves are so thin they look like needles; in fact, *acerosa* means needle-like. Each of the countless flowering heads has four to six white ray flowers and bright yellow disk flowers. Once flowers are done, the rays turn dull white but remain on the plant for a long time like a second bloom.

Prairie Verbena

Glandularia bipinnatifida

Bloom Period and Seasonal Color
Spring to fall, purple, lavender, pink

Mature Height x Spread
6 to 16 in. x 8 to 18 in.

Botanical Pronunciation
ver-BEE-nah bye-pin-ah-TIFF-ih-dah

If you love to attract butterflies to your garden, you need to include generous amounts of prairie verbena (syn. *Verbena bipinnatifida*) into your planting scheme. These durable natives are magnets for many species of butterflies as well as graceful summer-flowering plants. Prairie verbena is a low, spreading mat-forming perennial with narrow gray-green to bright green leaves. Each leaf is marked by deep lobes, each of which is also lobed. The overall effect is of a fern. All verbenas have tiny flowers jammed into round or thimble-shaped heads. Prairie verbena has tiny, purple to lavender flowers crammed into a rounded head. Flowers continue to form up the flowering stalks through the flowering season. Eventually, what began as a rounded flower head ends the season looking like an elongated thumb.

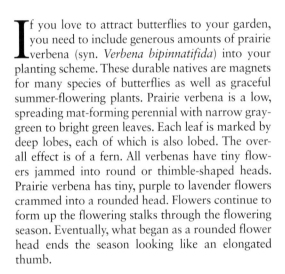

When, Where, and How to Plant

Set out transplants in fall or spring in warm winter areas. Plant in early spring in colder zones. Choose a site in full sun, although in extremely hot areas prairie verbena grows well in light, filtered shade. Prairie verbena prefers alkaline soils that are rocky or otherwise extremely well drained. If the soil is heavy or otherwise poorly drained, add generous amounts of gravel, compost, or other additions to increase the drainage.

Growing Tips

Apply a slow-release fertilizer in the spring once growth resumes. Formulations for roses are ideal. Water often enough to prevent the soil from completely drying out, especially when in bloom. In hot areas this may be once a week, much less often in cooler zones. Rely on natural rainfall in the winter in all zones.

Regional Advice and Care

The tops of prairie verbena will die in a freeze, but the roots are hardy. Prune any cold damage in early spring after all danger of frost is past. Lightly tip prune in summer to keep plants tidy or remove spent flowering heads. Prairie verbena is not susceptible to pests or disease.

Companion Planting and Design

Use prairie verbena as a colorful groundcover in areas that require little regular maintenance. It is an excellent addition to wildflower or meadow plantings. Its mat-forming habit makes it a good choice for erosion control on gentle or rocky slopes. They are also attractive in hanging pots or the edge of large planters. Plants typically last about three years, but reseed freely.

Try These

Goodding's verbena (*Glandularia gooddingii*) has moss green leaves and lavender to pink flowers with wide, gray-green leaves. Sandpaper verbena (*Verbena rigida*) is a South American species that gets its common name from the raspy feel of its deep green leaves with deep purple flowers in elongated heads. 'Polaris' has silvery leaves and lavender flowers. Moss verbena (*G. pulchella*) is a cold-tender, low-growing plant with finely cut leaves and deep purple or white flowers. It is remarkably drought tolerant in warm winter zones.

Rosemary

Rosmarinus officinalis

Bloom Period and Seasonal Color
Spring, blue, purple, white, pink

Mature Height x Spread
3 to 6 ft. x 3 to 8 ft.

Botanical Pronunciation
roz-mah-RINE-us oh-fis-si-NAL-is

Zones 8 to 10

Many gardeners only know rosemary for its culinary qualities, but it is a valuable addition to ornamental gardens throughout the state. The deep green, evergreen leaves are covered with sticky, resinous oil. This oil produces the sharp, clear fragrance when the leaves are touched and the rich flavor when they are cooked. The fragrant leaves are a delightful addition to fresh or dried arrangements. The blue flowers of rosemary are small and crowded on the stems. Beekeepers prize the honey made from these blossoms. Numerous cultivars are identified for upright, trailing, and bushy forms and for flower color and taste. If you intend to cook with the rosemary, taste it before you buy it; the range of flavors is astounding.

When, Where, and How to Plant
Plant in fall or spring in warm winter areas. Plant only in spring, once the soil has warmed and all danger of frost is past, in cold winter zones. Select a spot in full sun. Rosemary grows best in rocky, alkaline soils but will tolerate any well-drained soil that is not too wet or too acidic.

Growing Tips
Rosemary needs no supplemental fertilization. This extremely drought-tolerant species grows on natural rainfall in most regions of the state. However, to keep plants at prime vigor, water during extended hot or dry spells or at least once a month in summer.

Regional Advice and Care
Prune lightly through the growing season to maintain shape and encourage tender, new stems. Remove dead or damaged wood in late fall in warm areas or early spring in colder ones. Rosemary often gets a dead zone in the middle of the plant when grown with too much water or fertilizer. Prune back to within 1 to 2 feet of the ground every two or three years to prevent this problem. In humid areas spider mites may be a problem, but otherwise rosemary is not susceptible to pests or disease.

Companion Planting and Design
Plant rosemary as a low hedge or border plant. Its deep green color makes it a stunning background for bulbs, perennials, or annual plantings. Its heat tolerance makes it a good choice against a hot wall, around a pool or patio, or in other areas where reflected heat is intense. Many of the trailing forms are reliable groundcovers or erosion control on steep slopes. Place near a walkway where the foliage can brushed often to release the fragrance.

Try These
'Arp', introduced by the late Texas herb grower Madalene Hill, is a vigorous, cold-hardy selection. A sport of it with finer leaves, 'Hill's Hardy' is equally hardy. Both are upright, shrubby plants. 'Tuscan Blue' is upright with dark blue flowers. 'Spice Island' is upright, lush, and extremely flavorful. 'Lockwood de Forest' is a graceful trailing form with pale blue flowers, as is 'Irene' but with darker flowers.

Russian Sage

Perovskia atriplicifolia

Bloom Period and Seasonal Color
Late spring to frost, blue, indigo

Mature Height x Spread
3 to 4 ft. x 3 to 4 ft.

Botanical Pronunciation
per-OV-skee-ah at-trih-pliss-ih-FOE-lee-ah

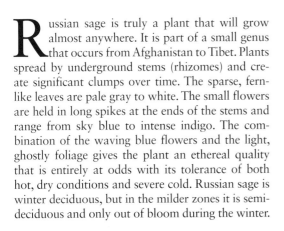

Russian sage is truly a plant that will grow almost anywhere. It is part of a small genus that occurs from Afghanistan to Tibet. Plants spread by underground stems (rhizomes) and create significant clumps over time. The sparse, fern-like leaves are pale gray to white. The small flowers are held in long spikes at the ends of the stems and range from sky blue to intense indigo. The combination of the waving blue flowers and the light, ghostly foliage gives the plant an ethereal quality that is entirely at odds with its tolerance of both hot, dry conditions and severe cold. Russian sage is winter deciduous, but in the milder zones it is semi-deciduous and only out of bloom during the winter.

When, Where, and How to Plant
Plant in fall or spring in mild winter zones. In colder zones, plant in spring after all danger of frost is past and the soil has warmed. Russian sage does best in full sun in all zones, although in areas with extreme heat it requires filtered shade. Russian sage is tolerant of almost any type of soil as long as the drainage is very sharp. Adding generous amounts of compost or other organic matter to the backfill when planting helps plants establish well.

Growing Tips
In mild winter areas, apply fertilizer annually in early fall. In colder areas, apply in late spring after growth has resumed. Water two or three times a month in summer. In extremely hot weather, water weekly. Rely on natural rainfall in winter. In all areas, a 4-inch layer of mulch through the summer helps maintain sufficient soil fertility and keeps the soil from drying out completely.

Regional Advice and Care
Prune to within 1 to 2 feet of the ground in early spring to remove winter-damaged stems or reinvigorate the plant. Cut dead flowering stalks regularly to prolong the bloom. Russian sage is not susceptible to pests or disease.

Companion Planting and Design
Add Russian sage to any mixed perennial planting for the contrast its delicate foliage provides. Plant generously to create a loose, informal border or fill a barren spot in the garden. Russian sage is particularly effective planted around hard features like statues or fountains.

Try These
'Blue Spire' is the most commonly offered form with dark, nearly violet, flowers. 'Longin' has gray-green leaves and a less spreading habit. 'Filagran' is an upright plant with deeply dissected, silvery foliage. 'Blue Haze' has sky blue flowers with uncut leaves, as does the light blue 'Blue Mist'. *Little Spire* is a dwarf form growing to 2 feet. Russian sage is widely grown, but many horticulturists consider that some or perhaps all of these forms may actually be hybrids between this species and the closely related and similar *Perovskia abrotanoides*.

Scarlet Rose Mallow

Hibiscus coccineus

Bloom Period and Seasonal Color
Late summer to fall, red

Mature Height x Spread 4 to 7 ft. x 3 to 4 ft.

Botanical Pronunciation
hy-BIS-kus kok-SIN-ee-us

Zones 8 to 10

Scarlet rose mallow, also called Texas star hibiscus, is a stunning plant that dominates the garden when it is in flower. Tall enough to be considered a shrub, it is not in fact woody, but does grow many stems. Plants die to the ground in freezing temperatures but are root hardy. The plant sends up new shoots each spring that flower the following summer. The deep green leaves with five distinct segments are themselves an attractive addition. But the flowers are sensational. Six inches or more across, they are deep, perfect red with split petals that are wide open. These scarlet stars wait until it is very hot to make their best showing, often waiting until July to bloom. Believe me, it is worth the wait.

When, Where, and How to Plant
Plant in spring after all danger of frost is past and the soil has warmed. Although established plants are root hardy, young or newly planted individuals can be destroyed by a late freeze. Plant in full sun everywhere for best performance. Grow scarlet rose mallow in any moderately fertile, well-drained soil, but this *Hibiscus* will also grow in seasonally flooded areas.

Growing Tips
Apply a balanced fertilizer, such as is formulated for roses, in early spring as growth resumes. In most areas that is all the fertilizer that is required. Water regularly, particularly when it is hot or dry. In coastal areas or where there is regular summer rainfall, scarlet rose mallow grows well on natural rainfall. Rely on natural rainfall in all areas in the winter.

Regional Advice and Care
Plants are winter deciduous and stalks can be cut down in late fall before they freeze back. Otherwise, cut winter-damaged stalks to the ground in early spring just as the plant resumes growth. Light tip pruning through the summer keeps them tidy, but take care to not overdo it, plants bloom on new growth. Scarlet rose mallow has no significant pest or disease problems.

Companion Planting and Design
Use scarlet rose mallow in the back of a mixed perennial planting for late season color. Because of its size, this is a good screening plant when planted close together or in mass. Use it in front of a hot window to calm the summer sun and provide a colorful view.

Try These
Common rose mallow (*Hibiscus moscheutos*) is an equally tall species, widely grown for its big, lush, pink, red, or white flowers and does best in moist, acidic soils. There are many hybrids and cultivars of this species including 'Flare' with bright pink flowers, 'Lord Baltimore' with deep red flowers, and 'Peppermint Flare' with red streaks on white petals. Heartleaf hibiscus (*H. martianus* syn. *H. cardiophyllus*) is a short, bushy plant with carmine red flowers. This species is more tolerant of hot, dry conditions and dry soils than are the other two. It is hardy only to the warmest parts of Zone 8.

Sedum

Hylotelephium spp.

Bloom Period and Seasonal Color
Spring to fall, yellow, red, pink, pink-purple, bronze-pink

Mature Height x Spread 4 to 18 in. x 12 in.

Botanical Pronunciation
HIGH-low-tell-ee-fee-um

Zones 7 to 9

Sedum, or stonecrop, (formerly *Sedum* species) is a name used for a wide number of species and cultivars that have fleshy, gray-green to bright green leaves and flower prolifically. These succulent perennials represent some excellent choices for cooler areas and provide outstanding drought tolerance. Most sedums grow best in the northern half of Texas where the summers are mild, not fiercely hot, and the fall and spring are cool. Winter hardiness depends on the species, but many are hardy to 0 degrees Fahrenheit. Garden sedums are typically mound-forming plants that fit in well with any perennial planting. Butterflies are drawn to their nectar, and because most bloom in the late summer and fall, they attract numerous migratory species. The garden species have been cultivated for centuries.

When, Where, and How to Plant
Set out transplants in the early spring after all danger of frost is past and the soil has warmed. In mild winter areas, plants can be set out in early fall as well. Choose a location in full sun for best form and flowering in the coldest areas but provide relief from afternoon sun where it is hotter in the summer. Sedums need excellent drainage and moderate fertility.

Growing Tips
Water carefully to avoid rotting the roots. Sedums prefer intermittent deep soaks rather than continuous light watering. Avoid overhead watering using a garden hose, soaker hose, or drip irrigation to avoid damaging the leaves. In all areas, rely on natural rainfall in the winter unless the weather is exceptionally hot or dry.

Regional Advice and Care
Prune flowering heads as they fade. Tip prune through the early summer to keep plants bushy. These tips cuttings will form roots quickly. Sedums are generally not bothered by pest or disease.

Companion Planting and Design
Because of their need for outstanding drainage, sedums are a traditional component of rock gardens. They blend well with other perennials where growing conditions are similar. Use along walkways or in mass in corners of the garden to maximize their late flowering.

Try These
Showy sedum (*Hylotelephium spectabile*) is a hardy, deciduous, free-flowering plant with large pink to red flowering heads in late summer. Orpine (*H. telephium*) has dense heads of small pink, red, or occasionally white flowers through fall. A hybrid between these two, 'Autumn Joy' is a 2-foot mounding plant with flowers that begin pale pink to white and fade to russet. Its round, succulent form and late summer to fall flowering make it an ideal companion for ornamental grasses. The low-growing 'Gold Moss' has bright yellow flowers in the summer. 'Ruby Glow' is up to a foot tall with fleshy blue-green leaves with a purple to reddish cast and deep rosy-red flowers. *Sedum palmeri* is a Mexican species brought into horticulture by YuccaDo Nursery. It is a spreading plant with bright yellow flowers and is well suited to southern gardening conditions.

Shrimp Plant

Justicia brandegeeana

Bloom Period and Seasonal Color
Spring to fall, red, red-orange, yellow

Mature Height x Spread
2 to 3 ft. x 2 to 6 ft.

Botanical Pronunciation
jus-TIS-ee-a bran-dee-gee-AH-na

Zones 8 to 10

Shrimp plant is a sprawling perennial with brittle stems holding widely spaced thin leaves. The tubular white flowers are densely clustered at the ends of the stems. Each is surrounded by big, showy bracts that range in color from light brown to reddish brown, occasionally dark maroon or light chartreuse. The whole array looks precisely like the tail of a shrimp and is the source of its fanciful common name. Despite its delicate appearance, shrimp plant grows best in areas with high summer heat, making it particularly reliable in the southern half of the state. *Justicia* is a largely tropical genus, but this species is among the most cold hardy of those commonly grown. Leaves are damaged in the mid-20s but plants are root hardy to 10 degrees Fahrenheit.

When, Where, and How to Plant
Plant in spring after all danger of frost is past and the soil is warmed. With attentive care planting can continue through early summer. Plants achieve their best form in full sun or half-day sun but tolerate and bloom well in light shade. Shrimp plant tolerates a wide range of soils, including alkaline ones, but does best in moderately fertile soils that are well drained.

Growing Tips
Apply a balanced fertilizer, such as rose food, in early spring as growth resumes. Reapply two or three times during the growing season. Water every seven to ten days, depending on temperatures, although this species tolerates short dry spells well. Mulch heavily to extend the time between waterings.

Regional Advice and Care
Prune to within a few inches of the ground in the spring to remove dead or damaged stems and reinvigorate the plant. Light pruning through the summer keeps the plant tidy. Shrimp plant has no significant pests or disease. Plants grown in too much shade or with consistent overhead spray can develop leaf fungus diseases. Prevent these problems by watering from below.

Companion Planting and Design
With its sprawling stems, shrimp plant is a fine choice for a corner or any place that needs to be filled up. Use it under woody shrubs or small trees or in the wells of fruit trees as a companion planting or groundcover. It is also a beautiful addition to any mixed perennial planting. Hummingbirds are strongly attracted to its flowers.

Try These
'Mutant' has deep red bracts. 'Fruit Salad' has bright chartreuse bracts, white flowers with a pink lip, and green foliage. 'Yellow Queen' and 'Chartreuse' both have bright chartreuse bracts, but the flowers are entirely white. There are numerous forms with deep red to maroon bracts that are unnamed. Mexican honeysuckle (*Justica spicigera*) has light green leaves and bright orange flowers. Both species are hardy only to the mid-20s. The infrequently offered Runyon's water willow (*J. runyonii*) has deep blue to purple flowers and leaves that turn burnished copper-red in fall.

Square-Bud Primrose

Calylophus berlandieri

Bloom Period and Seasonal Color
Late spring to fall, yellow

Mature Height x Spread
4 to 16 in. x 10 to 16 in.

Botanical Pronunciation
kal-LEE-low-fuss ber-land-ee-AIR-ee-eye

Zones 8 to 10

Square-bud primrose, also called sundrops, grows as a low, spreading perennial. The dusky, dark green leaves are smooth with slightly toothed margins. The prolific bright yellow flowers have tissue-thin petals; you imagine you can see through them. Each flower lasts only one day, but a continuous stream of them runs through the blooming season. Flowers have variable amounts of dark purple to brown at the base of the petals, a feature that is much sought after in selections that are offered for sale. This species is often considered a groundcover for its ability to run along and cover a lot of space quickly. I find it equally delightful as low, or sometimes mounding, addition to the front of a perennial garden or set among boulders and rocks.

When, Where, and How to Plant
Plant in spring after the soil has warmed. Flowering is best in full sun, particularly in the northern parts of Texas. In the southern half, plants also flower well in morning sun locations. Square-bud primrose is not particular about soil type as long as there is excellent drainage. Choose a site that does not hold water or stay consistently wet.

Growing Tips
Square-bud primrose does not require supplemental fertilization. Water to keep the soil evenly moist but not so much that it is water logged or consistently wet. In most areas this means watering two or three times a month in summer, and relying on natural rainfall in the winter. Water more frequently if it is exceptionally hot or dry.

Regional Advice and Care
Plants can be short-lived, but runners root readily. Remove or replace decrepit plantings in the spring by lifting rooted stems and replanting them. Otherwise, no pruning is required. Flea beetles cause superficial damage in early spring but are a short-lived and simply cosmetic problem.

Companion Planting and Design
Square-bud primrose is an excellent groundcover for new gardens or areas with steep slopes. It is a good rock garden plant and softens the rough edges of a rocky area. Use it in a mixed planting of perennial and annual flowering plants for a long season of color. Its low, spreading form makes it a good choice to line a walk or driveway.

Try These
Sundrops (*Calylophus hartwegii*) is even more of a running plant than square-bud primrose. It has larger flowers that lack the dark spot at their base. In bud the two are easily distinguished; square-bud primrose buds have prominent ribs on four sides, making them look square, whereas those of sundrops are rounded. Both square-bud primrose and sundrops are easily confused with many yellow flowering forms of primrose like yellow evening primrose, (*Oenothera macrocarpa*) or beach evening primrose (*O. drummondii*). To tell them apart, look at closely at the stigma. In *Calylophus* it is shaped like a club or a knot, in *Oenothera*, like a cross.

Texas Rock Rose

Pavonia lasiopetala

Bloom Period and Seasonal Color
Spring to frost, pink

Mature Height x Spread
1 to 3 ft. x 1 to 3 ft.

Botanical Pronunciation
pah-VOH-nee-ah lass-ee-oh-PET-al-lah

Zones 8 to 10

Texas rock rose is one of those plants that I think has a place is nearly every garden in the southern part of the state. This charming Texas native is a particularly good plant for regions with limestone soils, even thin or rocky ones, and its intense, pink flowers continue to open intermittently almost all year, making it an easy choice. Plants grow numerous, irregular stems rising from a woody base and have dark green, three-lobed leaves. The small, solitary, pink flowers open daily in the morning, closing by afternoon. Texas rock rose is a short-lived perennial, living for three to six years. It does, however, reseed readily in congenial conditions, so there is often a ready supply. It is also easy to propagate from cuttings.

When, Where, and How to Plant
Plant Texas rock rose in spring once all danger of frost is past and the soil is warm. Plants flower best in full sun in almost all areas, but in extremely hot regions it also grows and flowers well in light, filtered shade. Texas rock rose does best in alkaline, often highly alkaline, soils with moderate fertility. The addition of compost or other organic matter at planting is therefore optional, depending on your garden's soil. It is important to provide excellent drainage.

Growing Tips
In areas of extreme summer heat or during extended dry spells, water weekly in the summer. Otherwise, it grows well on watering once or twice a month or on natural rainfall. Rely on natural rainfall throughout the winter.

Regional Advice and Care
The erratic branching habit makes this a challenging perennial to prune. It is best to prune lightly through the early spring, taking only the tip to encourage a tighter form. Plants do not recover well from shearing or severe pruning. Tip pruning also encourages a longer and more prolific blooming season. Texas rock rose is not susceptible to pests or disease.

Companion Planting and Design
Use Texas rock rose in any mixed perennial planting for its color and long season of bloom. It blends well with succulents such as agaves or yuccas, providing color and contrast to these strong-leaved plants. Used generously, Texas rock rose makes a fine low border. This is another good choice to fill in a dry, sunny corner or other areas that do not receive regular maintenance.

Try These
Spearleaf swampmallow (*Pavonia hastate*) is another beautiful member of this genus. This species has bright white flowers with a dark, rose red center and as the name suggests long, linear leaves. It is sometimes offered as *P. peruviensis*, a name with no botanical standing. It has been grown in Australia for so long that it is often described as an Australian native. However, it is probably native to South America and naturalized in Australia long ago. Regardless, it is gorgeous growing with the same care as Texas rock rose.

Trailing Lantana

Lantana montevidensis

Bloom Period and Seasonal Color
Spring to fall, lavender, white

Mature Height x Spread
1 to 2 ft. x 3 to 6 ft.

Botanical Pronunciation
lan-TAN-na mon-TAY-vie-den-sis

Zones 8 to 10

Trailing lantana is a low-growing perennial with seemingly endless flowers through the summer. Although originally from South America, trailing lantana has naturalized through the warm winter areas of the United States, including Texas, Central America, and the West Indies. The long stems root along as they grow, particularly in fertile soils. The small purple, occasionally white, flowers are in fact a congested, round head of tiny flowers. Many species of butterfly find the flowers irresistible and feed regularly on them as they migrate through in the spring and the fall. Plants are at least semi-deciduous in cold weather when the leaves turn purple to brown. Trailing lantana is root hardy in normal winters as far north as Zone 7 with a heavy mulch.

When, Where, and How to Plant

Plant in spring once all danger of frost is past and soils are warm. Planting may continue through early summer. The best flowering and form is in full sun, but trailing lantana also grows well in light, filtered shade. It's not particular about soils, growing well in dry or alkaline ones as well fertile, well-amended ones.

Growing Tips

Trailing lantana does not need supplemental fertilization unless it is growing in soils with extremely low fertility. For these soils, amend with good-quality compost and mulch heavily. Water two or three times a month in summer. This species has good drought tolerance once established and will survive on much less frequent watering in mild summer areas.

Regional Advice and Care

Cut back severely in early spring as growth resumes to remove dead or winter-damaged stems. If plants become too large or unruly, prune back the stems in the summer. Whitefly can infest this plant where they are common, but otherwise it has few disease or pest problems.

Companion Planting and Design

Trailing lantana is a charming groundcover for a large barren area. It mixes with other low-water-use plants like agave or native shrubs. The long flowering stems make it a good choice for a raised planter or hanging basket so they fall over the edge. Its habit of rooting as it grows along also makes it a good choice for erosion control. Containers are an excellent way to enjoy this plant in areas where it might be too cold to use it in the ground.

Try These

'White Lightnin' is pure white, 'Imperial Purple' is purple with a prominent white eye, and 'Lavender Swirl' has flowers that begin white and fade to purple or lavender. There are numerous hybrids with shrubby lantana (*Lantana camara*). Some are small, bushy plants, whereas others are trailing. Spreading forms include 'New Gold' with garish gold-yellow flowers, 'Silver Mound' with white flowers and a golden eye, 'Lemon Drop' with pale yellow flowers, 'Malan's Gold' with yellow variegated foliage and deep rose-red flowers, and 'Red Spreading' as the name suggests.

Turk's Cap

Malvaviscus arboreus var. *drummondii*

Bloom Period and Seasonal Color
Spring to fall, red, pink, white

Mature Height x Spread 2 to 6 ft. x 3 to 8 ft.

Botanical Pronunciation
mal-vah-VISS-kus ar-BOR-ee-us druh-MUN-
dee-eye

Zones 8 to 10

Turk's cap lurks at the intersection of perennial and shrub; often large and woody at the base, but not quite to the stature or woodiness of a shrub. It is big, spreading, and heftier than most perennials. But this charming Texas native, by any designation, is an effortless winner in the garden. Numerous stems rise from its base, and each holds the dark green heart-shaped leaves. The abundant flowers are upright, brilliant red with petals that are wrapped together to form a closed flower that someone thought looked like a turban, hence the common name. There is a lot of variation in the species especially in both plant and flower size, but all are long-season splashes of bright color that are irresistible to hummingbirds.

When, Where, and How to Plant
Plant in spring once all danger of frost is past and the soil has warmed. Planting can continue through the early summer. In almost all of the state, it does best in full sun, but in the deserts provide relief from afternoon sun.

Growing Tips
Turk's cap needs no supplemental fertilization. In areas with long, hot summers water every seven to ten days. Turk's cap grows in most areas on natural rainfall, needing watering only during extended dry spells. Extend watering periods by heavy applications of mulch around the root zone.

Regional Advice and Care
Prune in spring to tidy up winter-damaged stems or correct errant growth. Lightly prune through summer to encourage a tighter form.

Companion Planting and Design
Use Turk's cap in a mixed perennial bed with other summer-flowering species. Because it spreads well, it fills in or accents a sunny corner. Hummingbirds are constant visitors to these plants, so situate Turk's cap where you can enjoy these winged visitors. It is heat tolerant enough to use against hot walls or around a pool.

Try These
There is a vast and long-lived confusion over the naming of Turk's cap. Plants can be called by *M. arboreus*, *M. drummondii*, *M. penduliflorus*, or *M. penduliflorus* var. *drummondii*, depending on where you live. However, *M. arboreus* is wide-ranging, tropical species that is found from Mexico to Central America as well as the Gulf Coast states. It is extremely variable, with flowers that are erect or drooping and larger than those of variety *drummondii*, which grows throughout south central Texas on into Mexico. Naturally growing plants of this variety grow along streambeds, and this smaller variety is also more cold hardy. Texas horticulturist Greg Grant took one of the big drooping tropical forms and crossed it with a smaller, upright one, and the result is an intermediate between the two he calls 'Big Momma'. This plant is large and woodier than the typical Turk's cap, with large, upright flowers. He then crossed 'Big Momma' with a smaller, white-flowered form to get the salmon-pink 'Pam Puryear'.

Western Mugwort

Artemisia ludoviciana

Bloom Period and Seasonal Color
Summer to fall, yellowish white

Mature Height x Spread 1 to 4 ft. x 3 to 5 ft.

Botanical Pronunciation
ar-tuh-MEE-zhah loo-doh-vee-see-AH-nah

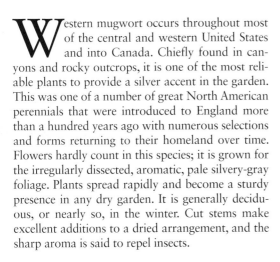

Western mugwort occurs throughout most of the central and western United States and into Canada. Chiefly found in canyons and rocky outcrops, it is one of the most reliable plants to provide a silver accent in the garden. This was one of a number of great North American perennials that were introduced to England more than a hundred years ago with numerous selections and forms returning to their homeland over time. Flowers hardly count in this species; it is grown for the irregularly dissected, aromatic, pale silvery-gray foliage. Plants spread rapidly and become a sturdy presence in any dry garden. It is generally deciduous, or nearly so, in the winter. Cut stems make excellent additions to a dried arrangement, and the sharp aroma is said to repel insects.

When, Where, and How to Plant
Plant container-grown plants in early spring. Clumps can also be divided and replanted in spring. Plant in full sun or filtered shade. Western mugwort grows in virtually any kind of well-drained soil. However, it does best in soils that are not too fertile and that do not stay consistently moist.

Growing Tips
Western mugwort needs no supplemental fertilizer. Water two to three times a month in summer, depending on temperatures and natural rainfall. In most of Texas, Western mugwort thrives on natural rainfall. Rely solely on natural rainfall in winter while it is dormant. It gets floppy and leggy in deep shade or when overwatered.

Regional Advice and Care
Prune to the ground in early spring to remove winter-damaged stems and reinvigorate. Western mugwort is not susceptible to pests or disease, although overwatered plants, or those growing with poor drainage, may develop root rots.

Companion Planting and Design
Western mugwort mixes well with perennials that also thrive in a dry garden. Western mugwort's tolerance of full sun, ability to grow in rocky soils, and minimal watering requirements make it ideal for succulent gardens or outer areas of the garden that receive minimal care. Its spreading habit makes it a good choice for erosion control on steep slopes.

Try These
'Silver King' is a 3-foot-by-3-foot erect perennial with linear, uncut silver leaves. This is one of the oldest selections and was bred in England. It spreads quickly and can be aggressive when water is abundant. It is usually sold as a cultivar in the United States, but the Royal Horticultural Society considers it a common name of the subspecies *mexicana* of Western mugwort. 'Silver Queen' is similar but not quite as large with leaves that are noticeably softly hairy and generally widely dissected. 'Valerie Finnis' grows only to 2 feet or less and spreads much less quickly than the others. The leaves are silver, softly hairy, and wider and longer than the other forms. This cultivar and the unselected species are the easiest to use in small gardens.

Wild Foxglove

Penstemon cobaea

Other Name Showy beardtongue

Bloom Period and Seasonal Color
Spring, lavender, purple, white

Mature Height x Spread
12 to 18 in. x 4 to 6 in.

Botanical Pronunciation
PEN-steh-mon co-BAY-ah

Native from the Midwest into East Texas, wild foxglove is a stunning perennial for all Texas gardens. The long, glossy green leaves grow near the ground. Flowering stalks tower over the leaves, and the flowers are held in congested clusters. An individual flower is an inch-long tube with a wide flare at the end. The lightly fragrant flowers have prominent purple nectar guides in the interior and are excellent cut flowers. *Penstemon* is an immense genus that occurs in a wide range of habitats. This is a boon to gardeners because there are at least a few, sometimes many, that will grow in your area. Wild foxglove rarely lives over four years, but it reseeds freely and will cross with other species when grown together.

When, Where, and How to Plant
Plant seed or transplants in fall in warm winter areas. In cold zones, plant in early spring as soon as the soil can be worked. *Penstemon* seed germinates readily but may slow down growth in cool temperatures then resume quickly when the weather warms. Choose a site in full sun (light shade only in desert or other hot zones). Wild foxglove does best with a fertile, well-amended soil that has excellent drainage. Add generous amounts of compost or other organic additives to the bed before planting.

Growing Tips
Wild foxglove does not require supplemental fertilization if grown in a fertile soil. Water regularly while it is growing and flowering. Reduce water in summer to no more than it takes to keep it from wilting. Rely on natural rainfall in winter.

Regional Advice and Care
Seedlings are abundant in this short-lived species, so leave the stalk to allow seed to mature. Prune off flowering stalks as soon as all flowers have opened if you wish to prevent seed production. Wild foxglove has no pest or disease problems.

Companion Planting and Design
Use generously in a mixed perennial planting or within a wildflower or meadow garden. This species is tall and is most effective toward the back of a border or bed. In hot areas it is a good choice for color in light shade.

Try These
Rock penstemon (*Penstemon baccharifolius*) is endemic to the Hill Country and does best in alkaline, rocky soils. The rosy red flowers are abundant in the summer even in desert areas. Scarlet bugler (*P. barbatus*) has thin, scarlet flowers and is cold hardy enough to grow throughout the state. Hill Country penstemon (*P. triflorus*) has glossy, green leaves and rosy red flowers that are held to one side of the stalk. Cardinal beardtongue (*P. cardinalis*) from the mountains of West Texas flowers in summer with large, spectacular scarlet flowers. In the Panhandle, try Palmer's penstemon (*P. palmeri*), which has large, pink to lavender, highly scented flowers, or sand penstemon (*P. ambiguous*), with its rounded form and abundant pinkish white flowers.

Winecup

Callirhoe involucrata

Other Name Poppy mallow

Bloom Period and Seasonal Color
Spring through fall, purple, magenta, white

Mature Height x Spread 1 to 2 ft. x 2 to 4 ft.

Botanical Pronunciation
kal-uh-ROH-uh in-voh-loo-KRAH-tah

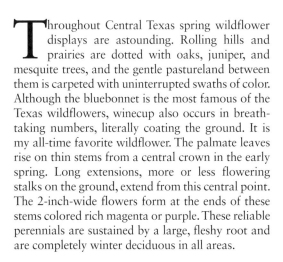

Throughout Central Texas spring wildflower displays are astounding. Rolling hills and prairies are dotted with oaks, juniper, and mesquite trees, and the gentle pastureland between them is carpeted with uninterrupted swaths of color. Although the bluebonnet is the most famous of the Texas wildflowers, winecup also occurs in breathtaking numbers, literally coating the ground. It is my all-time favorite wildflower. The palmate leaves rise on thin stems from a central crown in the early spring. Long extensions, more or less flowering stalks on the ground, extend from this central point. The 2-inch-wide flowers form at the ends of these stems colored rich magenta or purple. These reliable perennials are sustained by a large, fleshy root and are completely winter deciduous in all areas.

When, Where, and How to Plant
Plant transplants from the garden or container-grown plants in spring once the soil has warmed. Planting may continue through early summer. Winecup may also be planted from seed sown in fall. Winecup is adaptable to a wide range of soils but grows best in well-drained, alkaline but fertile soil. Prepare the soil by adding compost, composted manure, or a blend of organic matter to the soil. Be careful not to plant where water ponds or collects.

Growing Tips
Winecup needs no supplemental fertilizer. Water established plants weekly in summer if it's exceptionally hot or dry. In areas with regular summer rainfall, winecup grows well on natural rainfall. Provide a 4-inch layer of mulch around the roots to keep soil from drying out completely. In cold winter areas, mulch the roots heavily in fall to protect the crown.

Regional Advice and Care
Remove dead flowers anytime. Plants increase by runners and can create a dense mat over time. Rooted stems can be lifted and potted or moved in spring if they become too crowded or messy. Winecup is not susceptible to pests or disease.

Companion Planting and Design
Winecup is delightful mixed with other low-growing, summer-flowering perennials such as gaillardia or chocolate flower. Because it is short and spreading, it is useful as a border in front of larger perennials and shrubs. Use this effortless plant to fill barren gaps in the garden or to provide quick color for a new garden. Winecup grows well in containers or planters where the long running stems can spill over an edge. It can be used for erosion control on steep slopes.

Try These
The lovely purple poppy mallow (*Callirhoe involucrate* var. *lineariloba*) has five narrow leaf segments that are deeply lobed at the ends. Flowers tend to be light lavender with white accents. *C. digitata* is a somewhat smaller plant with narrow leaf segments that are deeply lobed at the ends. It blooms purple, magenta, and white and is a charming addition to any garden despite being less commonly grown than its cousin.

Yarrow

Achillea millefolium

Bloom Period and Seasonal Color
Spring to early fall, white, yellow, pink

Mature Height x Spread
6 to 36 in. x 8 to 36 in.

Botanical Pronunciation
ah-KILL-ee-uh mill-ee-FOH-lee-um

Yarrow has a long history of cultivation in its native range from southern Europe through Asia. Revered by the Greeks for the healing properties of the leaves, the genus takes its name from the warrior Achilles, who allegedly used it to treat his soldier's wounds. Yarrow is a tall, erect perennial with fern-like, fragrant leaves. They are graceful plants with these light green leaves abundant along the tall stems. The flowers are held in wide, flattened heads. Both the ray flowers and the disk flowers are white, yellow, pink, red, or combinations of these colors. Yarrow is a splendid cut flower and an even better dried flower. When cutting flowers to dry them, it is best to cut the flowering heads before they open.

When, Where, and How to Plant
Yarrow can be started from seed or from transplants. Sow seed in spring after all danger of frost is past and the soil is warmed. Set out transplants at the same time. Plants grow and flower best in full sun, but will tolerate light, filtered shade, particularly in areas with long, hot summers. Yarrow grows well in a wide range of soils from acid to alkaline, heavy or sandy, and is renowned for its performance in dry soils. Regardless, drainage should be excellent. Prepare the bed by removing all grass or other weeds and work in a light application of compost or mulch.

Growing Tips
Yarrow rarely needs supplemental fertilization. Water often enough to prevent the soil from drying out completely. Take care not to overwater or allow water to pond or stand around the plants. Water with a soaker hose, garden hose, or drip irrigation rather than overhead sprinklers.

Regional Advice and Care
Remove dead flowering heads regularly to prolong flowering. Yarrow dies back after the first frost, and stems can be cut to the ground at that time. Yarrow spreads by underground stems (rhizomes). To reduce the size of the clump, divide the rhizomes in fall.

Companion Planting and Design
Yarrow is an effortless choice in any part of the garden. Yarrow is tall enough to grace the back of a bed or anchor a corner of the garden that does not receive regular maintenance. Yarrow is highly attractive to many species of butterflies and makes a colorful addition to a butterfly garden.

Try These
Fern-leaf yarrow (*Achillea filipendulina*) is up to 5 feet tall with yellow flowers and dark green leaves. Its hybrids 'Coronation Gold' and 'Gold Plate', with its 6-inch heads, are widely grown. The hybrid 'Moonshine' is yellow with gray-green leaves, 'Cerise Queen' is deep pink, and 'Paprika' is red with yellow disks and ages to copper-red. *A. tomentosa* has hairy leaves on a low-growing plant, to 1½ feet. This species reportedly does particularly well in the acid soils of East Texas Piney Woods.

Zexmenia

Wedelia texana

Bloom Period and Seasonal Color
Spring to fall, yellow, gold

Mature Height x Spread
1 to 3 ft. x 1 to 3 ft.

Botanical Pronunciation
weh-DEEL-ee-ah TEX-an-uh

Zones 8 to 10

Zexmenia (formerly *Zexmenia hispida*) is one of the easiest native flowering perennials to grow throughout central and southern Texas. Numerous spreading branches rise from a woody base. Plants often look ungainly or erratic usually because it is grown in too much shade. The dark green leaves are rough to the touch and are densely held on the plant. The daisy-like flowering heads have up to 10 yellow or golden ray flowers and golden disk flowers. Each flowering head is held individually on a thin stalk that rises high over the foliage. Zexmenia is a long-lived plant that increases modestly in size over time. It is evergreen in the south, and even when it dies back, recovery is quick. Butterflies are strongly attracted to this plant.

When, Where, and How to Plant
Plant in spring once all danger of frost is past and soils are warm. Continue planting into early summer. Choose a location in full sun for tightest form, although zexmenia does well in light, filtered shade in very hot areas. Zexmenia grows best in fertile, well-drained soils. Amend the area with ample amounts of good-quality compost or other organic matter prior to planting.

Growing Tips
Zexmenia does not need supplemental fertilization. In most zones, water once or twice monthly. If the weather is especially hot or dry, water weekly. In areas with regular summer rainfall, zexmenia thrives on natural rainfall alone. Natural rainfall in winter is sufficient in all zones.

Regional Advice and Care
Cut back severely in early spring as growth resumes to remove winter damage or reinvigorate leggy or overgrown plants. Light tip pruning in summer helps maintains good form. Zexmenia is not susceptible to pests or disease.

Companion Planting and Design
Butterflies are extremely fond of its nectar, making this a splendid addition to a butterfly garden. The long season of bloom, especially the fact that it extends well into the fall, makes it valuable as part of a mixed perennial planting. It is also useful around patios or pools where its brilliant color can be enjoyed. I don't think this plant has ever quite caught on, which is a shame. It has a lot going for it: a long blooming season, rugged tolerance to dry conditions, resistance to pest or disease, and appeal to numerous species of butterfly. What more could we want in a plant?

Try These
Creeping wedelia (*Sphagneticola trilobata*) was once commonly grown as a groundcover and erosion control in warm winter or nearly frost-free zones. However, in those areas where water was abundant and frost infrequent, it became an invasive pest and is no longer recommended for these areas. In less congenial areas, it is still a useful groundcover when it does not get sufficient natural rainfall to become a pest. In desert zones, it is one of the few flowering groundcovers for deep shade.

ROSES

oses have been a part of gardens throughout the world for centuries. Chinese and European gardeners brought them into gardens from the wild hundreds, if not thousands, of years ago. Bred, hybridized, selected, and transformed, thousands of varieties are offered today in a host of styles and forms. The delicate, layered petals that open generously against the deep, green foliage demand attention and garner admiration. The unlikely contrast of the thorny stems and the gentle flowers has inspired poets and dreamers since ancient times. But the most memorable and evocative part of roses is their smell, that heady, sweet unmistakable scent, often with spicy accents, that adds immeasurably to both the mystique and the pleasure of roses in the garden. Like many people, the first thing I do when I see a rose is lean over and smell it, and those without scent are just a tiny bit disappointing.

Rosa 'Sombreuil' with daylilies

A Rose for Every Garden

Even in the hottest areas of the state, with the combination of careful selection and attention to the details of their cultivation, roses can be glorious garden plants. Whether you grow them in dedicated beds and care for them like doting parents or choose to blend them into a more diverse planting, if you want a rose, there is one available to suit your taste and your needs. I like roses best mingled with other perennials or placed where they become a colorful part of the garden. Large uniform rose beds are best reserved for demonstration and teaching gardens; at home I want a lot more diversity and interest.

I am especially drawn to the so-called heirloom or old garden roses and am amazed at how many varieties thrive in the withering heat of the summer, as well as the winters of the colder zones. Many of these varieties are very old, with lineages of up to two hundred years or more. Others are of entirely unknown parentage. They are found in old gardens among the bulbs and perennials or have been handed down in a family, one generation after another. Some come to us from cemeteries.

They share a heritage of toughness and endurance after living so long with

Bush and climbing roses

minimal care. They have found their own way, growing in neglected conditions and without the tender care of a gardener, and this life has tempered them into rugged, care-free plants in the garden. Many are exuberant shrubs growing much larger and in a less refined fashion than their modern hybrid kin. The profusion of varieties and classes attests to the bounty of these roses and their possibilities in all zones of the state.

Modern hybrid roses are generally sold bare root. This is a great way to buy roses and get them established in the garden. Take a bare root rose home wrapped in moist packing and plunge it in a bucket of water in the shade for a day or two. This process helps rehydrate the plant after shipping and greatly decreases transplant shock. Opinions vary on whether or not to put in fertilizer or other soluble treatments in the water.

Rose Care

Care of roses can be as complicated or straightforward as you choose and greatly depends on the combination of variety and zone in which it is grown. Choosing well-suited varieties simplifies their cultural requirements immensely, so check with local rose societies or growers for guidance for your particular area.

Roses grow best in fertile soil with even moisture throughout the year. Because roses are heavy feeders, a regular fertilization program is best, but most thrive with any all-purpose fertilizer. Organic amendments like compost, mulch, and alfalfa meal also work very well.

Pruning is an art form that is best learned by the doing. Most rose societies provide free pruning demonstrations. Take advantage of the offer and learn how to prune roses properly from the pros in your area.

Climbing

Rosa spp.

Bloom Period and Seasonal Color
Spring and summer, white, red, pink, lavender, blends, bicolors

Mature Height x Spread
6 to 15 ft. x 10 to 30 ft.

Botanical Pronunciation
ROW-suh

I find climbing roses irresistible and romantic. Strolling, or better yet lunching, under an arch loaded with their fragrant blooms makes me feel as if I have walked back to a more graceful, leisurely age. They are the very essence of an old-fashioned cottage garden with their long canes draped around the front door and their blossoms and fragrance welcoming you inside. The large flowers of climbers bloom either once a year or repeat through the year, depending on the variety. These roses grow long, sturdy canes and need an equally strong support or wall to hold them up. Over time some of the initial canes enlarge and form the frame of the plant. The smaller secondary canes emerge annually, and flowers arise from these new shoots.

When, Where, and How to Plant
Plant bare-root roses in January or February when the soil can be worked. Container-grown plants can be planted through late spring. Roses grow best in full sun or with a minimum of six hours. All roses need fertile, well-drained soil for best growth and flowering. Dig a hole that is three to four times wider than the container but just as deep. Add generous amounts of compost to the soil and work it in thoroughly. Set in the rose, making sure the bud union is well above the soil line. Mulch the root zone but prevent mulch from touching the plant.

Growing Tips
Apply balanced slow-release fertilizer formulated for roses or organic rose fertilizer every month while the plants are actively growing. In hot summer areas reduce or eliminate fertilization in summer, and in all zones discontinue fertilization in fall and through the winter. Water deeply to achieve the equivalent of 1 inch of rain a week or completely soak the root zone down 2 or 3 feet, depending on the size of the plant.

Regional Advice and Care
Remove dead or damaged wood in late summer. Save heavy pruning for January in the south and early February in the north. Leave the large, framing canes unpruned until they are as long as desired. Annually prune the secondary canes to create the desired growth pattern. Check local sources for varieties in your area with resistance to rose diseases.

Companion Planting and Design
Use against a wall or trellis to create a dramatic focal point. Allow the plant to climb over an archway, ramada, pergola, or trellis to form an entry to a building or areas of the garden.

Try These
'Fourth of July' has red-and-white striped petals and brilliant yellow stamens. 'Altissima' has fragrant, velvet red flowers held in clusters, whereas the very hardy 'Don Juan' has lacquer red single blooms against shiny, green foliage. 'Improved Blaze' and 'Climbing Pinkie' are other excellent choices. Check with the local rose society for the varieties that are recommended for your area.

Floribunda

Rosa spp.

Bloom Period and Seasonal Color
Spring and summer, pink, red, white, yellow, bicolors, blends

Mature Height x Spread 4 to 8 ft. x 3 to 5 ft.

Botanical pronunciation
ROW-suh

Floribunda arose as a class of roses in the early years of the twentieth century through the efforts of a Swedish breeder named Dines Poulsen. He introduced 'Rodhatte' in 1912, which was a cross between a hybrid tea and a polyantha. It was hit, and Poulsen kept at it. Ultimately, Jackson & Perkins saw this as a great new type of rose, coined the term floribunda, and introduced 'World Fair' at the 1939 World Fair in New York. For the next 50 years, Jackson & Perkins continued to create and introduce many of the classic floribundas in the trade. Floribundas are distinguished by having groups of three and seven large blossoms on each stem. They also have a long and continuous flowering through summer into fall.

When, Where, and How to Plant
In warmer areas, plant bare-root plants in January or February. In cold regions, plant in March. Container-grown plants can be planted until March in warm areas and May in colder zones. Select a site in full sun. Dig a hole three to four times wider than the container and just as deep. Add generous amounts of compost to the soil and work it in thoroughly. Be sure the bud union is well above the soil line. Mulch the root zone but do not allow the mulch to touch the bark.

Growing Tips
Apply slow-release rose fertilizer or organic rose fertilizer every month while actively growing. Most growers suggest no fertilizer when it is hot or during the winter; but many maintain monthly fertilization year-round. Water deeply to a depth of 2 to 3 feet and do not let the plants dry out. This can be as often as twice a week in the summer when it is hot. In most areas, monthly deep watering in the winter is sufficient.

Regional Advice and Care
Prune to remove dead wood and summer-damaged stems in early fall. Save hard pruning for February in warm areas and March in colder ones. A hard prune is removing up to one-third of the bush, including all dead or damaged canes and twiggy growth, leaving eight to 12 healthy canes. Roses are susceptible to powdery mildew, cane borers, and aphids.

Companion Planting and Design
Floribunda is a particularly good rose for landscape use either in mass or in mixed beds of perennials and bulbs. Use generously around walkways, seating areas, courtyards, or patios to enjoy the long and fragrant blooms.

Try These
'Betty Boop', 'Angel Face', 'Europeana', and 'Iceberg' are favorite floribunda varieties. Grandifloras are a cross between hybrid tea and floribunda with the long stems and floral style of the former and long bloom and hardiness of the latter. The first grandiflora was 'Queen Elizabeth', but others include 'Tournament of Roses', 'San Antonio', and 'Fame'. Check with local rose society for varieties best suited to your area.

Heirloom

Rosa spp.

Bloom Period and Seasonal Color
Spring to summer, white, pink, red, purple, lavender, bicolors, blends

Mature Height x Spread 3 to 12 ft. x 3 ft.

Botanical Pronunciation
ROW-suh

Heirloom roses are a polyglot group of species, hybrids, and cultivars in which there are a bewildering number of classes. Their common bond is that all of the classes were in existence before 1867, although some authorities move that date up to 1920. Most set a profusion of flowers, and although some bloom only once, others are continuous. Roses of this type tend to have open flowers with few petals and often an intoxicating fragrance. They are frequently found and regrown from plants in old gardens, cemeteries, or abandoned farmsteads. The Antique Rose Emporium in Independence abounds with these roses, particularly in late spring. The remarkable Tyler Rose Garden in Tyler displays a wide array of these sturdy beauties alongside their more modern hybrid kin.

When, Where, and How to Plant
Plant bare-root roses in late winter, which is January or February in the south and March farther north. Container-grown plants can be planted until early summer in all zones. Many heirloom roses are cold hardy enough to be planted in the fall, especially in the southern half of the state. Most heirlooms are not particular about soil as long as it is well drained. A soil amended with ample compost or other organic matter does increase vigor and bloom, however.

Growing Tips
Apply balanced slow-release or organic fertilizer every month when roses are actively growing. These plants tend to slow their growth in hot weather, and expanding the time between waterings and ceasing

fertilization during this time is advised. Growth will resume as the weather cools. While growing water every ten days to two weeks depending on the weather—no more than twice a month during hottest part of summer or during winter.

Regional Advice and Care
Many heirloom roses are shrubs with complicated branching patterns and do not need an annual heavy prune as do the modern hybrids. It is better to prune lightly following the spring bloom to shape or control growth. Flowers are set on new wood, so take care not to prune too late in the year and therefore arrest the spring bloom. These roses are tolerant of extremes of heat and cold and often resistant to rose disease and pests, but vigilance counts. Catch problems early, treat quickly, and keep the plants healthy for best results.

Companion Planting and Design
Smaller varieties can be intermingled with other perennials or with shrubs. Use along a border or fence line to block a view or hide an unsightly fence. Rambling or climbing varieties look wonderful against a wall, to cover an arbor, or on a post or trellis.

Try These
'Mutabilis' begins yellow and fades to orange, pink, and crimson. Other good selections include 'Martha Gonzalez', 'Zephirine Drouhin', 'Cecile Brunner', 'Katy Road Pink', and 'Old Blush', an extremely old variety. Check with your local rose society or rose garden for good selections for your area.

Hybrid Tea

Rosa spp.

Bloom Period and Seasonal Color
Spring to summer, red, pink, white, yellow,
purple, lavender, blends, bicolors

Mature Height x Spread 3 to 5 ft. x 2 to 4 ft.

Botanical Pronunciation
ROW-suh

Hybrid tea is a class of roses that came into being with the introduction of '*LaFrance*' in 1867. It and all subsequent hybrid teas are a complicated stew of crosses and recrosses between hybrid perpetuals, bourbons, and teas. Hybrid teas make outstanding cut flowers because there is one blossom at the end of each sturdy stem. In addition, hybrid teas have attractive, tightly furled buds. In some varieties buds last almost as long as the flower. This is the rose of the floral trade and probably the single most widely grown class of roses around the world. Hybrid teas are not long-lived plants, with a typical life span of around tenyears. But they are reliable bloomers and give a lot during that time.

When, Where, and How to Plant
Hybrid teas become available in the winter in the southern part of the state as bare-root plants. Choose plants with three sturdy canes and ample roots. After purchasing a bare-root plant, put it in a bucket of water for a day or so before planting to hydrate it. Plant bare-root roses in January or February in warm areas and March in northern parts of the state. Be sure that the planting hole is well amended with compost and/or other organic matter and that plants are set in with the bud union high above the soil line.

Growing Tips
Apply balanced slow-release rose food or organic fertilizer every month when actively growing. In the hottest areas, it is best to cease fertilization in the summer, resume the schedule in September, and then stop again from November to January. In the colder zones, do not fertilize in the coldest part of the winter. Hybrid teas should not be allowed to dry out completely. Water up to weekly during summer and up to every ten days in winter—twice a month in winter in colder areas.

Regional Advice and Care
In cold winter areas or when freezing temperatures last for days, protect hybrid teas with a thick blanket of mulch. Prune heavily in February in warm areas and March in northern zones. This pruning is dramatic; take out half the bush, leave four to eight healthy canes, and then strip off the leaves. Roses are susceptible to powdery mildew, cane borers, and aphids; use appropriate controls quickly to keep infestations in check.

Companion Planting and Design
Hybrid teas are vertical, shrubby plants that mix well with other shrub-type roses and perennials. They are stunning when grown in groups or in mass to line a walkway or frame a seating area, courtyard, or patio. Although all roses are good cut flowers, these and floribundas are among the best.

Try These
There are hundreds of hybrid tea varieties and more every year. Old favorites include 'Tropicana', 'Mister Lincoln', 'Peace', 'Olympiad', and 'Touch of Class'. Newer varieties include 'Grande Dame', 'Mellow Yellow', and 'Memorial Day'.

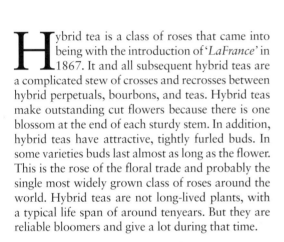

Lady Banks'

Rosa banksiae

Bloom Period and Seasonal Color
Spring, yellow, white

Mature Height x Spread
10 to 20 ft. x 10 to 40 ft.

Botanical Pronunciation
ROW-suh BANK-see-eye

Alongside my parents' house was a large empty lot. To hide it and provide privacy, my mother planted a row of Lady Banks' rose. Not only did they hide the view, they tried to hide that entire side of the yard. This old variety, introduced in 1807, sends out long, virtually thornless shoots with dark green leaves. Lady Banks' rose is more tolerant of hot, dry conditions than most hybrid roses. There are famously huge and long-lived specimens of this species, one of which in Tombstone, Arizona, covers over 8,000 square feet and is still growing. This Chinese species, grown since the 1790s, is named for Dorothea Banks, wife of Sir Joseph Banks, legendary English naturalist, plant explorer, and head of the Royal Horticultural Society.

When, Where, and How to Plant
Plant from late winter to early spring. For the best bloom, choose a location where the canes are in full sun but roots are shaded. Older plants will eventually shelter the roots themselves. Lady Banks' rose is not particular about the type of soil growing well even in highly alkaline ones. Amend the hole with compost or other organic matter and be sure it is well drained. Place near a fence or other support, and mulch the root zone with a 4- to 6-inch layer of mulch.

Growing Tips
Apply balanced slow-release rose fertilizer or a 4- to 6-inch layer of good compost every other month when actively growing. Do not fertilize in summer or from November to January. Water deeply,

soaking the root zone to 3 feet, every week in summer and every ten days in winter. Large, established plants can tolerate less frequent watering. Mulch heavily to conserve moisture in summer.

Regional Advice and Care
Just as growth resumes in spring, cut out canes that are too long or are growing in the wrong direction. Cut as close to the base of the plant as possible. At the same time, prune secondary branches to train them along the support. Prune carefully; this rose blooms on old wood. Lady Banks' rose is not susceptible to most common rose pests or disease.

Companion Planting and Design
Plant against a trellis, wall, sturdy fence, or arbor as a focal or specimen plant to show off its dramatic spring flowering. Use against a hot wall or anywhere that reflected heat is intense. Plant for erosion control on steep slopes where there is sufficient space.

Try These
'Alba Plena' is a white-flowered variety. *Rosa rugosa* is a reliable species with its dense foliage, rose-red flowers, strong fragrance, and great cold hardiness. Another Asian species, *R. wichuraiana*, is a fountain-like shrub with pink to white flowers. Native roses include the white-flowered *R. foliolosa*, *R. arkasana* with deep pink flowers and colorful fruit, the dark pink Wood's rose, *R. woodsii*, and the trailing pink-flowered prairie rose, *R. setigera*.

Miniature

Rosa spp.

Bloom Period and Seasonal Color
Spring and summer

Mature Height x Spread 2 to 3 ft. x 1 to 2 ft.

Botanical Pronunciation ROW-suh

I have a lifelong friend who is a serious rose breeder and who loves roses in way I can only admire but never emulate. When I got married, he could not come to the wedding but sent over a few dozen of the miniature 'Holy Toledo' instead. They were a huge hit as table centerpieces and as presents to relatives and friends. This memorable miniature and a later gift, the luscious white 'Gourmet Popcorn', just about rounded out my rose growing for a long time. I loved these miniatures for their riot of bloom over a long period of time, contentment in a large container, and of course the memories. Miniatures are smaller versions of hybrid tea, floribunda, or grandiflora, and there are even tiny climbers.

When, Where, and How to Plant
Miniatures are usually sold in containers and can be planted anytime they are available in the nursery. The optimal time to plant is February in warm areas and March in cold zones, but anytime through spring will work. Plant in full sun, amending the hole with generous amounts of compost, alone or in combination with composted manure and other organic matter. Be sure it is a well-drained location. Set the plant in the hole slightly high so that the bud union is above the soil line. Water in well and mulch the root zone taking care not let mulch touch the plant.

Growing Tips
Apply balanced slow-release rose food or organic fertilizer every month when actively growing. Miniatures often rest or decline in the summer,

particularly in hot climates. If the plant continues active summer growth, continue to fertilize regularly. In very hot weather, and through the winter, cease fertilization. Water regularly to keep the soil from drying out completely. In the warm areas this is often as much as once or twice a week in summer and once a week in milder climates. In the winter, twice a month is sufficient if there is little natural rainfall.

Regional Advice and Care
Prune heavily in January in warm areas and March in cooler zones. Cut out up to a third of the bush, removing dead or damaged canes and twiggy growth, leaving eight to twelve healthy canes. Lightly prune during the summer to keep tidy. Apply up to 4 inches of mulch annually to help retain moisture in the summer and protect from freezing in the winter.

Companion Planting and Design
Plant generously in front of larger roses, to fill in barren spots, or as a colorful hedge. Miniatures are outstanding in containers where they can be moved to favorable locations throughout the year. Mix with spring- or summer-flowering perennials to extend the season with their long-lasting bloom.

Try These
'Red Cascade' is red climber. 'Acey Deucy', 'Minnie Pearl', the old variety 'Petite Pink Scotch', pink bicolor 'Magic Carousel', and the yellow 'Fairhope' are good choices.

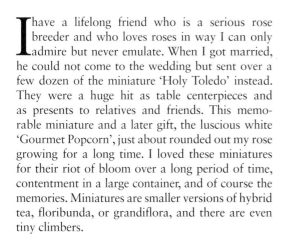

SHRUBS

S hrubs are the backbone of almost all gardens. They give form and substance to even the most minimal gardening efforts. Evergreen shrubs in particular are deeply valued as both foundation plants and to form hedges along the edge of a garden. This is probably the oldest use of shrubs—setting the living definition of where one garden ends and another begins.

Shrubs also divide large gardens into smaller spaces, providing a visual screen between one section of the garden and another. In small gardens using well-placed shrubs to hide one area from another makes the garden seem larger and more interesting. Shrubs also hide unsightly sheds, fences, buildings, views, or neighbors. They keep out noise, cut down on dust, and serve as nest and roost sites for countless birds. Many provide colorful flowers or fruit as well.

Shrubs also play an important role in keeping our homes cooled against the heat of summer. When planted close to a hot wall, shrubs absorb and reflect tremendous amounts of heat and radiation from the sun. Deciduous shrubs are especially useful against southern or western windows where the summer leaves keep out the hot sun and the bare limbs of winter allow in the welcome winter sunlight.

What a shrub *is* exactly has baffled horticulturists and gardeners for a long time. In this book, I consider a shrub to be a woody plant with many, rather than one, central or dominant large branches from which secondary branches arise. This definition is handy and makes size irrelevant, although it is true that most shrubs are considerably less than 20 feet tall.

Shrub Planting and Care Tips

Planting shrubs is straightforward. Dig a hole that is three to five times as wide as the rootball and just as deep. After removing the plant from the container, set it in the hole, making sure that the stems are no deeper in the ground than they were in the pot. Backfill gently, pressing only slightly to firm the soil and water the entire area well. In poorly drained soils, it helps to plant the shrub slightly higher than the surface to account for any sinking after planting.

Pruning shrubs is too often poorly done. The first rule of good pruning is to be sure to prune with a purpose in mind and then only when necessary. The ridiculous and all-too-common practice of shearing and close pruning on a timetable, rather than for a purpose or effect, would be outlawed in a perfect world. It does not improve the looks of the plants, it emphatically diminishes the health and vigor (and sometimes the bloom) of the plants, and it serves no real purpose.

To remove unruly or wayward limbs or reduce the size of a shrub, cut the offending branch back as far into the shrub as possible. Continue this way until the shrub

Evergreen Azalea, 'Mino Crimson'

is the size or shape you want. You are in effect pruning from the inside out with the intent of keeping the form of the shrub rather than just removing the outer layer of the shrub.

What Role Will Your Shrubs Play?

When choosing a shrub keep in mind what function you want it to perform in the garden and how large it will ultimately grow. Too many small urban yards have been inundated by massive hedges of privet or ligustrum. A hedge can provide plenty of privacy without sacrificing scale by selecting plants that fit the size of the space. Blending evergreens with deciduous shrubs, spring flowering shrubs with summer blooming ones, or any combination that inspires you creates a vivid border that adds interest and vitality to a garden.

Although shrubs have many practical uses, some are planted just for their great beauty, long blooming season, wonderful fall foliage, or graceful form. Planting for the sheer beauty and wonder of the plant should always be a consideration in any garden no matter how large or how small.

Abelia

Abelia x *grandiflora*

Other Name Glossy abelia

Bloom Period and Seasonal Color
Spring to fall, white, pink

Mature Height x Spread
3 to 10 ft. x 3 to 12 ft.

Botanical Pronunciation
ah-BEE-lee-ah ex gran-dih-FLOOR-ah

Zones 7 to 9

Abelia is a widely grown Asian shrub that has graced American and European gardens for more than a hundred years. This one is a hybrid between *A. chinensis* and *A. uniflora* that is attributed to an Italian nurseryman in the late nineteenth century. This intricately branched shrub has glossy, deep green leaves and is often known as glossy abelia. Through the long flowering season it is covered with lavender to pink bell-shaped flowers. Each flower has an orange to yellow throat and is delicately fragrant. In northern gardens, abelia is deciduous with bronze leaves in the fall. In southern parts of the state, it is semi-deciduous. It can die to the ground in a severe winter, but recovery is quick, and it typically blooms the following summer.

When, Where, and How to Plant
Plant in early fall or spring in all but the coldest areas. In those regions it is best to plant in spring as early as soil can be worked. Pick a spot that has full sun for the best form and color, but in hotter areas it can be grown in light, filtered shade. Abelia needs moist, rich soil that drains well. Add generous amounts of compost or other organic matter before planting. In heavy or poorly drained soils, raise the planting area slightly or amend with gravel.

Growing Tips
Fertilize in spring just as growth resumes with any well-balanced formulation. Rose and lawn fertilizers work well. Fertilize again in early fall but before the leaves begin to drop. Water deeply but at regular intervals for best results. In all but the hottest areas, twice a month is sufficient. Apply a 4- to 6-inch layer of mulch to keep the soil evenly moist and extend the watering frequency.

Regional Advice and Care
Abelia blooms on new wood so perform any severe pruning as early in the spring as possible, ideally just as growth resumes. Light tip pruning after initial flowering, through late spring and early summer, maintains good form and encourages reblooming. Abelia is not susceptible to pests or disease.

Companion Planting and Design
Abelia makes a charming background for a mixed perennial planting. Butterflies flock to the flowers, so consider using it as a backdrop or component of any butterfly garden. Abelia makes a good small hedge, or border in the garden.

Try These
'Edward Goucher' is a semi-evergreen, pink-flowering hybrid between *A.* x *grandiflora* and *A. shumannii* that was introduced in 1911. It grows to 5 feet tall. 'Prostrata' grows to only 3 feet tall, and 'Sherwoodii', although also short, growing 2 to 3 feet tall, has graceful arching branches. 'Sunrise' has cream and pink variegation on the leaves, and 'Francis Mason' is also variegated with wide yellow margins. 'Golden Anniversary' is a dense, rounded plant that grows to 3 feet tall with bright green leaves with yellow to golden margins.

Almond Verbena

Aloysia virgata

Bloom Period and Seasonal Color
Spring to fall, white

Mature Height x Spread 5 to 15 ft. x 6 to 8 ft.

Botanical Pronunciation
ah-LOY-see-uh vir-GAH-tuh

Zones 8 to 10

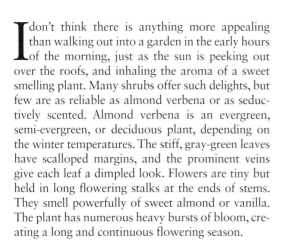

I don't think there is anything more appealing than walking out into a garden in the early hours of the morning, just as the sun is peeking out over the roofs, and inhaling the aroma of a sweet smelling plant. Many shrubs offer such delights, but few are as reliable as almond verbena or as seductively scented. Almond verbena is an evergreen, semi-evergreen, or deciduous plant, depending on the winter temperatures. The stiff, gray-green leaves have scalloped margins, and the prominent veins give each leaf a dimpled look. Flowers are tiny but held in long flowering stalks at the ends of stems. They smell powerfully of sweet almond or vanilla. The plant has numerous heavy bursts of bloom, creating a long and continuous flowering season.

When, Where, and How to Plant
Plant in fall or spring in warmer zones. In colder areas, plant in spring after all danger of frost is past and the soil can be worked. Sweet almond is more vigorous and blooms best in full sun, but it can tolerate light, filtered shade or a morning sun location. Provide well-drained, enriched soil for best results. Amend the bed or backfill generously with compost, composted manure, or other organic material before planting.

Growing Tips
Almond verbena needs no supplemental fertilizer. Water established plants weekly in summer, more often if the weather is very hot or dry. Water monthly or rely on natural rainfall in winter. Apply a 4- to 6-inch layer of mulch to maintain even soil moisture and extend the time between waterings.

Regional Advice and Care
In Zone 8, almond verbena may freeze to the ground in severe winters. Prune off remaining stems in spring once all danger of frost is past. In all other zones, it may only have minor stem damage, which can be removed in spring. In all zones, remove dead wood in spring. Almond verbena is not susceptible to pests or disease.

Companion Planting and Design
The intoxicating aroma of almond verbena makes it a good choice near a pool, patio, or other seating area where the fragrance can be enjoyed. Bees and other insects, including butterflies, are strongly attracted to the flowers, so consider its location if these insects are of concern. Mix with other perennials or shrubs in a perennial planting or mixed hedge. It also forms a good background for a meadow or wildflower garden.

Try These
The native Wright's bee bush (*Aloysia wrightii*) has minute leaves that smell like oregano and tiny, white, sweetly fragrant flowers. It thrives in rocky, alkaline soils and is immune to heat. Whitebrush (*A. gratissima*) is similar but up to 10 feet with 3-inch flowering spikes. Mexican oregano (*A. graveolens* syn. *Lippia graveolens*) is a cold-tender species with tiny, rough, highly pungent leaves and sparse, tiny flowers. It is the Mexican oregano of commerce.

American Beautyberry

Callicarpa americana

Other Name French mulberry

Bloom Period and Seasonal Color
Spring, pink, magenta berries

Mature Height x Spread 4 to 6 ft. x 5 to 8 ft.

Botanical Pronunciation
kal-eh-KAR-pah ah-mare-eh-KAH-nah

Zones 8 to 10

My in-laws live in the woods of East Texas, and whenever we are there in the fall the American beautyberry shine in the woods. American beautyberry is so open and spreading you can fail to notice it in the chaos of a wooded area. There are pink flowers in the spring, but they are small and insignificant. But come fall the stems are stacked with clusters of round purple to magenta berries. Birds go wild for them, and it pays to keep an eye on your plants if you want to enjoy the best show. This is a plant for those difficult areas beneath evergreen trees, where shade dominates. American beautyberry thrives under those conditions and lights the dark corners of such a site.

When, Where, and How to Plant
Plant in fall or early spring after the soil has warmed. Locate American beautyberry in partial or deep shade, but definitely where it has protection from afternoon sun. American beautyberry grows well in any well-drained soil, whether it has been amended or not. If you choose to amend the soil, apply a light layer of compost, composted leaves or manure, or other organic matter before planting.

Growing Tips
American beautyberry does not require supplemental fertilization. Water regularly in all zones. In the warmer parts of the state, this may be as often as weekly, less often where it is cooler or there is regular rainfall. Do not allow the soil to dry out completely. This is especially critical during the hottest part of the summer. Natural rainfall is sufficient in winter in all zones. Use a thick layer, 4 to 6 inches, of mulch to help maintain even soil moisture and extend the time between waterings.

Regional Advice and Care
Prune in early spring just as growth resumes. This plant has a loose-limbed, spreading form that can be ruined with aggressive or continuous pruning. It is best to let it take its own shape and remove only those stems that are dead or decrepit. Avoid pruning after flowering so that the attractive fruit is able to form. American beautyberry has no serious pests or susceptibility to disease.

Companion Planting and Design
Plant American beautyberry in groups beneath large, evergreen trees such as oaks or pines to form an understory. In areas with significant shade, American beautyberry makes a good focal or accent plant. It is tall enough to plant ferns or other shade-loving plants beneath it.

Try These
C. acuminate has almost black, dark purple fruit. There are also white-fruited forms. In my estimation, they are a pale imitation, lacking the feature that is most desirable in this species—its vividly colored fruit. Many gardeners report the white-fruited forms are weaker and not as hardy as the species.

Anacacho Orchid Tree

Bauhinia lunarioides

Bloom Period and Seasonal Color
Summer, white

Mature Height x Spread
6 to 12 ft. x 6 to 10 ft.

Botanical Pronunciation
baw-HIN-ee-uh loo-NAIR-ee-oi-deez

Zones 8 to 10

I am particularly drawn to this genus of woody plants, and Anacacho orchid tree is among the best for South Texas gardens. This is an upright, multi-trunked shrub or small tree. The leaves are paired, joined at the base, and look like a hoof; this is the distinctive leaf shape in all species of *Bauhinia*. The small flowers are pure white or pink with five open petals and extended stamens. The stems are brittle, and wind damage is common in almost all bauhinias, but this is the sturdiest of the group. Anacacho orchid tree's spring flowers are often in layers up the branches and look like dryland dogwoods. The most common ones in nurseries are white-flowered, but pink flowers are more common in nature.

When, Where, and How to Plant

Plant in spring when the soils are warm and all danger of frost is past. Hardy to about 18F18 degrees Fahrenheit, Anacacho orchid tree can be used in the warmer parts of Zone 8, needing protection in only the harshest winters. Plants in full sun have the best form and flowering. In extremely hot areas, Anacacho orchid tree tolerates light, filtered shade. This shrub grows well on rocky, alkaline soils but does equally well in a wide variety of soils as long as the drainage is extremely good.

Growing Tips

Anacacho orchid tree does not need supplemental fertilization. In almost all areas, established shrubs grow well on natural rainfall. If it is exceptionally hot or dry, or in the deserts of west West Texas, water deeply twice a month in summer. Natural rainfall is sufficient in winter in all zones. Mulch the root zone to maintain sufficient soil moisture.

Regional Advice and Care

Prune out any dead or damaged stems in late spring just before the first flush of bloom. In older plants the tallest stems often die out after a few years, leaving numerous smaller stems at the base. Prune out these dead stems anytime, and the other stems will grow quickly to restore the shape of the plant. Anacacho orchid tree is not susceptible to pests or disease.

Companion Planting and Design

Anacacho orchid tree is lovely as an understory plant near or on the edge of a group of larger trees. It is small enough to use in tight patios for its burst of spring color. This species is immune to heat and is a good choice against a hot wall, around a pool, or in other areas where reflected heat is intense.

Try These

Mexican orchid tree (*Bauhinia divaricata*) is a spreading shrub or small tree with small white to light pink flowers that end in a distinct point. Chihuahuan orchid tree (*B. macranthera*) is an openly branched tree to 20 feet with large, dark pink flowers in loose clusters along the top of the branches. Both have brittle stems that need protection from strong winds.

Apache Plume

Fallugia paradoxa

Bloom Period and Seasonal Color
Spring to fall, white

Mature Height x Spread
5 to 6 ft. x 4 to 6 ft.

Botanical Pronunciation
fah-LOO-jee-ah pare-ah-DOX-ah

Zones 7 to 9

Apache plume is an irregularly branched shrub that is found naturally throughout the western United States. It is a plant of two colors. In the spring and early summer, the somewhat rounded shrub is covered with its solitary, flattened, pure white flowers. In the rose family, flowers look like miniature old-fashioned roses. Later clusters of tiny fruit form, and each sports a feathery, pinkish white appendage—that is the plume. The result is arresting; the entire plant looks like a cloud that came to ground. To add another spurt of color, the fruit turns from pale green to dark rosy pink in the fall. The small leaves are green to gray-green. Young twigs are coated with gray hairs but as they age turn a rich, dark brown.

When, Where, and How to Plant

Plant in fall or spring in warm winter areas. In colder zones, plant in spring as early as the soil can be worked. Both growth and bloom is best in full sun, but plants tolerate light shade in areas with extremely hot summers. Apache plume tolerates any well-drained soil from fertile, garden soils to rocky, native ones, but does poorly in heavy clays or where water ponds around the plant. Plant on a slight mound, or add generous amounts of gravel, if planting in heavy or poorly drained soils. Generally, East Texas and areas along the coast are poor locations. Add a thin layer of compost or mulch to the backfill when planting.

Growing Tips

Apache plume requires no supplemental fertilizer. Water established plants every two to three weeks in summer where summers are hot or rainfall is unreliable. In cooler areas or with ample summer water, natural rainfall is sufficient. Rely on natural rainfall in winter. Water monthly if it is unusually warm or dry during winter. Provide a generous layer of mulch to keep soil from drying out too quickly.

Regional Advice and Care

Prune to remove dead or damaged wood in spring. Apache plume benefits from a hard prune every three or four years to keep it in good shape and to provide a new flush of growth, which increases flowering. Annual hard pruning is not advised; it reduces vigor and may impede bloom. Apache plume has excellent natural form and only needs this intermittent pruning to maintain its shape. This species is not susceptible to pests or disease.

Companion Planting and Design

Mix Apache plume with dark, evergreen shrubs to form an informal hedge or boundary planting. The bloom and subsequent plumed fruit is attractive enough to use the plant as a specimen or focal plant. Plant Apache plume in outlying areas of the garden that receive minimal care or as part of a naturalistic garden. It serves as a good background for colorful annual wildflower displays.

Try These

Fallugia is a monotypic genus, meaning there is only this species.

Azalea

Rhododendron spp.

Bloom Period and Seasonal Color
3 to 10 ft. x 3 to 8 ft.

Mature Height x Spread
Spring, red, coral, salmon, pink, white, lavender

Botanical Pronunciation roe-doe-DEN-dron

Zones 7 to 9

Our house in New Orleans was typical with crepe myrtle, old roses, and a hedge of azalea along the front. In the spring when all those azaleas flowered, it seemed the entire city came into bloom. These were the big, old-fashioned, lush flowering ornamental Asian azaleas. These dense, evergreen shrubs have been in cultivation since at least the mid-nineteenth century. They have flowers in many colors, mainly pastels, and flowers are held in full, more or less rounded heads at the tip of the stems. Recent breeding efforts have produced smaller plants that bloom over a longer time, including through the summer. But I doubt I will ever be won over by them in the same way as I was by those exquisite old-fashioned giants.

When, Where, and How to Plant

Plant in spring as soon as the soil can be worked and there is no danger of frost. The warmer the summer, the more shade azalea requires, but all do well in morning sun or light shade. In the coldest zones, choose a location in full sun or with light, filtered shade. For best results, grow azalea in well-drained, highly organic, acid soil. These conditions are generally met in East Texas and down to Houston. Amend the soil with abundant amounts of organic matter including compost before planting. Azalea also grows well in containers.

Growing Tips

Fertilize in spring after flowering is complete and twice more through the growing season. Use a fertilizer formulated for azaleas for best results. Water to maintain even soil moisture and never let the plants dry out completely. Maintain a thick organic mulch over the root system to retain soil moisture and increase soil fertility.

Regional Advice and Care

Prune if necessary right after flowering is complete. Azalea blooms on new wood, therefore do not prune after late summer. Azalea can be susceptible to a number of pests and chlorosis. These problems chiefly occur when it is grown in conditions outside those described here. Otherwise, it is pest and disease free.

Companion Planting and Design

Larger varieties of azalea make excellent hedges or borders. Because it grows and blooms well in light shade, use azalea in woodland garden or along the border of large trees. Azaleas have shallow roots, so take care not to plant them where there will be continuous soil disturbance.

Try These

There are countless hybrids, forms, and series from which to choose. 'Coral Bells', 'Hino-Crimson', 'Flame', and 'Snow' grow in deep shade. In warmer areas try 'George L. Tabor', 'Fielder's White', or 'Formosa'. Satsuki hybrids include 'Higasa', 'Macrantha', 'Gumbo Pink', and 'Pride of Mobile'. Native azalea include wild azalea (*Rhododendron canescens*) with large, showy white flowers, Texas azalea (*R. oblongifolium*), with tubular white flowers, early azalea (*R. prunifolium*), with light pink to lavender flowers, and swamp azalea (*R. viscosum*), with large, open clusters of white blooms.

Butterfly Bush

Buddleia davidii

Bloom Period and Seasonal Color
Summer, lilac, dark purple, white, pink, yellow

Mature Height x Spread
3 to 8 ft. x 4 to 6 ft.

Botanical Pronunciation
BUD-lee-uh DAY-vid-ee-eye

Zones 7 to 9

There was a large butterfly bush outside my parents' house that seemed to be in flower every time I visited. It was splendid, as butterfly bush always is, replete with huge, congested heads of deep purple flowers. This plant endured minimal care, bright sun, and some extremely harsh winters and looked fabulous every summer. I became fond of that plant; it looked so full of hope and cheer, and I spent a lot of time admiring it and the blizzards of butterflies that descended on that plant each year. Butterfly bush came to us from Asia. Plants are open-branched deciduous shrubs with linear, gray-green leaves. The flowers are individually tiny, but hundreds are jammed into the long, flowering stalks at the ends of branches.

When, Where, and How to Plant
Plant in spring as soon as the soil can be worked and all danger of frost is past. Choose a site in full sun or one with at least six hours of sun. Plants become leggy and bloom poorly when grown in too much shade. Butterfly bush tolerates any moderately fertile, well-drained soil. It does not grow well in soils that are poorly drained or those that stay consistently wet. Amend the soil with compost, composted manure, other organic matter, or a blend of these before planting.

Growing Tips
Butterfly bush should be fertilized once in spring just as growth resumes and again about two months later. Use any well-balanced or slow-release fertilizer. Water to maintain even soil moisture—once or twice monthly in summer unless it is exceptionally hot or dry. Mulch well to maintain even soil moisture and to expand the time between waterings.

Regional Advice and Care
Prune hard in early spring, as it begins to regrow to enhance its natural form and encourage good flowering. Lightly tip prune in summer by deadheading spent flowering stalks to encourage repeat bloom. Butterfly bush is not susceptible to pests or disease.

Companion Planting and Design
Use butterfly bush near patios, seating areas, or a pool to enjoy the nearly continuous visits by butterflies as well as its sweet fragrance. This is a good choice for a focal point on a small patio. It blends well with other flowering shrubs and perennials for long-season summer color. Its height makes it a good background for a butterfly garden.

Try These
'Black Knight' has flowers that are so dark they are virtually black. 'Ile de France' is an old selection with violet flowers with a yellow throat that fades to lavender. 'Pink Delight' has deep pink bloom, whereas those of 'Royal Red' are magenta. 'White Bouquet' is a spreading plant that flowers white with an orange eye. 'White Profusion' has pure white flowers, and both the plant and the flowering stalks are upright. 'Harlequin' has yellow leaf margins and purple flowers.

Camellia

Camellia sasanqua

Bloom Period and Seasonal Color
Fall and winter, pink, red, white

Mature Height x Spread
2 to 15 ft. x 3 to 8 ft.

Botanical Pronunciation
kuh-MEE-lee-a suh-SAN-kwuh

Zones 7 to 9

Camellia flowers are an iconic image of the Old South. Old plantation homes as well as modern gardens are full of these deep green shrubs with their perfectly formed flowers. Of the three in common cultivation, *Camellia sasanqua* is my favorite. This camellia has leathery, deep green leaves that are smaller than those of the other widely grown camellia, *C. japonica*. Sasanqua camellias begin blooming in fall and continue through winter. This is a faster-growing shrub and more drought tolerant than japonica camellias, and the late flowering (or early, depending on your perspective) means there is handsome color in the garden when little else may be in flower. Flowers look like a painted plate with their flat, radiating petals surrounding prominent, upright yellow stamens.

When, Where, and How to Plant
Plant in fall through early spring while the soils are cool. Camellia prefers light, filtered shade or locations with only morning sun. Camellia requires a moist, acidic soil to grow best. This is best found in the eastern third of Texas. In other areas, if it is cool enough, they may be more successful in large containers. Amend the soil with good-quality compost or pine bark mulch before planting. These are shallow-rooted plants, so take care not to compact the soil around their roots.

Growing Tips
Fertilize camellia only if they appear to be losing leaves or leaves turn yellow. A good acidic fertilizer blend, such as for azaleas, works well. Water to keep evenly moist throughout the year. In much of

East Texas, natural rainfall is sufficient except during the driest part of summer. Then water weekly. Be careful not to overwater or have too much ponded water around the plants or they can develop root rots.

Regional Advice and Care
Prune only to remove dead or damaged limbs. Camellias have excellent natural form and rarely need pruning for shape. Scale insects commonly occur. Examine the undersides of leaves often and treat quickly. Brown or deformed flowers are caused by camellia flower blight. Remove affected blooms and discard in the trash.

Companion Planting and Design
Camellia is a perfect choice for a hedge or border planting for both privacy and definition. Blend among large evergreen trees to provide winter color and textural contrast. The winter flowering makes them a charming addition to a small garden or patio where it can be an accent or focal plant.

Try These
'Hana Jiman' a semi-double with white petals edged in pink, 'Yuletide' a deep rosy red with brilliant yellow stamens, 'Shishi Gashira' is a bright, hot pink semi-double, and 'Setsugekka' has white flowers with ruffled edges. 'White Dove' has perfectly formed, semi-double white flowers. *Camellia japonica* is similar but has larger, less shiny leaves and generally larger flowers with hundreds of named cultivars. The beverage tea is the leaves of *C. sinensis*, which has small white flowers.

Cenizo

Leucophyllum frutescens

Other Name Texas Ranger

Bloom Period and Seasonal Color
Late summer to fall, blue, purple, rose, white

Mature Height x Spread
5 to 10 ft. x 4 to 10 ft.

Botanical Pronunciation
loo-koh-FILE-um froo-THE-senz

One of the most extraordinary natural blooms in the western Hill Country and South Texas is the burst of pink, lavender, and purple flowers of cenizo after a summer rain. Entire hillsides erupt with the flowers of this shrub, and it is no wonder that has become a reliable and durable part of Texas gardens for more than 30 years. This species and all its relatives are immune to heat and drought and thrive in highly alkaline soils. Cenizo leaves are covered with fine hairs, giving them a light gray-green color hence its common name cenizo, which means ash in Spanish. Lightly fragrant flowers are in short clusters at the nodes and open after any significant rain. Plants repeat bloom regularly after big rains or deep waterings.

When, Where, and How to Plant
Plant in fall or spring in warm winter areas. In colder zones, plant in spring as soon as the soil can be worked and has warmed. Choose a location in full sun, even reflected heat is fine. Cenizo grows in any soil except heavy clays or those that are poorly drained. It is not necessary to add amendments to the soil before planting.

Growing Tips
Cenizo does not require supplemental fertilizer. Water carefully; plants fail quickly in consistently moist soils. It is best to water at long intervals, but soak the area thoroughly, rather than frequent, shallow watering. In most areas, monthly watering in summer is sufficient for established plants. Rely on natural rainfall in winter in all zones.

Regional Advice and Care
Cenizo has an excellent natural form, and plants rarely need pruning for shape. Prune to remove dead or damaged wood in spring. If plants become leggy or have too many erratic branches, cut back in spring to 2 or 3 feet to rejuvenate. Cenizo is susceptible to cotton root rot and chlorosis when grown in heavy or poorly drained soils.

Companion Planting and Design
Mix cenizo into hedge or border plantings at the edge of a garden or in areas that do not receive routine maintenance. Its tremendous heat tolerance makes cenizo particularly effective against hot walls, around pools or patios, or in other areas where reflected heat is intense.

Try These
'Green Cloud' has green leaves and magenta flowers, 'White Cloud' has gray leaves and white flowers, and the smaller 'Thundercloud' has whitish leaves and deep purple flowers. 'Bert-star' Silverado Sage™ both grow to 5 feet with light purple flowers. 'Rain Cloud' is a hybrid between cenizo and Big Bend silverleaf (*Leucophyllum minus*) with profuse congested purple flowers. *L. candidum* 'Silver Cloud' is a large, white-leaved plant with intense purple flowers, and the 3-foot 'Thunder Cloud' is similar. *L. langmaniae* 'Lynn's Legacy' has bright green foliage and heavily congested violet flowers. Fragrant rain sage (*L. pruinosum*) has fragrant, purple flowers, whereas blue rain sage (*L. zygophyllum*) has dark violet flowers.

Cotoneaster

Cotoneaster spp.

Bloom Period and Seasonal Color
Spring, white, pink

Mature Height x Spread 1 to 8 ft. x 3 to 10 ft.

Botanical Pronunciation
kah-TONE-ee-as-ter

Zones 7 to 8

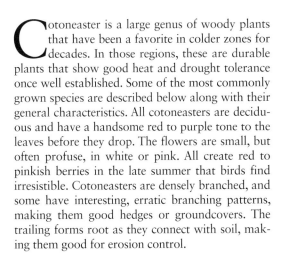

Cotoneaster is a large genus of woody plants that have been a favorite in colder zones for decades. In those regions, these are durable plants that show good heat and drought tolerance once well established. Some of the most commonly grown species are described below along with their general characteristics. All cotoneasters are deciduous and have a handsome red to purple tone to the leaves before they drop. The flowers are small, but often profuse, in white or pink. All create red to pinkish berries in the late summer that birds find irresistible. Cotoneasters are densely branched, and some have interesting, erratic branching patterns, making them good hedges or groundcovers. The trailing forms root as they connect with soil, making them good for erosion control.

When, Where, and How to Plant
Ideally plant in fall, but with attentive care cotoneaster can be planted anytime. Choose a location in full sun for the best flowering and form but avoid areas of intense, reflected heat. Prepare the bed well by adding generous amounts of compost or composted manure.

Growing Tips
Fertilize after all danger of frost is past in spring. Reapply fertilizer in fall. Water regularly in summer to maintain even soil moisture, although some species are reasonably drought tolerant once established. Mulch the root zone heavily to maintain soil moisture and spread out watering frequency. Natural rainfall is sufficient in winter.

Regional Advice and Care
Prune in spring to maintain shape or to remove dead or damaged wood. Cotoneaster is susceptible to the bacterial disease fire blight. Prune out infected areas quickly and burn or remove them to the trash.

Companion Planting and Design
Spreading forms are good accent plants along walls or walkways. Use for erosion control on steep slopes or as a woody groundcover. Shrub forms are good low borders, or they can be used to form a background for perennial plantings.

Try These
Peking cotoneaster (*Cotoneaster acutifolius*) is a 6- to 10-foot shrub with dull green leaves that performs well in poor soils. Spreading cotoneaster (*C. divaricatus*) grows to 6 feet with bright, glossy green foliage and large red berries. Creeping cotoneaster (*C. adpressus* 'Tom Thumb') is less than 12 inches tall with bright green foliage that turns red in fall. This plant is sold under many names, including *C. apiculatus* 'Tom Thumb'. Pyrenees cotoneaster (*C. congestus*) is 3 feet tall with dense, matted stems and is among the most heat and drought tolerant. Gray-leaved cotoneaster (*C. glaucophyllus*), which is well suited to alkaline soils, and rock cotoneaster (*C. horizontalis*), which spreads to 6 feet with profuse red berries, are 3 feet tall. Bearberry cotoneaster (*C. dammeri*) grows to 2 feet with larger flowers, and its 'Coral Beauty' has coral berries. Willow-leaved cotoneaster (*C. salicifolius*), growing to 18 inches, is a semi-deciduous, fast-growing, drought-tolerant groundcover, and cranberry cotoneaster (*C. apiculatus*) is small with large red berries.

Esperanza

Tecoma stans

Other Name Yellowbells

Bloom Period and Seasonal Color
Spring to fall, yellow

Mature Height x Spread
6 to 25 ft. x 3 to 15 ft.

Botanical Pronunciation ta-COE-muh STANS

Zones 9 to 10

The first time I saw esperanza was in Key West, where its large clusters of bright yellow flowers draped invitingly over a clapboard fence. It never occurred to me that it might be a native plant, but this wide-ranging species is native in Texas and Arizona south to Argentina. This huge range gives esperanza a lot of natural variation. The common U.S. variety is *angustata* with thin, serrated leaves and narrow yellow flowers. It is root hardy to around 10 degrees Fahrenheit. The more tropical variety *stans* is a small tree with deep green leaves, large clusters of bright yellow flowers but is hardy to only the high 20s. Most of the esperanza sold are some variation of these two varieties or a cross with *Tecoma alata*.

When, Where, and How to Plant
Plant in spring after all danger of frost is past and the soil is warm. Planting may continue through summer. Pick a location in full sun. Esperanza grows well where reflected heat is intense, such as a western wall or around a pool deck. Esperanza tolerates any well-drained soil from fertile, garden soil to rocky ones, but does poorly in heavy clays.

Growing Tips
Apply slow-release or organic fertilizer annually in spring just as growth resumes. Water established plants regularly to maintain good form and continuous bloom. This is up to once a week in extremely hot weather, or as little as every two or three weeks when temperatures are milder. Esperanza is quite drought tolerant, but will lose leaves and quit blooming if it gets too dry. Recovery is quick once water is available. Rely on natural rainfall in winter.

Regional Advice and Care
Prune in spring after all danger of frost is past to remove winter damaged stems or dead wood. Esperanza can be pruned through summer to shape or remove stems that have grown too tall or leggy. Esperanza is not susceptible to pests or disease.

Companion Planting and Design
Mix with other summer-flowering shrubs for long seasonal color. Use as an informal hedge or boundary plant. Tree forms make a spectacular focal or specimen plant for small gardens or patios. Esperanza has the heat tolerance to shade western walls or windows or to be used in areas of reflected heat such as around a pool.

Try These
'Gold Star' is extremely heat tolerant and flowers extravagantly and early. 'Sunrise' has yellow flowers backed with deep orange. 'Orange Jubilee' is a hybrid between *Tecoma stans* and the Argentine *T. alata*, with clustered tubular flowers that are mainly orange, as is 'Burnt Out', with deep orange flowers and a compact, shrubby habit. *T. alata* has slender, tubular orange flowers that flare at the end. Cape honeysuckle (*T. capensis*) is a frost-tender shrub with deep green leaves and bright orange tubular flowers that occur nearly year-round. There is also a yellow-flowered form.

Evergreen Sumac

Rhus virens

Bloom Period and Seasonal Color
Summer to fall, white

Mature Height x Spread 7 to 8 ft. x 5 to 10 ft.

Botanical Pronunciation RUSE VYE-rens

Zones 8 to 10

Evergreen sumac is one of those shrubs that fades into the background until its fuzzy red fruit are formed. Then it is a delight, colorful and rich, with birds visiting constantly for the delicious berries. The glossy, deep green leaves are held in opposite pairs on a stiff stem. They are delicately pink when new in the spring and have a maroon caste in the fall. The leaves remain on the plant through the winter, but drop shortly before new leaves emerge. The tiny white flowers form a loose cluster at the tips of the branches and are followed by the bright red fruit in the fall. Deer are known to browse on new plants or new growth, so some protection would be advisable.

When, Where, and How to Plant
Plant in fall or spring in warm winter zones, otherwise plant in spring after all danger of frost is past. Evergreen sumac needs a well-drained soil but is not particular about soil type. But it can fail quickly in soils that are heavy or poorly drained.

Growing Tips
Evergreen sumac does not need supplemental fertilization. Water carefully. It is best to water this plant with slow, deep soaks at long intervals rather than shallow, frequent waterings that keep it constantly moist. Overwatering, or poor drainage, kills plants quickly.

Regional Advice and Care
Prune to remove dead or winter-damaged stems in the spring once growth resumes. Take care not to prune late in the spring. Flowering is on new wood, and you can lose a season's bloom if you prune too late. Evergreen sumac is not susceptible to pests or disease other than deer.

Companion Planting and Design
Plant generously to form an informal hedge either singly or in combination with other drought-resistant shrubs. In the warmer parts of the state, it can be planted in light shade to fill in under evergreen trees or to create a woodland feel. Birds love the fruit, so plant where their continual visits can be enjoyed.

Try These
The variety *choriophylla* is considered by some botanists to be merely a variant of this species. It looks similar, but ranges from southern Arizona into Baja California and is even more drought resistant than is evergreen sumac. Fragrant sumac (*Rhus aromatica*) is a deciduous shrub with blue-green leaves that turn reddish in the fall. Its dark red berries persist through early spring. Smooth sumac (*R. glabra*) forms extensive colonies from underground stems with deep red fruit in a congested pyramid and brilliant red fall leaves. Skunkbush (*R. trilobata*) is a deciduous, spreading shrub with fuzzy red fruit that makes a delicious beverage and gold to red fall leaves. Little-leaf sumac (*R. microphylla*) has tiny, deep green leaves on widely spreading branches. This species grows well on rocky, alkaline soils and has bright red fuzzy fruit in the fall.

Firebush

Hamelia patens

Other Name Scarlet bush

Bloom Period and Seasonal Color
Spring to fall, red-orange

Mature Height x Spread
3 to 10 ft. x 3 to 10 ft.

Botanical Pronunciation
ha-MEL-ee-ah PAT-enz

Zones 8b to 10

The first time I saw firebush I fell completely under its spell. It was a newcomer to Arizona gardens at the time and won me over with its long, spectacular bloom through the intense heat of a desert summer. It is just as wonderful in my South Texas garden. This tidy shrub has large, deep green leaves that turn a burnished copper in cool weather. The thin, tubular, orange flowers are clustered at the tip of each branch. This is true heat seeker; flowers routinely wait to open until it becomes really hot in the late spring or summer. Hummingbirds are delighted to feed on the flowers throughout the summer. Black berries follow in the fall that are equally attractive to birds such as phoebes and mockingbirds.

When, Where, and How to Plant
Plant in spring after all danger of frost is past. Choose a location in full sun for best flowering and form, but firebush tolerates growing in light, filtered shade as well. Firebush grows best in a deep, well-drained, fertile soil and is tolerant of high alkalinity.

Growing Tips
Apply slow-release or organic fertilizer annually in spring. Water to keep the soil from drying out completely, although I have seen plants recover from extreme water loss quickly with a deep soak. In summer, apply a deep mulch to maintain soil moisture and to keep the plants from drying out too quickly. Water once a month in the coldest parts of the winter.

Regional Advice and Care
Prune dead or winter-damaged wood in spring just as the leaves emerge. If necessary, plants can be severely pruned to within a foot of the ground. Firebush will lose its leaves at or near freezing and sustain stem damage in the mid-20s. Recovery is quick, however, and plants bloom the following summer. Lightly tip pruning firebush in the summer helps maintain its tidy, rounded shape. Firebush is not susceptible to pests or disease.

Companion Planting and Design
Mix firebush with summer-flowering perennials and shrubs such as lantana, hibiscus, red bird of paradise, and salvias. Firebush can be used as specimen or focal point for patios, courtyards, or seating areas. Firebush is a reliable choice in areas of intense reflected heat such as pools or against hot walls or windows. Firebush grows quickly and flowers early, making it a fine choice for use in a large container or as an annual with a long floral season in areas where it is too cold to grow it in the ground. Hummingbirds visit the flowers all summer, and the fruit attracts many species of birds in the fall.

Try These
There are dwarf forms of firebush that grow to only 3 feet tall but bloom just as prolifically. There is also a form with variegated foliage. Neither of these forms has a recognized name.

Forsythia

Forsythia x *intermedia*

Bloom Period and Seasonal Color
Spring, yellow, gold

Mature Height x Spread 6 to 8 ft. x 6 to 10 ft.

Botanical Pronunciation
for-SITH-ee-ah in-ter-ME-dee-ah

Zones 7 to 9

*F*orsythia x *intermedia* is a hybrid between *F. suspensa* and *F. viridissma* first introduced in 1880. Since then, there have been an overwhelming number of hybrids developed from these first plants. It is not a wonder. Forsythia flower early, before the bright green leaves have emerged. They are a welcome burst of color especially where winter is long and bleak. The numerous thin stems are smothered with bell-shaped, bright yellow to gold flowers. These flowers last up to two weeks until the beginning of leaf growth. It is one of a number of old-fashioned reliable plants that don't seem to be much in favor by today's gardeners. But this is an excellent plant, easy to grow, sturdy, and long-lived, that deserves a renewal in Texas gardens.

When, Where, and How to Plant
Plant in fall or as early in the spring as soil can be worked. Forsythia is not particular about soil type as long as it is well drained. It does poorly in low spots that collect water or in soils that are consistently moist. Site it in full sun for best flowering, although plants tolerate light, filtered shade.

Growing Tips
Fertilize in early spring as growth resumes. Reapply again in two or three months and again in fall. Use any well-balanced or slow-release fertilizer. Water to maintain even soil moisture. Apply a 4- to 6-inch layer of mulch to maintain soil moisture and extend the frequency of waterings.

Regional Advice and Care
Prune in spring once bloom is complete to remove any dead or damaged stems. Some gardeners cut back forsythia severely to increase young stems, whereas others choose to remove only the oldest stems annually.

Companion Planting and Design
The stunning floral show is best enjoyed when forsythia is planted at the front of a large perennial or shrub bed. It also makes a good accent or focal point with its early spring flowering. Use it generously to set off a corner of the garden or to form a background for art or other hard features.

Try These
'Lynwood Gold' an older variety with upright stems and brilliant yellow flowers. 'Spring Glory' is similar but is a slightly more spreading shrub with bright yellow flowers. 'Arnold Giant' is a large, rigidly upright shrub with profuse amounts of golden flowers. 'Beatrix Farrand' is a vigorous, heavy bloomer from the Arnold Arboretum that may be hard to locate but is stunning. 'Gold Tide' is a dwarf to 20 inches with golden flowers. 'Golden Peep' is a prostrate form with dark, golden flowers. Both of these cultivars are the result of French experiments with irradiating 'Spring Glory' and growing out the resulting seed. Green stem forsythia (*Forsythia viridissima*) has green stems and pale yellow to yellow-green flowers. This variety grows well in warmer zones. 'Bronxensis' is a low, flat-topped plant with light yellow flowers.

Gardenia

Gardenia jasminoides

Bloom Period and Seasonal Color
Spring, white

Mature Height x Spread
2 to 8 ft. x 2 to 4 ft.

Botanical Pronunciation
gar-DEEN-ya jazz-min-OY-dees

Gardenia is a short shrub, with deep green leaves framing the waxy, white flowers. I have heard it said that scent is the most powerful reminder of places, events, or people of all our senses. I believe it. When I smell a gardenia I am instantly transported to our time in New Orleans or to the perfume some old aunts used to wear. In the deep South it is easy to grow, but in Texas it is tricky. Most of the state is too hot for it, soils in many areas are too dry and alkaline for it, and some zones are too cold for it. This leaves it to the tender mercies of East Texas gardeners, where it thrives and is a reliable bloomer.

When, Where, and How to Plant
Plant in spring once the soil can be worked. Choose a location that receives good filtered light or morning sun only. Gardenia does *not* do well in full sun, reflected heat, or afternoon sun. Gardenia grows best in a well-drained, rich, highly acidic soil. Although soil amendments can greatly improve drainage, nothing improves acidity for long. If you don't have these soils, consider planting it in a pot.

Growing Tips
Fertilize with a formulation designed for azaleas or gardenias or a combination of fish emulsion and bloodmeal. Apply once in spring and again in early summer. Do not fertilize in fall. Water regularly, usually weekly, throughout the summer. Apply a heavy mulch, ideally of pine straw, but any organic matter will do, to maintain an even soil moisture.

Regional Advice and Care
Prune in spring once the weather is warm but before the heat of summer. Most gardenias have excellent natural form and require no more than light tip pruning to tidy them up. Remove spent flowers anytime. Gardenia has the most problems when it is grown outside the conditions named here, although whiteflies can be bothersome in the late summer.

Companion Planting and Design
The deep evergreen leaves make a good foundation or background plant. Use gardenia near a seating area or patio to define an area and to best enjoy the alluring scent. Flowers make good cut flowers if picked just before they completely open, but they bruise easily so handle with care. Gardenia grows well in large containers, and this is often the best way to meet their exacting cultural requirements.

Try These
Native to China, it reached Houston in the late nineteenth century. 'Martha Turnbull' is a single-flowered form that is an abundant bloomer. 'Radicans Variegata' grows to 2 feet with cream on the foliage. The South African white gardenia (*Gardenia thunbergia*) is hardy only in Zone 10 but requires much the same cultural conditions as gardenia. It grows to 15 feet with highly fragrant, showy tubular white flowers that end with a spreading wheel of narrow petals.

Guajillo

Acacia berlandieri

Bloom Period and Seasonal Color
Spring to fall, white

Mature Height x Spread
6 to 15 ft. x 6 to 6 to 15 ft.

Botanical Pronunciation
ah-KAY-shuh ber-land-ee-AIR-ee

Zones 8b to 10

Guajillo is a deciduous to semi-evergreen native shrub with numerous stems that rise from its base. Branches are gray to white and darken as they age. The leaves are double compound and up to 6 inches long with tiny individual leaflets creating an overall effect of a fern-leaved, delicate shrub. Nothing could be further from the truth for this species. It is immune to heat and is a reliably drought-tolerant choice. The flowering head is a rounded, fragrant, puffball made up of numerous, minute flowers with no petals but prominent, creamy white stamens. An outstanding honey is made from the flowers. *Acacia* species are most easily distinguished by their pods. Guajillo pods are flat, dark brown, and up to 6 inches long with bulging seeds.

When, Where, and How to Plant

Plant in fall or spring in all areas. In areas where it is marginally cold hardy, plant in spring after all danger of frost is past. Choose a location in full sun for best flowering and form, although in extremely hot areas guajillo will tolerate light, filtered shade. Guajillo grows in almost any well-drained soil and requires no special amendments before planting.

Growing Tips

Guajillo needs no supplemental fertilization. In areas of extreme heat or dryness, or if there is an extended hot, dry spell, water every two to three weeks. Otherwise, guajillo grows well on natural rainfall. Rely on natural rainfall in the winter in all areas.

Regional Advice and Care

To form guajillo into a small tree prune selected branches in the spring. Be careful to take no more than 25 percent of the mass of the tree in any year. Rabbits are attracted to small or recently set out plants. Cage or otherwise protect plants until the woody base forms. Guajillo is not susceptible to other pests or disease.

Companion Planting and Design

Guajillo makes an excellent focal point with its abundant spring flowering. Use in a mixed hedge or to form a light background for a perennial or butterfly garden. Its great heat and drought tolerance make it a good choice for areas without regular irrigation or at the edge of the garden as well locations with intense reflected heat, such as around a pool.

Try These

Catclaw acacia (*Acacia greggii*) is a larger, more densely branched shrub to small tree. The stems of this species are covered with small recurved spines. Flowers are similar creamy white puffballs, but the leaflets are rounded and more widely spaced. Pods of catclaw acacia are highly twisted and contorted. There is an uncommon hybrid between these species known as *Acacia emoryana* that has an elongated flowering head but otherwise resembles catclaw acacia. Prairie acacia (*A. angustissima*) is much smaller, growing to 3 feet. This species spreads by rhizomes and forms extensive colonies over time. The pods are reddish brown, flat, and only 2 to 3 inches long.

Japanese Barberry

Berberis thunbergii

Bloom Period and Seasonal Color
Spring, yellow

Mature Height x Spread
3 to 6 ft. x 3 to 7 ft.

Botanical Pronunciation
BER-ber-is thun-BER-gee-eye

Zones 7 to 9

Japanese barberry is part of a large genus of woody plants that are some of the most reliable shrubs for gardens throughout Texas. This one is small and grows in a spreading rounded shape. The leaves are round and held in tight clusters along the stem. There are sharp spines at the axils of the leaves, a feature that is wise to notice when you go to prune the plant. Flowers are bright yellow followed by deep red berries that birds find irresistible. But it is in the fall that Japanese barberry truly comes into its own. The leaves turn crimson, red, or amber as they begin to drop. The colors are intense, and in certain lights the plant appears to be ablaze.

When, Where, and How to Plant

Plant in fall or spring in warm winter zones. In colder zones, plant in spring after all danger of frost is past. Choose a location in full sun for best form and color. Japanese barberry grows well in any type of well-drained soil. Add lots of compost, composted manure, organic matter, or a blend of these to the bed or the backfill when planting. This species does not do well in consistently dry soils.

Growing Tips

Japanese barberry does not need supplemental fertilization when grown in fertile, well-amended soils. Water to maintain consistent soil moisture. Established plants show good drought tolerance, particularly where summers are not extremely hot. Mulch the root zone heavily, particularly in summer, to prevent the soil from drying out.

Regional Advice and Care

Japanese barberry flowers on new wood. Therefore, prune early to allow the growth of ample new flowering stems. Prune in spring to shape or remove diseased or damaged wood. Japanese barberry is not susceptible to most pests but can be vulnerable to scale, fungal disease, and rust particularly.

Companion Planting and Design

Use Japanese barberry as an accent plant in corners or small areas of the garden for its powerful impact in fall. It is small enough to blend into a mixed perennial bed.

Try These

In the Northeast in particular, this species has become invasive, although there are no records of such problems in Texas. 'Atropurpurea' and 'Rose Glow' have purple-red fall foliage, and 'Aurea' is yellow. 'Monomb' and 'Crimson Pygmy' have bright red fall foliage. *Berberis xmentorensis* is a hybrid with *B. julianae* that has yellow to orange fall color. The related Oregon grape (*Mahonia aquifolium*) is an evergreen, 6-foot shrub with glossy, leathery leaves and bright yellow flowers followed by clusters of blue fruits. New growth is bronze to copper red. Agarita (*B. trifoliolata*) is an evergreen Texas native with deeply split, three-part leaves tipped with sharp spines like holly. Immune to heat and growing well in dry, alkaline soils, agarita is also highly drought tolerant. Jellies of great renown are made from its fruit.

Loquat

Eriobotrya japonica

Bloom Period and Seasonal Color
Fall, white, yellow

Mature Height x Spread
10 to 25 ft. x 10 to 15 ft.

Botanical Pronunciation
err-ee-o-BOT-tree-uh juh-PON-ih-kuh

Zones 8 to 10

There was a large loquat outside the front door of the house where I grew up. I didn't give it much thought other than as a quick snack, but I have come to appreciate this attractive evergreen shrub to small tree for its ease of culture, lush, tropical look, and tasty fruit. The long, leathery leaves are deep green above with a felty white or rust color on the underside. The small flowers are unremarkable but are held in a tight cluster at the tip of the stems, and the effect is of a series of bouquets covering the plant. The fruit is oval and golden yellow, and when left on the plant until it softens, it has great flavor fresh or as jam.

When, Where, and How to Plant
Plant in spring when all danger of frost is past and the soil has warmed. Choose a location in full sun or light, filtered shade. Protect plants from high winds in the winter. Loquat will grow in almost any well-drained, moderately fertile soil. It does not, however, do well in soils that are consistently dry.

Growing Tips
Apply a well-balanced fertilizer formulated for roses once in spring and again in fall. Water to maintain steady soil moisture in the summer, but be careful not to overwater or overfertilize the plants. Apply a thick layer of mulch to prevent the soil from drying out too quickly.

Regional Advice and Care
Prune in spring to remove any damaged or dead stems. Loquat has excellent natural form and rarely needs pruning for shape. In moist conditions it can be susceptible to the bacterial disease fire blight. Scorched-looking leaves indicate this infection. Remove the entire limb and burn or discard in the trash to remove infected limbs from the garden.

Companion Planting and Design
Loquat makes a fine choice for an accent or focal plant in a small garden or patio. It is not a good choice near a pool, however, because of the fruit drop. Add to a mixed border or boundary planting for its textural contrast and to entice birds into the garden.

Try These
When grown for the fruit there are numerous varieties with orange flesh. They include the following: 'Big Jim', vigorous and highly productive; 'Early Red', an old variety that is early, juicy, and sweet; 'Gold Nugget', later ripening and a good keeper; 'Mogi', smaller fruit; 'Strawberry,' notes of strawberry; 'Tanada', ripening as late as May, vigorous and sweet; and 'Wolfe', good for cooking. White-fleshed varieties include these: 'Advance', to 5 feet tall and resistant to fire blight; 'Champagne', late ripening, large fruit; 'Victory', sweet large fruit; and 'Vista White', small, very sweet fruit. 'Coppertone' is a hybrid between this species and Indian hawthorn (*Rhaphiolepis indica*) with reddish new leaves and shorter stature. This hybrid is also sold as *Eriobotrya* 'Coppertone' and *R. indica* 'Majestic'.

Narrow-Leaf Rosewood

Vauquelinia corymbosa

Bloom Period and Seasonal Color
Summer, white

Mature Height x Spread
9 to 15 ft. x 10 to 15 ft.

Botanical Pronunciation
vaw-kwah-LIN-ee-ah Kor-rim-BOW-suh

Zones 8 to 10

Narrow-leaf rosewood, also called Nuevo Leon rosewood, is a large shrub to small tree with deep green, narrow leaves. Each leaf is serrated along its edge and attached to the stem by a reddish petiole. Leaves tend to form loosely hanging clusters, and the plant appears to be vacant in the middle but round and full on the exterior. This makes it a big attraction to ground-dwelling birds like quail. Flowers are tiny but held in big, round heads at the ends of the stems. These flowering heads are profuse and literally hum with bees seeking their nectar and pollen. Bloom is followed by small, tan woody capsules that hold onto the plants for months.

When, Where, and How to Plant
In warm winter areas plant in either spring or fall. In colder zones, plant in spring as soon as the soil can be worked and all danger of frost is past. Choose a location in full sun that accommodates the large spread of the shrub. Plants become lanky and bloom poorly in too much shade. Narrow-leaf rosewood tolerates a wide range of soils from highly alkaline to moderately fertile ones. Good drainage is essential and plants can fail in heavy clays or where there is too much consistent moisture.

Growing Tips
Narrow-leaf rosewood does not need supplemental fertilization. Water only once or twice a month in summer, even in the hottest weather. It is best to water this plant with a slow, deep soak at long intervals rather than consistent, shallow watering. Rely on natural rainfall in winter everywhere.

Regional Advice and Care
Prune after flowering to remove unruly, dead, or damaged stems. Plants bloom on new wood so be careful not to prune too late in the year or anytime in spring. Narrow-leaf rosewood has no significant pests and is not susceptible to disease.

Companion Planting and Design
Use narrow-leaf rosewood as part of a mixed border or boundary hedge with plants of similar scale. This species is an excellent choice to screen an unfortunate view or hide an ugly building. It is also useful in areas of the garden that receive minimal maintenance. It is best to plant away from seating areas or pools because of its strong appeal to bees.

Try These
There is vast taxonomic stew around this species. Most plants sold are the variety *heterodon*. There is a subspecies *angustifolia*, also considered by some botanists as the species *Vauquelinia angustifolia*, which has extremely narrow leaves and blooming heads that are only 3 to 4 inches wide. Arizona rosewood (*V. californica*) is a handsome shrub with shorter and wider, deep green, upright leaves that are pale gray on the underside. Hardy to about 15 degrees Fahrenheit, Arizona rosewood has bright white flowering heads that are 4 to 6 inches wide.

Oakleaf Hydrangea

Hydrangea quercifolia

Bloom Period and Seasonal Color
Late spring to early summer, white

Mature Height x Spread
6 to 7 ft. x 6 to 8 ft.

Botanical Pronunciation
hy-DRAN-jah kwer-sih-FOE-lee-ah

Zones 7 to 9

Gardeners that have a lot of shade are presented with a number of challenges. I think the most difficult is to find plants that provide color in the shade, whether from flowers or leaves. Southern gardeners have long turned to the native oakleaf hydrangea for its ease of culture, rounded form, textural contrast, and stunning flower and leaf color. Oakleaf hydrangea, as the name suggests, has large, coarse, three-lobed leaves that resemble massive oak leaves. Flowers are held in either conical or flattened heads atop the foliage. They begin light chartreuse, turn white and then a deep purple as they age. The leaves turn a burnished gold before they drop in the fall. Like most hydrangeas, it spreads by long, extended stems (stolons) forming small clumps.

When, Where, and How to Plant
Plant oakleaf hydrangea in the fall or the spring. Choose a location in at least half-day shade with no direct afternoon sun or reflected heat. Oakleaf hydrangea needs a rich soil, amply amended with compost or other organic matter but that is well drained.

Growing Tips
Fertilize in spring with any well-balanced fertilizer. Apply again after flowering. Water to maintain consistent soil moisture. To assure ample soil moisture, apply a thick, 4- to 6-inch layer of mulch annually.

Regional Advice and Care
Prune in spring after flowering. Cut stems back nearly to the ground at least every other year in the spring, annually if plants show a lot of unruly growth. Oakleaf hydrangea has no serious pest or disease problems.

Companion Planting and Design
Use where the natural spreading habit can be an asset rather than a problem, such as beneath large evergreen trees or at the back of large border or hedge planting. The flowers and leaves are so colorful they are useful as a mass planting where conditions are favorable.

Try These
'Snow Queen' (also offered as 'Flemygea') is a big shrub with large leaves and 8-inch conical flower heads. The foliage produces outstanding fall color, and the flowers take on purplish pink hues when dried. 'Alice' is upright with a broad rounded habit and large, arching flower heads. It has good disease resistance and superior fall color. 'Sike's Dwarf' grows to only 3 feet tall with smaller leaves and flowering heads and spreads less aggressively. 'Pee Wee' is also compact with a rounded habit and is very similar to 'Sike's Dwarf'. Big-leaf hydrangea (*Hydrangea macrophylla*) is a familiar shrub in southern gardens that has been cultivated for a long time. There are two general flowering styles; big, rounded flowering heads, and the so-called lacecaps with a flattened head. It has the same general light and watering requirements as oakleaf hydrangea, but tolerates more consistent moisture as well as full sun. There are numerous selections, cultivars and hybrids, and flower color ranges from pastel to deep pink, blue to lavender, and white.

Oleander

Nerium oleander

Bloom Period and Seasonal Color
Spring to fall, white, pink, red, mauve, and yellow

Mature Height x Spread
6 to 30 ft. x 4 to 12 ft.

Botanical Pronunciation
NEAR-ee-um oh-lee-AN-der

Zones 8 to 10

I am deeply fond of oleander's tantalizing summer flowers that open continuously through the hottest or driest summers. Oleander is a dense, multistemmed shrub with numerous long, dark green leaves, making the plant virtually impenetrable. Oleander is from North Africa and into India, and there are two distinct strains as a result. The African ones tend to have vivid colors and lack fragrance, whereas the Indian ones are larger and noticeably fragrant. Countless crosses between the two have resulted in hundreds of varieties of single, double, or ruffled flowers as well as plants from 30 feet tall to dwarfs 5 to 6 feet tall, occasionally less. Oleander was brought to Galveston in 1841, and that city still has huge public and private collections.

When, Where, and How to Plant
Plant oleander in spring after all danger of frost is past and the soil is warm. You can still plant through summer. Choose a location in full sun for best flowering and form; oleander tolerates almost any type of soil, including heavy clays and those that are intermittently soggy.

Growing Tips
Oleander does not need supplemental fertilizer. Water plants carefully; the amount of water greatly determines the size of the plant. Water every two to three weeks in summer when young, every month or less once mature. Rely on natural rainfall in winter.

Regional Advice and Care
Prune in summer to shape, reduce, and remove dead or damaged wood. Note: use adequate protection.

All parts of the plant are poisonous if ingested, and the sap causes contact dermatitis, so take care when pruning to use gloves and eye protection. Do not put oleander prunings in a compost bin or burn it; even the smoke can cause intense irritation. Hardiness is highly variable, and most show tip damage at 20 degrees Fahrenheit, whereas others die. Oleander gall is common but rarely more than a cosmetic problem. Otherwise, oleander is not susceptible to pests or disease.

Companion Planting and Design
Use as a hedge or screen alone or mixed with other shrubs. Plants can be trained to a single trunk to serve as a focal point for smaller garden. Oleander is an excellent choice to shade a hot wall or near pools where reflected heat is intense. All varieties do well in large containers, but the dwarfs are particularly good in pots.

Try These
'Little Red', 'Hardy Red', and 'General Pershing' are good choices for colder zones and flower in shades of red. 'Hardy Pink', 'Hardy White', and the red 'Cherry Ripe' are generally hardy to Zone 8. The deep red 'Marrakesh' and the yellow 'Mathilde Ferrier' both have moderate cold hardiness. For warmer zones try the salmon 'Mrs. Roeding', 'Sister Agnes', white with a yellow interior, or 'Algiers', a deep red, among countless others. Look also for the Turner varieties, chiefly dwarfs, from Ted Turner of Corpus Christi.

Rose of Sharon

Hibiscus syriacus

Other Name Althea

Bloom Period and Seasonal Color
Summer, pink, mauve, purple, red, and white

Mature Height x Spread
10 to 12 ft. x 3 to 6 ft.

Botanical Pronunciation
hi-BIS-kus si-ri-AH-kus

Zones 8 to 10

Each of the houses in which I grew up had a rose of Sharon outside the doorway. The lush, ruffled blooms in shades of rose and purple greeted us every day throughout the long Texas summer. This is a reliable summer-flowering, deciduous shrub for virtually the entire state. Related to tropical hibiscus, the flowers have thin, often ruffled petals and generally occur in pastel shades. A deciduous shrub, rose of Sharon is yet another of those old-fashioned plants that have been in cultivation so long they are often found on old homesteads or around derelict farms. In fact, it comes from Asia where it has been cultivated for thousands of years. In Texas it has been around since the end of the nineteenth century.

When, Where, and How to Plant
Plant rose of Sharon in spring after all danger of frost is past in full sun or partial shade. Where winters are mild it can also be planted in the fall. Rose of Sharon grows well in any well-drained soil, but avoid areas that are either extremely dry or consistently wet. Select a location that receives at least six hours of full sun, but avoid deep shade.

Growing Tips
Apply slow-release or organic fertilizer in spring after growth has resumed. Follow up with applications every six to eight weeks with the last application a month before the average frost date. When hot or dry, water every other week, with regular rainfall or milder temperatures, water less frequently. Rely on natural rainfall in the winter unless exceptionally then, water monthly.

Regional Advice and Care
Prune in spring before leaves emerge to remove dead or damaged wood or to reinvigorate the plant. As plants mature they become more open and spreading and are easily trained to a small single-trunked tree by removing the lowest three or four branches each spring. Rose of Sharon is not susceptible to pests or disease.

Companion Planting and Design
Plant rose of Sharon as part of a large flowering shrub border or perennial bed. Either as a shrub or a small tree, rose of Sharon makes a striking specimen or focal plant in small courtyards or to provide long season color around seating areas, patio, or pools.

Try These
'Aphrodite' has rosy pink flowers and deep red eye, 'Helene' has white flowers and red eye, and 'Minerva' has ruffled lavender flowers and red to purple eyes. Doubles include 'Blushing Bride', a pastel pink, and 'Collie Mullens', deep pink. Single-flowered cultivars include 'Admiral Dewey', pure white, 'Blue Bird', dark lavender with a red throat, 'Rubis', deep rose-pink with dark throat, and 'Hamabo', white with long, striking red markings on the petals. The similar but more cold-hardy swamp rose mallow (*Hibiscus moscheutos*) has white flowers with deep rose throat. Numerous hybrids and cultivars of this species are offered.

Scarlet Buckeye

Aesculus pavia

Bloom Period and Seasonal Color
Spring, red, yellow, bicolor

Mature Height x Spread
10 to 40 ft. x 5 to 10 ft.

Botanical Pronunciation
ESS-kah-lus PAH-vee-ah

Scarlet buckeye is a spreading shrub or small tree found along the creek sides and limestone ledges of central and eastern Texas. Trees in the Hill Country and the western part of the range are rarely over head high; with individuals much taller in East Texas and further east. The leaves are divided like a hand into five prominent segments, each of which has distinct veins that makes them look pleated. The overall effect is a vegetative umbrella. Tall spikes of the showy flowers rise up over the foliage. Flowers are most often scarlet red, but there is a yellow-flowered variety as well. Where they both occur you find orange, pink, and bicolor flowers. Hummingbirds feast on the nectar. The large, shiny seeds are highly poisonous.

When, Where, and How to Plant
Plant in fall or early spring. Scarlet buckeye grows best in light, filtered shade, or spots that receive full morning sun. Provide an enriched, moist soil that is well drained. Amend the soil with ample amounts of compost, composted manure, or a combination before planting. Although scarlet buckeye grows in clay soils, be sure that the drainage is excellent.

Growing Tips
Fertilize once in spring as growth resumes and again in fall. Use a well-balanced formulation such as rose fertilizer. Scarlet buckeye requires even soil moisture, and this is best achieved with deep, but infrequent soaks rather than constant light, frequent watering. Use a bubbler attachment or drip irrigation for good results. Mulch heavily to help maintain soil moisture and extend watering frequency.

Regional Advice and Care
This is a beautifully formed shrub that rarely needs pruning. Should pruning be needed, cut branches in early spring just before leaves emerge. Leaves can be sun scorched when planted with southern or western exposures. Scarlet buckeye has no serious pests, although anthracnose and leaf blotch cause a leaf drop at the end of the summer that is harmless to the plant.

Companion Planting and Design
In a large garden use scarlet buckeye as an understory planting among larger trees or on the edges of a heavily wooded area. In smaller gardens, plant as a focal tree for its spectacular bloom and attractiveness to hummingbirds. Alternately, site in the back of a bed where other plants mask its leafless stems in winter.

Try These
Texas yellow buckeye (*Aesculus pavia* var. *flavescens*) has the same large leaves and spreading form of scarlet buckeye but is generally shorter to only 15 feet or less. The flowers are pale to bright yellow. Ohio buckeye (*A. glabra*) is a small tree to 30 feet tall with the same attractive foliage, but is much showier in fall with leaves that turn bright orange. The fruit is the iconic buckeye; a nut enclosed in a splitting husk. The variety *arguta* is smaller and occurs in Texas.

Shower of Gold

Galphimia glauca

Other Name Thryallis

Bloom Period and Seasonal Color
Spring to fall, yellow

Mature Height x Spread 5 to 6 ft. x 4 to 5 ft.

Botanical Pronunciation
gal-FEE-mee-uh GLA-kuh

Zones 8b to 10

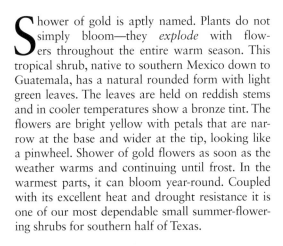

Shower of gold is aptly named. Plants do not simply bloom—they *explode* with flowers throughout the entire warm season. This tropical shrub, native to southern Mexico down to Guatemala, has a natural rounded form with light green leaves. The leaves are held on reddish stems and in cooler temperatures show a bronze tint. The flowers are bright yellow with petals that are narrow at the base and wider at the tip, looking like a pinwheel. Shower of gold flowers as soon as the weather warms and continuing until frost. In the warmest parts, it can bloom year-round. Coupled with its excellent heat and drought resistance it is one of our most dependable small summer-flowering shrubs for southern half of Texas.

When, Where, and How to Plant
Plant in spring once all danger of frost is past and the soil is warm. Planting can continue all throughout summer. Choose a site in full sun for best form and flowering, although plants can tolerate light, filtered shade. Shower of gold is not particular about soil type, but does need good drainage and is a good choice for sandy soils. Amend the soil with ample amounts of compost or other organic matter prior to planting.

Growing Tips
Fertilize once in spring as growth resumes. Use a well-balanced formulation or a slow-release product. Fertilize once or twice more in summer. Be careful not to apply fertilizer late in the season; new growth is highly susceptible to frost damage. Water well to establish, but once established plants need only moderate watering. In areas with regular summer rainfall, it grows well on natural rainfall. Water every 10 days when the weather is exceptionally hot or dry. Natural rainfall is usually sufficient in winter.

Regional Advice and Care
Prune in spring or early summer to tidy up or remove winter damage. Do not prune late in the season to avoid tender new growth that is more susceptible to freeze damage. At temperatures below 25 degrees Fahrenheit, shower of gold can die to the ground, but recovers quickly. It is not susceptible to pests or disease.

Companion Planting and Design
Shower of gold is a good choice for a low hedge or boundary planting in a large garden. The long-lasting color makes it a good choice to blend with other perennials or in the front of a large, evergreen hedge. Use it generously to create a groundcover for large areas, particularly ones that do not receive routine maintenance. It is also provides erosion control on hot, steep slopes.

Try These
Narrow-leaf goldshower (*Galphimia angustifolia*), a Hill Country native, is a short, rarely over 12 inches tall, perennial with orange to yellow flowers. Shower of gold is in the same family as Barbados cherry (*Malpighia glabra*) and yellow butterfly vine (*Callaeum macroptera*), and together they make a spectacular summer show.

Silverberry

Elaeagnus pungens

Bloom Period and Seasonal Color
Fall, cream

Mature Height x Spread
8 to 12 ft. x 8 to 10 ft.

Botanical Pronunciation
el-ee-AG-nus PUN-jenz

Zones 7 to 9

ilverberry is a big, sprawling Asian shrub that, when grown in full sun with ample space, is a rounded, highly symmetrical plant. But when closely spaced, the thorny young stems quickly intertwine with their near neighbors, creating a dense, tangled hedge. The thorns are actually young stems that begin as stiff spurs but eventually soften to stems. The new leaves are silvery and age to olive green. The clusters of bell-shaped flowers are small and unremarkable but have a potent gardenia-like fragrance. They are followed by hanging, red fruit that is coated with an unusual splatter of silver, giving them the look of an old-fashioned Christmas ornament. The fruit is technically edible, but hardly palatable; it is seedy and tart. Birds, however, find it irresistible.

When, Where, and How to Plant

Plant in fall for best results, although silverberry can be planted almost anytime. Choose a location in full sun, and give the plant enough room to grow without crowding into other species. Silverberry grows in almost any type of soil including sand, but consistently wet or poorly drained soils cause it to fail. Amend soil with moderate amounts of compost and composted manure to increase drainage in heavy soils.

Growing Tips

Apply slow-release or well-balanced fertilizer in spring after the danger of frost is past and again in fall. Water only when the soil has dried out. In many areas, there is sufficient natural rainfall to support this species. Silverberry withstands considerable

drought, and because consistent moisture will quickly kill the plant, err on the side of dry when watering.

Regional Advice and Care

Prune in spring to remove any dead or damaged stems. Silverberry responds well to pruning and can be trained to any desired shape. It is not susceptible to most pests and disease, particularly when grown in full sun and kept on the dry side.

Companion Planting and Design

This fast-growing evergreen shrub makes a quick hedge, boundary, or privacy screen. The stems tangle together easily, making it excellent cover for birds and other wildlife. It is best used in a garden large enough to allow it to grow naturally. In small gardens, it is in need of constant pruning. Silverberry makes a good choice for erosion control on steep slopes.

Try These

The nineteenth-century selection from Georgia, 'Fruitlandii', is still regularly offered. It has large, bluish green leaves with a wavy margin and grows as a large mound. 'Maculata' has leaves with a yellow midsection and green margins. 'Marginata' is the reverse with cream-colored leaf margins. There are various dwarf forms, often sold as 'Nana'. *Elaeagnus macrophylla*, also called silverberry, is similar. A hybrid between this species and *E. pungens*, *E. xebbengei*, is commonly available. It has large, leathery, deep green leaves with silver undersides and no spines. 'Gilt Edge' is its variegated form.

Sky Flower

Duranta erecta

Other Name Golden dew-drop

Bloom Period and Seasonal Color
Spring to fall, blue, purple, white

Mature Height x Spread
10 to 15 ft. x 6 to 15 ft.

Botanical Pronunciation
dur-AN-tuh ee-REK-tuh

Zones 9 to 10

Sky flower is native to the hot limestone soils along the Gulf Coast from Florida to Mexico. There is some controversy about whether it has simply naturalized in extreme south Texas or is truly native, but regardless this is a stunning, flowering shrub for all of southern Texas. The glossy, bright green leaves densely cover the long, fast-growing stems, which droop gracefully. Each stem is tipped with long clusters of small, sky blue flowers that are lightly fragrant. These are quickly followed by round, waxy, golden fruit that hangs on the shrub for months. I have grown skyflower in every garden I have had and find it a durable shrub that may be limited by cold, but not by heat, drought, or modest watering.

When, Where, and How to Plant
Plant in spring after all danger of frost is past and the soil is warm. It can be planted well into early summer. Choose a location in full sun or where there is at least six hours of sun. It is best to locate it with protection from cold winds, as well. Sky flower tolerates almost any soil from deep, well-drained, fertile soil to rocky ones. But it does best in soils with excellent drainage and moderate to high alkalinity.

Growing Tips
Apply slow-release or organic fertilizer annually in spring, especially for plants growing in dry soils. Water two or three times a month in the hottest part of the summer unless rainfall is abundant. Mulch the roots in summer to keep soil from drying out too quickly. Water established plants monthly in winter.

Regional Advice and Care
Prune in late spring or early summer to remove dead or damaged limbs. Lightly tip prune to remove spent flowering stalks. Sky flower will lose leaves in a freeze but is root hardy to at least 20 degrees Fahrenheit. It will also defoliate if severely drought stressed, but in both cases recovers quickly. Skyflower has no serious pest or disease problems.

Companion Planting and Design
Plant generously to create a colorful background for perennial or annual plantings. Use as a specimen or accent plant in small patios or courtyards. Mix sky flower with other shrubs to form an informal hedge, visual screen, or border planting. Sky flower's great heat tolerance makes it an attractive choice around pools or other areas where reflected heat is intense.

Try These
'Geisha Girl' has deep purple flowers with a white throat and white ruffled edges. It is probably the same as 'Sapphire Swirl' and 'Sweet Memory'. By whatever name, this selection is a vigorous bloomer, and the white-edged, deep blue to purple flowers are stunning throughout the summer. It makes little fruit, which is a shame; I find the fruit as attractive as the flowers. 'Alba' and 'White Sapphire' are white, 'Dark Skies' is intense blue; 'Variegata' and 'Gold Edge' are variegated.

Texas Kidneywood

Eysenhardtia texana

Bloom Period and Seasonal Color
Spring to fall, white

Mature Height x Spread
4 to 9 ft. x 3 to 6 ft.

Botanical Pronunciation
eye-zen-HAR-dee-ah TEX-an-uh

Zones 8 to 10

I think every garden needs a generous number of fragrant plants, and Texas kidneywood is one of my favorite choices. Texas kidneywood is a loosely branched shrub that is often wider than it is tall with a delicate appearance that belies its heat and drought tolerance. The dark green compound leaves smell of citrus when crushed. The tiny white flowers held in tall, conical spikes smell strongly of vanilla. Flowering is profuse and although intermittent through the year, is most prolific in the late summer. This West and South Texas native will often lose its leaves during drought or an unusually cold winter, but recovers from either condition quickly. Butterflies are strongly attracted to its nectar and swarm the plant in the late summer.

When, Where, and How to Plant
Plant in spring when soils are warm and all danger of frost is past. Texas kidneywood grows best in fast-draining soils with average to high alkalinity. However, it tolerates a wider range of soils as long as they are well drained. It is not strictly necessary to amend the soil before planting.

Growing Tips
Texas kidneywood requires no supplemental fertilization. Water established plants deeply once or twice a month in summer. Rely on natural rainfall in winter.

Regional Advice and Care
Prune spent flowering stalks anytime after bloom is complete. Prune dead or damaged stems, or those growing erratically, in spring as growth resumes.

Texas kidneywood is not susceptible to pests or disease.

Companion Planting and Design
Texas kidneywood blends well with other small shrubs to form an informal hedge or boundary. Use this species in a small garden or patio as an accent or focal plant. Plant near seating areas or other well-used parts of the garden to enjoy its strong, sweet fragrance. Its strong attraction for butterflies, particularly late in the summer, makes it a natural component of any gardener wishing to encourage these delightful visitors.

Try These
Kidneywood (*Eysenhardtia orthocarpa*) is a closely related species from southern Arizona and western Mexico. It is distinguished from Texas kidneywood by its height, to 20 feet tall, and more tree-like form. The leaves are gray-green and its gray to tan bark becomes shaggy with age. Texas kidneywood has deeper green leaves, and the bark typically remains smooth with age. The flowers also have an intense vanilla fragrance. Both species have short, flat pods, but on kidneywood the pods are persistent for months and look like small pagodas arranged along the stems of the tree. It has similar heat, cold, and drought tolerance. Mexican kidneywood (*E. polystachya*) is native from Durango to Oaxaca. Earlier treatments considered it the same as or perhaps a variation of *E. orthocarpa* but is now considered a distinct species. Mexican kidneywood is a large tree, growing up to 25 feet tall, but is otherwise similar to the American kidneywoods.

Texas Lantana

Lantana urticoides

Bloom Period and Seasonal Color
Spring to fall, yellow, orange, red

Mature Height x Spread
3 to 5 ft. x 4 to 8 ft.

Botanical Pronunciation
lan-TAN-ah ur-tih-COY-ee-deez

Zones 8 to 10

I have long admired lantanas. I find their cheerful heads of flowers in the face of relentless heat and poor soils encouraging. Although there are low-growing forms, it is the shrubs, like Texas lantana (syn. *Lantana horrida*), that really grab my attention. Texas lantana has the characteristic pungent, raspy leaves with a crinkled appearance. The rough texture comes from short hairs that are irritating to some people and should be kept away from your eyes. It is the flowering heads that make this such a beloved plant. All lantana have tiny tubular flowers with flared ends that are collected in rounded heads at the tips of the stems. Butterflies are drawn to these flowers, and plants can have as many butterflies as flowers in late summer.

When, Where, and How to Plant
Plant in spring after all danger of frost is past and soils are warm. Planting can continue through early summer. Choose a location in full sun, even one with reflected heat, for best form and flowering. Texas lantana is not particular about soil type and will grow well in any well-drained soil, even highly alkaline or rocky ones.

Growing Tips
Texas lantana needs no regular supplemental fertilization. If leaves yellow or fade in late summer, apply a light application of a well-balanced fertilizer. Established plants have excellent drought resistance, but for better and more consistent flowering, water enough to keep the soil from drying out completely. Rely on natural rainfall in winter.

Regional Advice and Care
Prune Texas lantana hard in the spring as growth resumes to remove dead or winter-damaged stems and rejuvenate the plant. Light tip pruning in the summer helps continue the blooming season and keep plants tidy. Texas lantana has no serious disease problems. Whiteflies can be a problem when they are abundant, but their damage is usually only cosmetic.

Companion Planting and Design
Blend Texas lantana into any perennial planting or the front of a hedge or border planting. This is a good plant to use in areas that do not receive routine maintenance. Because of its strong appeal to butterflies, plant Texas lantana generously near seating areas or pools where these visitors can be enjoyed. In zones where it is too cold for Texas lantana to overwinter in the ground, plant in large containers or planters for long summer flowering.

Try These
Most other lantanas offered are hybrids between the tropical common lantana (*Lantana camara*) and the trailing lantana (*L. montevidensis*). Common lantana is a shrub with flowers that cover a huge range of pinks, oranges, yellows, white, and combinations of all of these. Culture is much the same as for Texas lantana. Shrub forms include 'Irene' with deep pink and yellow flowers; 'Christine' with yellow, pink, and purple flowers; and 'Radiation' with rich orange blooms. Trailing or low-growing choices are numerous as well.

Texas Mountain Laurel

Sophora secundiflora

Bloom Period and Seasonal Color
Spring, purple

Mature Height x Spread 6 to 25 ft. x 5 to 15 ft.

Botanical Pronunciation
so-FORE-uh se-kune-dih-FLOOR-uh

Zone 8b to 10

I could grow Texas mountain laurel, also called mescal bean, just for its rounded, evergreen leaves and rugged resistance to heat and drought. But when you add in its superb, although brief, flowering, it becomes completely irresistible. Native to the Hill Country and on through eastern Mexico, this tall, upright shrub or small tree has deep green, rounded leaflets. The deep purple, highly fragrant flowers are shaped like oversized sweet peas and are collected in robust wisteria-like cascades at the ends of the stems. The flowers do not remain open long but are followed by round pods that persist for over a year. Pods hold the rock hard, scarlet seeds, but be careful—the seeds are toxic if eaten. But they are widely used in jewelry, especially in Mexico.

When, Where, and How to Plant
Plant in fall or spring in warm winter areas. In colder zones, plant in spring after the soil has warmed. Choose a location in full sun for best form and flowering, although Texas mountain laurel will grow in light, filtered shade. Plants grow in any soil, even highly alkaline ones, but need extremely sharp drainage. Heavy clays or other poorly drained soils cause plants to fail quickly. Although I have seen plants growing in acid, forest soils they are usually short-lived and rarely grow to full size.

Growing Tips
Texas mountain laurel does not need supplemental fertilizer. Water established plants at long intervals with a slow, deep soak. Plants accept regular watering in summer as long as the drainage is excellent. Rely on natural rainfall in the winter unless it is unusually hot or dry.

Regional Advice and Care
Prune in spring after blooming either to train it to a small tree or to remove dead or damaged stems. When grown as a shrub, Texas mountain laurel has excellent natural form and rarely needs pruning for shape. Tent caterpillars may infect the terminal buds in early spring. Remove them promptly by hand or prune out the tip. Plants that are overwatered or watered too shallowly become chlorotic. Otherwise Texas mountain laurel is not susceptible to pests or disease.

Companion Planting and Design
Use Texas mountain laurel as an evergreen hedge or screen either singly or mixed with other shrubs. The dark evergreen leaves make a fine background for colorful perennial plantings. When trained as a small tree it can be used as a specimen or focal plant in patios or courtyards.

Try These
'Silver Peso' has silvery white leaves. Arizona sophora (*Sophora arizonica*) is smaller, to 10 feet tall, with broad, rounded leaflets and lightly fragrant lavender to dark purple flowers. Yellow sophora (*S. tomentosa*) is an evergreen, upright shrub with gray-green foliage and bright yellow flowers growing to about 6 feet tall with hardiness to about 20 degrees Fahrentheit. This species is tolerant of consistent moisture and grows well along the coast.

Wax Myrtle

Morella cerifera

Bloom Period and Seasonal Color
Fall and winter, greenish white

Mature Height x Spread
12 to 20 ft. x 8 to 16 ft.

Botanical Pronunciation
mo-RELL-uh ser-IFF-er-ah

Wax myrtle is a handsome evergreen shrub with a range of delights. The olive green foliage has a spicy fragrance when crushed. Plants bloom in the winter with pale green male catkins, and female flowers that resemble a bump more than bloom. Pale blue-gray berries, much revered by birds, follow and are held in thick sets along the stems. Wax myrtle has a long tradition of use around the home, either by boiling off the waxy coating on the fruit to make fragrant candles or by using the leaves to repel insects, even cockroaches. Wax myrtle is a significant larval plant for a number of hairstreak butterflies. And in case that wasn't enough, the light gray bark on its numerous stems pales to nearly white in some individuals.

When, Where, and How to Plant
Plant in early spring or fall, although in all areas fall planting is optimal. Wax myrtle grows in almost any sun exposure, although flowering and fruiting are best in full sun. In the hottest zones, it is necessary to protect it from afternoon sun. Wax myrtle grows in almost any soil, including those that are poorly drained or suffer from intermittent flooding. It is not necessary to amend the soil before planting.

Growing Tips
Fertilize wax myrtle in spring with any well-balanced formula after the soils are warmed and growth resumes. Apply again twice during the year at regular intervals. Water sufficiently to keep soil evenly moist, which can be as often as once a week if the weather is exceptionally hot or dry. Established plants have good drought tolerance,

particularly in northern and eastern parts of the range noted above. Wax myrtle does well with long, deep soaks at long intervals rather than frequent, shallow, or overhead watering. Mulch the root zone to maintain even soil moisture and extend the time between waterings.

Regional Advice and Care
Pruning is optional because wax myrtle has excellent natural form. Plants increase from root suckers, and these can be removed anytime; other pruning should be done in the spring. Wax myrtle is not susceptible to pests or disease.

Companion Planting and Design
Use wax myrtle as part of a mixed hedge or boundary planting. It can be trained to a small tree for use in smaller gardens or as a focal plant. Wax myrtle tolerates extreme root crowding, so it is useful in tight or restricted spaces. Birds avidly eat the fruit, and I know one gardener who uses this plant solely to attract wintering myrtle warblers.

Try These
Dwarf forms of wax myrtle are sometimes sold as *Myrica pusilla*, but that name has no botanical standing. Dwarf forms look similar to the type but grow 5 to 6 feet tall and as wide. There are selections of dwarf wax myrtle that are occasionally offered that have slight differences in leaf or stem color.

Winter Jasmine

Jasminum nudiflorum

Bloom Period and Seasonal Color
Winter and early spring, yellow

Mature Height x Spread
4 to 10 ft. x 3 to 6 ft.

Botanical Pronunciation
JAS-min-num new-dih-FLOOR-um

Zones 7 to 9

Winter jasmine is a fountain of a plant with long, bright green stems that rise up to 4 feet tall then fall over, creating a big, rounded shrub. In some situations it can trail along the ground or can be trained as a vine. The leaves are bright, shiny green and are split into three parts. They are spread widely on the stems, but overall the plant is dense, almost impenetrable. Although deciduous, the bright green stems provide a welcome note of color in a winter garden. Unlike most other jasmines, the flowers of winter jasmine have no fragrance. The small bright yellow flowers are arranged along the stem and flower most abundantly in late winter when few other plants are in flower.

When, Where, and How to Plant

Plant in spring after all danger of frost is past and the soil can be worked. Winter jasmine grows and flowers best in full sun. In shady locations it becomes lanky with few flowers. Choose a site where there is ample room for the plant to spread out. Winter jasmine grows in most well-drained, moderately fertile soils.

Growing Tips

Fertilize winter jasmine with any well-balanced fertilizer in spring once the leaves have emerged. Reapply three more times through the year but quit about a month before the last frost date. Water to maintain even soil moisture. A heavy mulch of 4 to 6 inches of any good organic matter helps keep the soil moist and reduce the frequency of watering.

Regional Advice and Care

Prune winter jasmine almost to the ground every three to four years to keep it tidy and well formed. Otherwise, no pruning is necessary. Winter jasmine is not susceptible to pests or disease.

Companion Planting and Design

Winter jasmine is a good choice for erosion control on steep slopes. It is also attractive when planted above a retaining wall so that the long branches cascade over the wall. Winter jasmine can be trained to a sturdy trellis or wall as a vine.

Try These

'Aureum' has yellow blotches on the leaves, whereas 'Nanum' is a dwarf. Primrose jasmine (*Jasminum mesnyi*) looks much the same, but the yellow flowers are larger and this species is evergreen. Primrose jasmine grows well in areas of high heat and is well suited for the southern half of Texas. Showy jasmine (*J. floridum*) and Italian jasmine (*J. humile*) are similar. Pink (or white) jasmine (*J. polyanthum*) is a semi-deciduous vining shrub with a profusion of small star-shaped white flowers that are pink in bud. Arabian jasmine (*J. sambac*) has pure white, highly fragrant flowers intermittently through spring and summer. It grows best in filtered shade and areas with hot summers and is hardy only to Zone 9. Its petals are the flavoring for jasmine tea. 'Grand Duke of Tuscany' (also 'Flore Pleno') has double flowers.

Woolly Butterfly Bush

Buddleia marrubiifolia

Bloom Period and Seasonal Color
Spring to fall, orange

Mature Height x Spread
3 to 5 ft. x 4 to 5 ft.

Botanical Pronunciation
BUD-lee-uh mah-RUBE-ih-fole-ee-uh

Zones 8 to 10

Woolly butterfly bush captivates me for its soft, fuzzy, gray-white leaves topped by buttons of bright orange flowers. The white of the leaves is a dense coating of fine white hairs and is a clue to how drought and heat tolerant this shrub actually is. Hairs on leaves reflect heat and act like minute umbrellas to hold in precious moisture. This is a shrub with a tight, dense natural form; it has a natural ball shape. The flowers are tiny, and although they begin a pale yellow, they quickly fade to deep orange. They are crammed into tight whorls at intervals along the blooming stalk, like lollipops piled on top of each other. Butterflies are extremely fond of the flowers, finding them a rich source of nectar.

When, Where, and How to Plant
Plant in fall or spring in all zones. Although very cold hardy, woolly butterfly bush's need for dryness is more limiting than the cold. Plant in full, unrelieved sun, or even areas of high reflected heat. Woolly butterfly bush grows well in any well-drained soil from fertile, garden soils to rocky, native ones, but does poorly in heavy clays or in areas of consistently moist soils. It is not necessary to amend the soil before planting.

Growing Tips
Woolly butterfly bush requires no supplemental fertilization. Water carefully; this plant is killed quickly with too much watering or soils that do not drain sufficiently. Avoid overhead watering and use soaker hoses, garden hose, or drip irrigation for best results. Plants become overgrown, floppy, and subject to rot when overwatered. Water established plants every two to three weeks in the summer, less frequently if there is regular summer rainfall. In most zones, natural rainfall is sufficient in the winter, but even in dry winters do not water more than monthly in the winter.

Regional Advice and Care
Prune woolly butterfly bush in fall or very early spring to remove dead or damaged wood. Prune to within 1 or 2 feet of the ground every two or three years to maintain the shape of the plant and reinvigorate it. Woolly butterfly bush is not susceptible to pests or disease.

Companion Planting and Design
Woolly butterfly bush mixes well with other perennials or shrubs that favor growing in similarly dry conditions like many salvias, yellowbells, and other natives. Use this tidy shrub as an informal hedge or boundary planting particularly for areas of the garden that do not receive routine maintenance. The white foliage is cooling in a hot spot, and its excellent heat and drought tolerance make this a good choice around a pool or anywhere with strong reflected heat. Place near seating areas where the continuous stream of butterflies can be enjoyed, or add it to a butterfly garden. Because of its requirements for good drainage and minimal water, woolly butterfly bush blends well with cactus and succulents.

Yaupon

Ilex vomitoria

Bloom Period and Seasonal Color
Spring, white

Mature Height x Spread
12 to 20 ft. x 15 to 20 ft.

Botanical Pronunciation
EYE-lex vah-meh-TOR-ee-ah

Zones 7 to 9

Yaupon, or yaupon holly, is a plant that you fail to notice until its bright red berries form in the fall. Suddenly you realize it is common and it is everywhere, and in some parts of the state that is literally the case. Roadsides are lined with it and fence lines are punctuated by it, undoubtedly because its beautiful berries are a feast for many species of birds. This is a reliable species that is one of the least demanding evergreen shrubs for Texas gardens. The deep green leaves are prolific and well-grown plants are virtually impenetrable. The small white flowers are easy to disregard but on female plant they are followed by tight clusters of red to red-orange berries that remain on the plant through the fall and winter.

When, Where, and How to Plant
Plant in fall in all but the coldest zones. In those areas plant in spring as soon as the soil can be worked. Yaupon grows well in either full sun or partial shade. Avoid planting in deep shade, however. This shrub is not particular about the soil and is one of the best choices for areas that are poorly drained, or where fertility is minimal.

Growing Tips
Yaupon needs no supplemental fertilization. Water established plants sparingly; this species has excellent drought tolerance. In the hottest part of summer, water deeply, monthly if there has been inadequate rainfall. In most areas established plants do fine on natural rainfall. Rely on natural rainfall in winter in all zones.

Regional Advice and Care
Prune in spring to remove dead or damaged stems, or to shape the plant. Yaupon has good natural form and does not need annual pruning. This species has no pest or disease problems.

Companion Planting and Design
Plant generously to form a hedge or barrier at the edge of the garden. Plants grow deliberately at first but increase their rate of growth over time. This is a preferred addition to any native garden or one that favors attracting birds, who devour the fruit particularly after it freezes. Plants are dioecious with male and female flowers on separate plants.

Try These
'Hoskins Shadow' is an extremely hardy selection (down to minus 10 degrees Fahrenheit) with bigger leaves and abundant fruit set. 'Will Fleming' has finer leaves and a naturally columnar growth habit. This male selection makes no fruit. 'Pendula' is just the reverse—a female plant with small, fine leaves and a decided weeping habit. 'Stokes Dwarf' is a male selection that grows only to 3 feet tall and spreads about as far. 'Nana' is also dwarf but produces berries. Possumhaw (*Ilex decidua*) is a deciduous, native shrub with a horizontal branching pattern. After the dark green leaves drop, the female plants provide winter contrast with the light gray bark studded with abundant bright red berries that remain on the plant throughout the entire winter.

Yellow Bird of Paradise

Caesalpinia gilliesii

Bloom Period and Seasonal Color
Spring to fall, yellow

Mature Height x Spread
5 to 10 ft. x 4 to 6 ft.

Botanical Pronunciation
ses-al-PIN-ee-uh gil-EEZ-ee-eye

Zones 8 to 10

Yellow bird of paradise is a loosely branched, multitrunked shrub that is one of the cold hardiest members of this colorful genus. The bright green compound leaves are evergreen in warm winter areas but deciduous in colder zones or after a hard freeze. The remarkable flowers have large, butter yellow petals out of which 4-inch scarlet red stamens unfurl. Flowers are crowded into dense heads at the ends of the branches and truly look like birds ready to take flight. Native to Argentina and Uruguay, yellow bird of paradise has naturalized in parts of western Texas, southern New Mexico, southern Arizona, southern Florida, as well as Mexico. To prevent unwanted seedlings, trim off the long, flat seed pods as soon as they form.

When, Where, and How to Plant
Plant in spring as soon as the soil can be worked and all danger of frost is past. Choose a location in full sun, although in hot, desert locales yellow bird of paradise grows well in partial shade. This species tolerates any well-drained soil from fertile, garden soils to rocky, alkaline ones, but it does poorly in heavy clays. It is not necessary to amend the soil prior to planting.

Growing Tips
Apply slow-release or organic fertilizer annually in spring. Water enough in the summer to prevent the soil from drying out completely. Frequency will depend on temperatures, but in most zones every two weeks is usually adequate. Add a generous layer of mulch to keep soil from drying out too quickly.

Rely on natural rainfall in winter when the plant is all but dormant.

Regional Advice and Care
Cut back in spring after growth resumes to remove dead wood or winter-damaged stems. Leaf drop occurs in the mid-20s, but the stems are hardy to at least 10 degrees Fahrenheit, and recovery is quick. Continue light pruning through the summer to remove suckers, unruly branches, or spent flowering heads. Yellow bird of paradise can be trained to a small tree with careful pruning. Yellow bird of paradise is not susceptible to pests or disease.

Companion Planting and Design
Plant yellow bird of paradise in groups to highlight the spectacular color show. Use it against southern or western walls, in hot barren spots, or around pools where reflected heat is intense. When trained to a small tree it makes a splendid specimen or focal plant for courtyards, small gardens, or patios.

Try These
Mexican bird of paradise (*Caesalpinia mexicana*) is a large shrub or small tree native to far South Texas with deep green leaves and bright yellow flowers. Flowering from late spring through the summer, it is hardy to about 20 degrees Fahrenheit. Pride of Barbados (*C. pulcherrima*) is has a dense, almost round form and tall, pyramids of brilliant orange to brick-red flowers variously marked with yellow. Hardy to 30 degrees Fahrenheit, it recovers quickly from light freezes.

TREES & PALMS
FOR TEXAS

Trees preside over a garden rather than merely blend in and often set the garden's style and character. This makes selecting a tree and deciding on its location a matter for careful thought. Take your time; consider how tall and wide the mature tree will be and how it will affect your garden.

Trees

Trees have many uses in a garden, but none is more important than providing shade. Trees with open branching or small leaves create light filtered shade. Almost any plant grows well under this shade including most succulents, many cactus, shrubs, and perennials.

Trees that are evergreen, have intricate branching patterns, or grow large, dense leaves caste deep or full shade. Plants that need some cold protection, or are well adapted to deep shade, grow well under such trees.

Smaller trees or those with spectacular bloom make excellent focal plants or specimens. A smaller tree may be the only tree needed in small patio or courtyard.

Purchasing a Tree

Consider how tall and how wide a tree your garden can accommodate. Do not make the mistake of planning to keep cutting it back as this type of pruning only ruins the tree.

If you require shade for a patio or seating area choose a tree with a wide, spreading crown and plant it on the sunniest side. For heightened interest or drama, choose a tree with interesting bark or a dramatic branching pattern.

Near a pool, consider a palm, which has less litter or a tree with large leaves that won't clog a pool filter. Alternately, site the tree on the west and southwestern side of the yard to block the afternoon sun.

When selecting a tree, think small. Young plants endure transplant shock better than old ones and grow and establish quickly.

Don't be afraid to inspect the roots before you buy a tree. Roots should be about the size of a pencil, with a spreading network of fine, fibrous roots covering the entire root ball with no coiled or mangled roots at the bottom or roots growing outside the pot. Avoid trees that have grown into the ground, or where large roots are running out of the pot.

Planting a Tree

Begin by digging a hole that is three to five times wider than the container but just as deep. Remove any stakes or other constraints from the tree. Set the tree in the hole

White oak

with the soil line from the container even with the top of the hole. Backfill gently, filling up the spaces but without compacting the soil.

Watering Trees

Most trees are best watered with a slow, deep soak at long intervals. For newly planted trees, begin by watering in a circle around the perimeter of the plant. How often will depend on the soil and temperature. Use a probe to determine that you have soaked the root zone to at least 3 feet with each watering. Continue to expand the watering zone in a rough circle at the edge, or drip line, of the tree as it grows.

Tree roots grow in response to water and this ever increasing, moist, root zone encourages the roots to spread out, sink deeply, and form the anchor that is vital for the long-term health of the tree. Young trees that grow too fast, or have abundant top growth, are almost always being watered too often and too shallowly.

Drip irrigation is an excellent method for watering newly planted trees. Provide enough emitters to evenly soak the root zone at the drip line to a depth of 3 feet. After they about five years or when a tree is over 10 feet tall, it usually best to shift from drip to laying down a hose near the edge of the tree and letting it provide a slow, deep soak of the root system.

Basins built by mounding up a 4- to 6-inch berm around the drip line are also an effective way to water trees. Fill the basin with water and allow it to slowly percolate into the soil. Repeat if necessary to thoroughly wet the root zone. Basins also must be expanded as the tree grows.

Pruning Trees

Pruning should be performed only when it is actually necessary. Mature trees do not need to be pruned annually, except to remove dead wood, take out crossing branches, clean up wind, freeze, or disease-damaged limbs. Young trees, however, can be gently pruned to encourage a particular form or direction of growth.

To train young trees go at it slowly and do not prune anything for the first year. Then lightly prune annually, taking no more than one-fourth of the mass of the tree. Concentrate on pruning branches that are growing toward the ground, growing toward the center, or that are crossing or laying on each other. Do not try to get the final form of the tree all at one time, but shape the tree over many growing seasons.

Be sure to prune at the appropriate time of year for the species, and make sharp, clean cuts that do not cut into the branch collar. Above all remember that a chain saw is strictly for the initial cuts to remove large branches (final cuts should be made by hand), for removal of dead limbs or to cut down an entire tree.

Staking Trees

I am not a great fan of staking. I think it is done too often, left for too long, and almost always done badly. Few trees really need to be staked. Trees in areas with extreme or consistent wind can benefit from initial staking, but otherwise try to avoid staking. The action of bending and moving in the wind strengthens the trunk and allows a tree to grow strong and straight.

If you must stake a tree, begin by setting two stakes in the ground in line with the tree. Wrap tree tape around the tree 2 or 3 feet from the ground. Secure it to the stake, keeping it loose enough to allow the tree to move in the wind. Repeat about a foot higher on the tree, securing this section to the other stake. Be sure the stakes do not touch the tree and remove them within six months.

Palms

Palms are not woody plants, but are monocots related to grasses, bulbs, and agaves. This means they grow quite differently than woody plants. The large head of leaves that supports the plant throughout its life often takes years to fully form. During that time, palms are close to the ground as the leaves continue to increase in number and size.

Once the head is mature, the plant begins to grow the trunk, which is not wood but rather a compressed collection of vascular and other tissue. This growth is usually faster than that of the maturing head.

Pygmy date palm

Pruning Palms

The mature head of a palm is a fine balance between the older leaves that maintain photosynthesis and the newly emerging leaves that will replace them. As leaves age they transfer energy to the newer ones and serve as props to hold them up until they are firm enough to stand on their own.

Therefore, living leaves should never be removed from a palm. Pruning in palms is the removal only of completely dead leaves, blooming or fruiting stalks.

Dead leaves should be cut, never pulled, off the plant, leaving a small piece of petiole attached to the trunk. Dead leaves are best pruned in the summer, while blooming or fruiting stalks can be pruned any time.

Trees and palms are a commanding presence in any garden, often dominating the space. But one in just the right spot creates proportion and balance that is irreplaceable.

Anacua

Ehretia anacua

Other Name Sandpaper tree

Bloom Period and Seasonal Color
Summer to fall, white

Mature Height x Spread
15 to 20 ft. x 15 to 30 ft.

Botanical Pronunciation
eh-REE-tee-uh ah-NAH-koo-wa

Zones 8b to 10

I first saw anacua at the garden outside of Austin and mistook it for an oak. A closer look revealed that although this was no oak, it was a stunning tree with a dense canopy. The large evergreen leaves have smooth margins ending in a sharp tip. The top side is rough, hence the other common name. Delightfully fragrant white flowers are held in clusters at the tips of the branches. They are followed by tiny orange to dark yellow, fleshy, edible fruit. Old trees are striking specimens with gnarled, stocky trunks and branches marked by reddish, flaking bark. The name anacua is from *anachuite*, its Mexican name, which comes from two Nahuatl words meaning paper and tree, a possible reference to the peeling bark.

When, Where, and How to Plant
Plant in spring after all danger of frost is past and the soil is warm. Planting may continue through early summer. Choose a location in full sun for the best form, providing ample room for its ultimate size. Anacua grows best in alkaline soils, but adapts well to those that are neutral to slightly acid. It does require excellent drainage, so avoid areas of heavy clays or those that have frequent standing water.

Growing Tips
Anacua needs no supplemental fertilization. Water established plants deeply at long intervals. In most areas established plants grow on natural rainfall unless it is especially hot or dry. Under those conditions water deeply once a month. Rely on natural rainfall in winter.

Regional Advice and Care
Prune in late spring or early summer to remove dead or damaged wood. Trees tend be multitrunked. To reduce their number, remove one or two of the largest trunks a year until you have the desired number. Take care not to remove more than a quarter of the overall mass of a tree in one year. Anacua is not susceptible to pests of disease. New leaves are yellow, which causes some gardeners to believe they are diseased. This is natural, and they turn green on their own.

Companion Planting and Design
Plant as a specimen or focal tree, leaving sufficient room for both top and side growth. Use along the borders of a large garden for its striking form, dense, evergreen growth, and ease of care. Because of its heavy crown and evergreen habit, this is an excellent shade tree or a shelter for beds of tender succulents or perennials.

Try These
Although there are about fifty species in the genus, this is the only species native to the Americas. The other species are found in Asia and Africa. They are all equally striking woody plants but are rarely offered or grown in this country. Another large, white-flowered multitrunked woody plant is the native Texas olive (*Cordia boissieri*). This species has wide, smooth, evergreen leaves and pure white flowers in prominent clusters.

Bald Cypress

Taxodium distichum

Bloom Period and Seasonal Color
Spring, insignificant

Mature Height x Spread
30 to 60 ft. x 25 to 40 ft.

Botanical Pronunciation
tax-OH-dee-um DISS-tik-um

Zones 7 to 9

It is tempting to think of bald cypress as a plant only of the deep swamps of eastern Texas and the deep South. But these majestic trees also line the clear creeks and rivers that cut through the Hill Country of Central Texas. Bald cypress has a large, straight trunk that is often buttressed at the base. The deep brown or silvery bark peels away in long shreds over time. The regularly spaced horizontal branches flatten at the top in old trees. Deciduous, new needles are bright green and fade to brown or copper in the fall. Cones on the female trees are small, tight globes. Bald cypress has beautiful wood that is resistant to rot and has long been used in construction and furniture.

When, Where, and How to Plant
Plant in fall or spring in warmer zones. Plant in spring once the soil can be worked in cooler zones. Choose a site where the full height and spread of the tree can be accommodated. Although young trees grow well in light, filtered shade, mature trees often outlive other trees and rise high above them.

Growing Tips
Bald cypress never needs supplemental fertilizer. Despite growing in association with rivers and streams, bald cypress grows well on garden irrigation. In summer, water young trees weekly. Established trees should be watered two or three times a month with a long, deep soak during the summer. In areas with abundant summer rainfall, or if it is growing in a low or moist site, lessen the frequency of supplemental watering. Drought-stressed trees lose their leaves prematurely, but recover with a deep soak.

Regional Advice and Care
Bald cypress has excellent natural form and rarely needs pruning except to remove storm-damaged stems. This species resists almost all pests and disease.

Companion Planting and Design
Young trees make a good addition to a mixed woodland planting or along the boundary of a large garden. They are also striking as focal or accent trees. Eventually trees get very large, so plan accordingly.

Try These
Bald cypress live to great age, and an individual growing along the San Antonio River is known to be more than three hundred years old. Montezuma bald cypress (*Taxodium mucronatum*) is closely related and looks similar but is usually evergreen and not as cold hardy. Water tupelo (*Nyssa aquatica*) is an aquatic tree often found growing with bald cypress. It is, however, a flowering tree with bright yellow fall foliage but rarely grows without standing water. Black gum (*N. sylvatica*) is a tall, columnar tree often found near or around water in East Texas. Growing best in moist, acidic soils, this species is a reliable garden plant in its natural range. The glossy green foliage gives way to intensely red foliage in fall. Late in the summer, the tree forms abundant blue fruit that birds find irresistible.

Bur Oak

Quercus macrocarpa

Bloom Period and Seasonal Color
Spring, insignificant

Mature Height x Spread
60 to 80 ft. x 40 to 60 ft.

Botanical Pronunciation
KWER-kus mack-row-CAR-pah

Bur oak is a tall, straight tree with a heavy trunk and a rounded crown. It has the unusual (in trees) combination of being fast growing but extremely long-lived. The leaves are 6 to 9 inches long with deep, rounded lobes. Although it is deciduous, its fall color is insignificant. Acorns are one of the best indicators of which species of oak you have, and in this one it is a snap. They are the biggest of all our oaks, up to 1½ inches broad and almost entirely encased in a cup that is formed of coarse and curled scales. The entire thing looks like a nest for the acorn, and once I had a charming ornament with a bird sitting on eggs in this nest.

When, Where, and How to Plant
Plant in fall or in spring as soon as the soil can be worked. Choose a location in full sun and where both the height and crown spread of the mature tree can be accommodated. Bur oak grows in almost any type of soil from sandy, slightly acidic ones to rocky, limestone soils. Good drainage is important but not entirely critical.

Growing Tips
Fertilize young trees annually in spring using a formulation that has a low-nitrogen content. Once established, bur oak needs no supplemental fertilizer. Water maturing trees regularly, up to twice a month, in summer to assure a good root system. Established trees are quite drought tolerant and grow well on natural rainfall unless it is exceptionally hot or dry. During those times, a long soak once a month is more than ample.

Regional Advice and Care
Prune in spring or fall to remove dead or damaged limbs. Do not prune in the hottest part of the summer or in the depth of winter. Bur oak has excellent natural form and no further pruning should be required. Bur oak is not susceptible to most pests and disease. Plants that become infested with aphids or other insects are usually deeply water stressed.

Companion Planting and Design
This is a large tree that will be a commanding presence in any garden. Give it ample space and consider it as the principle shade tree in a modest-sized yard. Its height makes it useful to shade western walls or windows, as well as the roof.

Try These
Overcup oak (*Quercus lyrata*) has a similar acorn that is almost entirely encased in a frilly cup. The leaves are smaller and narrower, but the chief difference is overcup oaks' preference for moist, even wet, sites. Post oak (*Q. stellata*) grows slowly with gnarled or twisted branching and an upright, rounded form. Leathery, deep green leaves are slightly lobed, and the large acorns are barely covered by the smooth cap. Monterey oak (*Q. polymorpha*) grows to 60 feet with highly variable, dark green foliage and an upright, regular form.

California Fan Palm

Washingtonia filifera

Bloom Period and Seasonal Color
Summer, creamy yellow

Mature Height x Spread
40 to 50 ft. x 20 to 25 ft.

Botanical Pronunciation
wash-ing-TONE-ee-uh fa-LIF-ur-uh

Zones 8 to 10

California fan palm is a large, stately plant with a full, rounded crown of leaves. The bases of the leaves are not long lasting, which makes the light brown trunk smooth over time. The fan-shaped leaves are light green and prominently split at the ends with shreds of fiber hanging from the tips. Each leaf is over 6 feet long. Found in isolated but dense groves within the canyons and fault breaks of southern Arizona and southern California, this is the palm for which the city of Palm Springs was named. Some populations are thought to have been planted centuries ago by native peoples who valued the tree for construction, weaving, thatch, and the edible fruit. Today the small dark fruit is usually enjoyed only by birds.

When, Where, and How to Plant
Plant when soils are warm even during the hottest part of the summer. Like most palms, the root system is virtually dormant when temperatures are below 65 degrees Fahrenheit, and plants fail quickly when planted in cold weather. California fan palm is tolerant of a wide range of soils from very dry and rocky, to well-drained, fertile soils, even those that are nearly saturated. Choose a site in full sun and where there is ample room to accommodate the maturing head and the full vertical height.

Growing Tips
Apply slow-release or organic fertilizer annually, especially when plants are young. Fertilize established plants every other year. Water established plants every 10 to 14 days in summer, less often if summer rains are abundant or reliable. Plants become significantly drought tolerant as they age, and mature plants may only need monthly watering unless there is no rain. Rely on natural rainfall in the winter.

Regional Advice and Care
Prune dead leaves or blooming stalks anytime. Never prune living leaves unless they are severely damaged. Dead leaves remain on the plant for years and then suddenly begin to fall away in a process known as self-cleaning. These dead leaves can be removed with care but only if they come away easily in your hand. Never try to climb a tree to remove dead leaves. California fan palm is not susceptible to pests or disease.

Companion Planting and Design
Use in gardens that have the scale to support them, especially in groups or groves for shade. In hillside gardens, plant at the lowest point and enjoy peeking into the crown. Many birds, particularly orioles, nest in the leaves.

Try These
Mexican fan palm (*Washingtonia robusta*) has a thinner trunk, smaller head, and darker leaves, and old plants are over 80 feet tall. In California they are known as skyduster because of their height. Mexican fan palm is somewhat less hardy than California fan palm. There are countless hybrids between the two, and because they are difficult to distinguish when young, plants or hybrids are sold by either of these names.

Cedar Elm

Ulmus crassifolia

Bloom Period and Seasonal Color
Spring, insignificant

Mature Height x Spread
50 to 60 ft. x 40 to 60 ft.

Botanical Pronunciation
ULL-mus krass-ih-FOLE-ee-uh

Cedar elm is a commonly planted tree that is native throughout much of central and eastern Texas. It has an irregular form created by its drooping branches that arise low on the tree. Young branches have corky extensions, like wings, along the edges, and the bark of mature trees is gray and rough. The raspy leaves are serrated along the edges with deep, prominent venation. The flowers are not showy but interesting with a waxy, reddish corolla surrounded by small, extended, bright yellow stamens. They emerge directly from the stems in the fall. The leaves turn yellow or golden in autumn. In the southern parts of the state both planted and naturally occurring trees are frequently evergreen. Some people are allergic to the pollen.

When, Where, and How to Plant
Plant in fall or spring in all zones. Cedar elm adapts to almost any soil, including compacted or heavy soils and those with poor drainage. It is especially useful in disturbed or heavy soils. It is unnecessary, and some experts believe destructive, to add soil amendments when planting.

Growing Tips
Cedar elm does not require supplemental fertilization. Water young trees regularly to establish an adequate root system. Established trees accept almost any watering regimen, although water at least monthly in the summer if rainfall is erratic or lacking. Rely on natural rainfall in winter in all zones.

Regional Advice and Care
Prune dead or damaged stems in winter while the plant is dormant. Take care not to overprune; trees become stressed by aggressive pruning. Cedar elm is somewhat susceptible to Dutch elm disease, although it has not taken the toll on this species that it has on other elms.

Companion Planting and Design
Use it as a single, large shade tree especially where drainage or soils are inferior. Cedar elm effectively shades western windows, the side of a building, or the roof. This is a strong tree with good wind resistance, making is especially desirable in high wind areas.

Try These
American elm (*Ulmus americana*) was once a common tree throughout the eastern United States, including Texas. This tall, stately, vase-shaped tree was decimated by the Dutch elm disease fungus. Winged elm (*U. alata*), also known as wahoo, is another handsome native growing to 30 feet with a rounded, spreading crown. Unfortunately, it is also susceptible to this disease. Chinese elm (*U. parviflorus*) is one of the few elms that does well in extremely hot areas. Siberian elm (*U. pumila*) is widely planted for its fast growth and great cold tolerance, but it can become weedy and has become significantly overused in the northern part of the state. Both Chinese and Siberian elm are less susceptible to Dutch elm disease, and there is active work underway to develop hybrids or selections of native elms that are resistant to this disease.

Chaste Tree

Vitex agnus-castus

Other Name Monk's pepper tree

Bloom Period and Seasonal Color
Summer to fall, blue, purple, pink, white

Mature Height x Spread
10 to 25 ft. x 10 to 25 ft.

Botanical Pronunciation
VI-tex AG-nus-CAS-tus

Zones 7 to 9

Chaste tree is a spreading deciduous tree, often wider than it is tall. Leaves are dusky gray-green above and silver, composed of five to seven lance-shaped leaflets with a sharp aroma. Trunks are dark brown, almost black, and although naturally multitrunked, plants are routinely trained to a single trunk. Flowers are in a dense, terminal spike held high above the foliage. In older forms flowers are nearly pastel, but modern selections have deepened the color range from pastel blue to purple, with pink and white forms as well. Originally from China and India, chaste tree has been cultivated in this country since the seventeenth century. Both common names refer to the medieval belief that potions made from the berries helped monks maintain their vows of chastity.

When, Where, and How to Plant
Plant in spring once all danger of frost is past and the soil has warmed. Choose a site in full sun that will accommodate the tendency of the plant to be wider than it is tall. Chaste tree accepts a wide range of soils from rocky and dry to moist and fertile. It grows faster and lives longer when grown in well-drained, moderately fertile, alkaline soils.

Growing Tips
Apply slow-release or organic fertilizer in fall and early spring to young plants. Established plants don't need fertilizer. Water established trees two or three times a month in the summer in the warmest areas. Over much of Texas, chaste tree grows well on natural rainfall and is highly drought tolerant. Rely on natural rainfall in winter in all zones.

Regional Advice and Care
Prune in late spring, after all danger of frost is past, to remove dead wood or damaged limbs. Removing dead flowers of the first bloom encourages it to repeat bloom later in the summer. To create a single-trunked tree, begin by pruning the side shoots and the three or four lowest branches each spring. Continue this annual pruning until the crown is the desired height. Do not take off more than a quarter of the tree in any one year. Chaste tree is not susceptible to pests or disease.

Companion Planting and Design
Chaste tree complements any perennial planting with its colorful summer bloom, dark multitrunked habit and dusky green leaves. It is very effective near a small patio or seating area. Chaste tree creates less litter during the summer than some trees, therefore is useful near a pool.

Try These
The var. *latifolia* has no botanical standing but is applied to a shorter form with broader leaves and larger flowering stalks. 'Montrose Purple' has large densely congested flower spikes that are a vibrant dark purple. 'LeCompte' has congested spikes of lavender to light purple flowers. 'Shoal Creek' is a vase-shaped plant with loose heads of light lavender, fragrant flowers. 'Salinas Pink' has tall pink-flowering spikes, whereas those of 'Silver Spire' are white.

Chinkapin Oak

Quercus muhlenbergii

Bloom Period and Seasonal Color
Spring, insignificant

Mature Height x spread
50 to 90 ft. x 20 to 40 ft.

Botanical Pronunciation
KWER-kus muh-len-BERG-ee-eye

Oaks are arranged into three rough categories. White oaks have deeply lobed leaves with rounded tips, acorns that mature in the year they are formed, and light gray scaly bark with gray ridges. Red oaks have sharply lobed leaves with a spiny tip, acorns that mature in two years, and black or dark gray bark that forms ridges or blocks. Live oaks are more or less evergreen, losing their leaves as the new leaves emerge. One of the most useful and wide ranging of the white oaks is chinkapin oak with its 6- to 8-inch leaves that look as if they were cut with pinking shears. The 1-inch acorn is about half covered with the scaly cup. Fall color is either yellow or bronze.

When, Where, and How to Plant
Plant in fall or in spring once the soil can be worked. Choose a site that offers enough room for its mature height and crown spread in the full sun. Chinkapin oak grows in almost any type of soil with excellent drainage, even highly alkaline ones. Trees decline in soils that are poorly drained or where water ponds frequently.

Growing Tips
Young trees may be fertilized annually in spring with any well-balanced fertilizer that is not too high in nitrogen. Established trees need no supplemental fertilizer. Water to maintain consistent soil moisture, particularly for young trees, by providing a deep soak every two to three weeks in summer. Established trees are quite drought tolerant and need only intermittent deep soaks during exceptionally hot or dry conditions. Natural rainfall is sufficient in winter.

Regional Advice and Care
Prune in spring or early fall to remove dead or damaged limbs. Chinkapin oak is not susceptible to most pests and disease.

Companion Planting and Design
Chinkapin is a large oak that will be the main shade tree in a modest-sized garden. Plant it where the deep shade is needed, near patios, or to shelter a seating area. It is also useful to shade a western wall or window, even the roof.

Try These
Swamp chestnut oak (*Quercus michauxii*) is similar, but the leaves are longer with a rounder tip and the acorns are elongated with the cup covering less than half the nut. It does not do well in alkaline soils. Willow oak (*Q. phellos*) is a tall, upright, deciduous tree with long, narrow, deep green leaves that turn bright yellow in the fall. The acorns are small and nearly round. This tree grows best in the moist, acidic soils of East Texas. Another stunning large, deciduous tree for the eastern half of the state is white oak (*Q. alba*). The leaves are deeply lobed, almost filigreed, dark green in the summer, and turn bright red in fall. The paired acorns are up to 1 inch long and slightly covered by the scaly cap.

Crape Myrtle

Lagerstroemia indica

Bloom Period and Seasonal Color
Summer, white, pink, red, lavender, purple, magenta

Mature Height x Spread
18 to 25 ft. x 10 to 25 ft.

Botanical Pronunciation
lah-ger-STROH-me-uh IN-dih-kuh

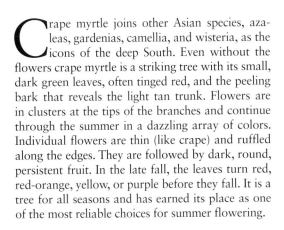

Crape myrtle joins other Asian species, azaleas, gardenias, camellia, and wisteria, as the icons of the deep South. Even without the flowers crape myrtle is a striking tree with its small, dark green leaves, often tinged red, and the peeling bark that reveals the light tan trunk. Flowers are in clusters at the tips of the branches and continue through the summer in a dazzling array of colors. Individual flowers are thin (like crape) and ruffled along the edges. They are followed by dark, round, persistent fruit. In the late fall, the leaves turn red, red-orange, yellow, or purple before they fall. It is a tree for all seasons and has earned its place as one of the most reliable choices for summer flowering.

When, Where, and How to Plant
Plant in fall or spring in warm winter zones. Plant in spring once all danger of frost is past and the soil is warmed in colder areas. Planting may continue through the early summer anywhere. Choose a site in full sun for best flowering and form, although plants adapt to light, filtered shade. Crape myrtle grows in almost any well-drained, moderately fertile soil. Amend the planting hole with generous amounts of compost or other organic matter before planting.

Growing Tips
Fertilize in spring just as the leaves emerge and again two more times ending in early fall. Water to maintain an even soil moisture. Although somewhat drought resistant when mature, crape myrtle flowers best if it does not dry out completely. Water twice a month in summer, more frequently if it is

particularly hot or dry. Natural rainfall is sufficient in winter.

Regional Advice and Care
Prune in late spring or early summer to reshape, remove dead or damaged limbs, or control growth. Crape myrtle is susceptible to powdery mildew in humid climates; select varieties with known resistance. Good air circulation also helps keep that fungus under control. Leaf cutter bees and harvester ants are a seasonal problem in some areas.

Companion Planting and Design
Use crape myrtle as a focal or accent plant in a small garden, patio, or courtyard, or incorporate it into a mixed hedge for its long season of bloom. Larger varieties make good specimen trees.

Try These
Numerous crape myrtles have been bred for disease resistance, color, and size. Check with local sources for those that perform best in your area. Some to consider are white 'Natchez' and 'Sarah's Favorite'; red 'Dynamite', 'Dallas Red', 'Red Rocket' and 'Arapaho', pink 'Biloxi', 'Comanche', 'Osage', and 'Sioux'; and purple 'Catawba'. There are also dwarf forms growing to 4 feet or less; 'Tightwad Red', 'Chica Pink', and 'Chica Red' are just a few. Japanese crape myrtle (*Lagerstroemia faurei*) is a stunning and much taller plant with larger leaves, spectacular cinnamon bark, and flowers in all the same colors as crape myrtle.

Date Palm

Phoenix dactylifera

Bloom Period and Seasonal Color
Summer, creamy yellow

Mature Height x Spread
6 to 50 ft. x 5 to 40 ft.

Botanical Pronunciation
FEE-nix DAK-tih-lif-er-uh

Zones 9 to 10

Date palm has fed, clothed, and sheltered desert peoples since the dawn of recorded history in its long association with the residents of the North African deserts. Date palm has straight, grayish trunks marked with a diamond pattern made of old leaf bases. Trees may be single trunked or sprout numerous offsets from near the base. The blue-gray leaves are up to 12 feet long and split into numerous, narrow leaflets. Long flowering stalks hold creamy white to yellowish flowers with male and female flowers on separate plants. The fresh fruit is yellow and crisp like an apple and delicious. If you plan to harvest the fruit, cover the stalk just as the fruit forms to keep birds and other animals from eating it all.

When, Where, and How to Plant
Plant in late spring or summer, when soils are warm to hot. Date palms handle a wide range of soils from very dry and rocky, to well drained, fertile soils, including those that are nearly saturated. Plant in full sun, allowing plenty of room for the mature crown of leaves. Be sure to plant so that the entire base of the trunk is aboveground.

Growing Tips
Apply slow-release or organic fertilizer annually in early summer. Date palms become very drought tolerant as they mature and can thrive on deep, monthly watering in summer. Reduce watering to every other month in winter.

Regional Advice and Care
Prune dead leaves or blooming stalks anytime. Never prune living leaves unless they are a danger or heavily damaged. Leaf bases are firmly attached to the stem and cannot be removed without damaging the plant. Date palms are not susceptible to pests or disease, although deeply stressed plants can show symptoms of crown rots.

Companion Planting and Design
These tall palms are spectacular in groves or groups for light, filtered shade. They are tall enough to provide light, filtered shade for perennials or succulents that require some shade. This is a good choice near pools because all parts are large enough not to cause filter problems.

Try These
Canary Island date palm (*Phoenix canariensis*) is also tall with a huge, spreading crown at maturity. The leaves are feather-shaped, dark green, and up to 20 feet long. The trunk is dark brown and somewhat smooth with age, although the leaf bases are persistent near the crown. Both this species and date palm are hardy to about 20 degrees Fahrenheit. The diminutive pygmy date palm (*P. roebellinii*) grows a mere 8 feet tall, and its 4-foot leaves curve gracefully around the trunk. This species is hardy only to 28 degrees Fahrenheit but makes a beautiful container plant. Senegal date palm (*P. reclinata*) is a multitrunked species to 25 feet tall with 13-foot leaves that curve and fall back toward the ground in a graceful reverse arch and is hardy to 25 degrees Fahrenheit.

Desert Willow

Chilopsis linearis

Bloom Period and Seasonal Color
Spring to fall, lavender, pink, rose, purple, white

Mature Height x Spread
10 to 20 ft. x 10 to 20 ft.

Botanical Pronunciation
Chi-LOP-sis lin-ee-AIR-us

Zones 7 to 10

Found in washes and along arroyos throughout the Southwestern deserts and into Mexico, desert willow is an unexpected delight in the summer. This deciduous, erratically branching tree is not a willow, but is in the family that also includes yellowbells and trumpet vine. This is a wide-ranging species that shows great variation is size, leaf color, and flower size and color. The long, thin, willow-like leaves are typically light green. The bell-shaped flowers have open, flared ends with or without ruffled edges. Each flower has prominent nectar guides, and both this feature and the corolla range from deep purple to lavender to pink or white. The flowers are sweetly fragrant, but the intensity varies by selection.

When, Where, and How to Plant
Plant in spring after all danger of frost is past. Planting can continue through early summer. Choose a location in full sun, but desert willows grows in light shade in the desert zones. This tree tolerates almost any soil condition from deep, well-drained, fertile soils to rocky, dry ones, but fails quickly in heavy clays or with poor drainage.

Growing Tips
Apply slow-release or organic fertilizer annually in spring to young trees. Mature plants do not need supplemental fertilizer. Water established plants deeply at long intervals. Allow it to dry out between waterings to promote continued waves of blooms. In most areas, natural rainfall is sufficient with a monthly soak during periods of prolonged drought. Rely on natural rainfall in winter everywhere.

Regional Advice and Care
Prune in early spring as the leaves emerge to remove dead wood and winter damage or to form a single-trunked tree. Seedpods may be pruned anytime. Desert willow is not susceptible to pests or disease and is highly resistant to cotton root rot.

Companion Planting and Design
Mix with other large shrubs or trees to form an informal hedge or border planting. Plant against hot walls or near a pool or patio where reflected heat is intense. Grow in containers in cold areas. Desert willow has performed well as far north as Kansas and Chicago in sheltered locations where it freezes to the ground but recovers rapidly to be a small, blooming shrub.

Try These
'Burgundy', 'Dark Storm', and 'Bubba' are dark purple to magenta; light lavender 'Lois Adams' is nearly podless, as are bright pink 'Art's Seedless™' and 'Timeless Beauty™' (patented as 'Monhew'), a dark pink to purple bicolor. 'Burgundy Lace' is two-toned white and pink, whereas 'Lucretia Hamilton' is purple with a white throat. 'Marfa Lace' is a semi-double pink, and the exceptionally hardy 'Hope' is white. *Chitalpa xtashkinensis* is a sterile hybrid between this species and *Catalpa bignonioides*. It is a tall, upright tree with big clusters of white to pink flowers. Chitalpa is hardy to 10 degrees Fahrenheit and also has good wind resistance.

Eastern Red Cedar

Juniperus virginiana

Bloom Period and Seasonal Color
Spring, insignificant

Mature Height x Spread
20 to 40 ft. x 20 to 40 ft.

Botanical Pronunciation
joo-NIP-er-us ver-jin-ee-AY-nah

Zones 7 to 9

Throughout the central parts of the state, you find cedar posts as standing relics of old fence lines. The wood of this tree has been revered since colonial times for its resistance to contact with the ground and bugs. I have a 50-year old cedar box that still smells sharp and clean every time I open it. In the ground, Eastern red cedar is an evergreen conifer with a slim, columnar crown and an angled, contorted, or buttressed trunk. The scale-like foliage is gray- or blue-green or dark green and provides ample winter cover for numerous species of birds. The bright blue-gray fruit of the female plants forms in the fall and winter, and some people are allergic to the pollen of the male plants.

When, Where, and How to Plant
Eastern red cedar can be planted anytime except summer, although fall is best anywhere but the most frigid zones. Choose a location that accommodates the ultimate size of the tree and is in full sun. Very young plants grow in the shade, but older ones do not thrive in shade. Eastern red cedar will grow in almost any soil but does best in those that are deep, moist, and well drained.

Growing Tips
Young Eastern red cedar can be fertilized up to three times a year beginning in late spring. Established trees do not need extra fertilization. Water twice a month, more if it is exceptionally hot or dry, when it is young. Mature plants should be watered deeply once a month during times of extended drought. Otherwise, rely on natural rainfall.

Regional Advice and Care
Eastern red cedar has excellent natural form and rarely needs pruning. To remove dead or damaged wood prune in spring and go deep into the tree to cut at a junction to preserve its form. Plants that are water or heat stressed are susceptible to spider mites. Bagworms are usually only a cosmetic problem. Cedar apple rust occurs on some trees, so it is best to avoid planting Eastern red cedar near apple trees.

Companion Planting and Design
Use Eastern red cedar as part of a mixed hedge or boundary planting. Individuals attain a picturesque stature in old age and make excellent specimen or focal plants in gardens large enough to support them.

Try These
Ashe juniper, locally known as mountain cedar (*Juniperus ashei*), is a smaller, shrub-like plant from the Hill Country. This plant also has blue berries in the fall on female plants and highly allergenic pollen for susceptible people. It, too, has aromatic wood that is resistant to rot and bugs. Ashe juniper is a better choice for rocky, alkaline soils and is not susceptible to cedar apple rust. The rare and local golden-cheeked warbler uses the peeling bark for its nests, and the bird is rarely found where this tree is not abundant.

Eastern Redbud

Cercis canadensis

Bloom Period and Seasonal Color
Spring, pink, white

Mature Height x Spread
6 to 20 ft. x 6 to 15 ft.

Botanical Pronunciation
SER-sis kan-uh-DEN-sis

There was a huge redbud in the yard of our house when I was raised. Every spring the barren, dark branches were smothered by deep pink flowers. They were our first signal of spring. I still find redbud to be an attractive, and often least used, early-flowering tree. Redbud and its varieties all show a wide range of variation in flower color and leaf size, color, shape, and texture. Some of that variation has resulted in named forms. If you care deeply about the color, it is best to buy the tree in flower. For most of the year, this small tree fades into the background waiting to impress us with one or the other of its seasonal shows. It is well worth the wait.

When, Where, and How to Plant
Plant in fall or spring in the warmer zones of the state. Plant in spring as early as the soil can be worked in colder areas. Avoid summer planting. Eastern redbud grows in a wide range of soils but does best in well-drained, deep, fertile soil. Amend planting holes with ample amounts of compost or other organic matter.

Growing Tips
Apply slow-release or organic fertilizer just as leaves emerge in spring and then three more times before fall. Water deeply twice a month in summer, more often when it is exceptionally hot or dry. Monthly watering, or natural rainfall, is sufficient in the winter. Maintain 4- to 6-inch mulch around the root zone to assure even soil moisture.

Regional Advice and Care
Prune during winter dormancy to remove dead or damaged wood. Redbud grows small shoots from the base regularly, and they can be removed in winter to retain the desired number of stems. Plants bloom on new wood, so prune carefully to preserve the blooms. Redbud is not susceptible to pests and disease.

Companion Planting and Design
Mix redbud with large perennials or shrubs for early spring color. Redbud grows well in shady locations and provides needed color and texture to shaded beds or beneath large evergreen trees.

Try These
Mexican redbud (*Cercis canadensis* var. *mexicana*) is the smallest variety, growing 10 to 15 feet tall. It has small, rounded, leathery leaves with wavy margins and light pink flowers. This variety tends to grow as a multitrunked shrub and is well suited to areas with great heat, aridity, and alkaline soils. Texas redbud (*C. canadensis* var. *texensis*) is found from Central Texas to Oklahoma, where it intergrades with Eastern redbud. This variety has a distinctive tree form with larger leaves than Mexican redbud. It also tolerates lean, alkaline soils but is not as drought tolerant as Mexican redbud. Western redbud (*C. occidentalis* syn. *C. orbiculata*) is a drought-tolerant, small tree with blue-green leaves, bright pink flowers, and yellow fall foliage that grows best with some winter chill in low-alkaline soils.

Eve's Necklace

Sophora affinis

Bloom Period and Seasonal Color
Spring, pink

Mature Height x Spread
15 to 30 ft. x 10 to 20 ft.

Botanical Pronunciation
so-FORE-uh ah-FIN-is

Zones 8 to 10

Eve's necklace is a lovely small tree, native to the Hill Country up into north central Texas. It has bright, shiny compound leaves that form a striking backdrop for the cascades of pink flowers each spring. Each pea-like flower is crowded into a large flowering head that hangs down like wisteria. This charming floral display is followed by long black pods that contain its black beans. With age the pod constricts around the bean so it looks like a necklace of dark pearls. A deciduous tree, Eve's necklace has yellow foliage in the fall. Plants like this often cause me to wonder how in the world plants get their names. I have no idea how Eve, or her possible necklace, came into this common name.

When, Where, and How to Plant
Plant in spring once the soil can be worked. In warmer zones, Eve's necklace may be planted in fall as well. This species grows in full sun or partial shade. Eve's necklace is not particular about the type of soil but does require excellent drainage. It is a good choice in alkaline soils.

Growing Tips
Eve's necklace does not require supplemental fertilization. Water established plants deeply at regular intervals. In summer, water two or three times a month, particularly when it is especially hot or dry. Rely on natural rainfall in winter or where summer rain is abundant. Older plants are quite drought tolerant.

Regional Advice and Care
Prune in spring just as leaves emerge to remove dead or damaged wood. Be careful not to prune off blooming branches too early in the season. Pods are persistent but can be removed at any time. Eve's necklace is not susceptible to pests or disease.

Companion Planting and Design
Plant beneath large trees as an understory planting for its spring color. Use Eve's necklace singly as a focal or specimen plant in a small yard, patio garden, or courtyard. Consider it as a background plant for mixed plantings where the colorful flowers, pods, and fall foliage add year-round interest.

Try These
Texas mountain laurel (*Sophora secundiflora*) is a related shrub that is evergreen with purple flowers in the spring. Pagoda tree (*Styphnolobium japonicum*, formerly *S. japonica*) is an Asian species that is widely grown there and throughout the United States. Growing to 50 feet, pagoda tree has pure white flowers in the summer, but its leaves remain green long into the fall and then simply fade to yellow before falling. Pagoda tree is extremely cold hardy, but does not do well in areas warmer than Zone 8. The East Texas native two-wing silverbell (*Halesia diptera*) is a deciduous tree to 15 feet with white, tubular hanging flowers. The leaves turn yellow in fall, and the striped or furrowed bark lends interest to a winter garden in wooded or moist gardens in the eastern part of the state.

Flowering Dogwood

Cornus florida

Bloom Period and Seasonal Color
Spring, white, pink

Mature Height x Spread
15 to 25 ft. x 10 to 20 ft.

Botanical Pronunciation
KOR-nus FLOR-eh-dah

Zones 7 to 9

Considered by many to be the most beautiful of all native flowering trees, it is easy to see how dogwood gained such favor. This is a delicate tree with wide, horizontal limbs that are packed with the prominent white or pink flowers every spring. The actual flowers are minute and tightly congested into a rounded head but are surrounded by large, showy, colorful bracts. My in-laws live amid the forests of East Texas, and when we are there in April the entire forest seems to be illuminated by these extraordinary flowering trees. Flowering is followed by clusters of brilliant red berries that are an ornamental sensation all their own. And if that wasn't enough, the leaves turn brilliant red in the fall.

When, Where, and How to Plant
Plant in early fall or early spring as soon as the soil can be worked. Dogwood prefers light, filtered shade but will grow in deep shade almost as well. Full sun is recommended only in the most northern zones. Dogwood requires rich, well-drained, acidic soil. Avoid heavy clays, areas that pond or hold too much water, or dry sites.

Growing Tips
Dogwood does not need supplemental irrigation. Water to maintain even soil moisture all year. Apply mulch thickly around the roots to maintain soil moisture and improve fertility.

Regional Advice and Care
Prune in spring only to remove dead or damaged wood. Dogwoods have a graceful, spreading form, and pruning should follow their natural shape. Plants become chlorotic in highly alkaline soils. Dogwood is susceptible to cotton root rot and borers if it is in poor condition or growing in unfavorable conditions.

Companion Planting and Design
Plant under large trees or among a grove of large shrubs for maximum impact. These trees are small enough to use as a focal or accent plant in small gardens, patios, or courtyards. Dogwoods need good air circulation for best results, so do not crowd them.

Try These
There are many selections of dogwood. 'Cherokee Chief' has deep rose red floral bracts with a white base and new foliage that is tinged red; 'Cloud Nine' has large, overlapping white bracts, abundant bloom, and rust-red leaves in the fall; 'White Cloud' has creamy white, spreading bracts and bronze fall foliage; 'Spring Song' has dark rose-red bracts shot with white; and 'First Lady' has white bracts and variegated foliage. Rough-leaf dogwood (*Cornus drummondii*) is a clump-forming, native shrub or small tree with prominent clusters of creamy white flowers and purplish red fall foliage. The fruit of this species is white and the stems are reddish brown. This is the best choice for areas with alkaline soils. Red twig dogwood (*C. sericea*) and bloodtwig dogwood (*C. sanguinea*) both have colorful red twigs that retain their color through the winter but are only suitable for cold winter areas.

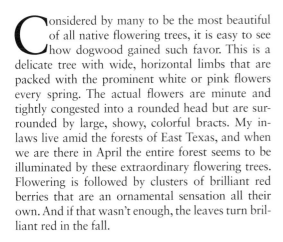

Fringe Tree

Chionanthus virginicus

Bloom Period and Seasonal Color
Spring, white

Mature Height x Spread
15 to 20 ft. x 10 to 25 ft.

Botanical Pronunciation
key-oh-NAN-thus ver-JIN-ih-kus

One of the glories of spring in East Texas is the flowering of many shrubs and trees. Dogwoods are the most often cited, but fringe tree is an outstanding part of this spring glory. A large shrub to small tree, fringe tree blooms right before or just as the leaves come out in the late spring. The small greenish white flowers are held in large clusters that look like a cloud over the plant. They are nicely fragrant without being overwhelming. As the glossy, dark green leaves emerge, they masquerade the blue fruit on female plants. But birds are not fooled and strip the fruit quickly once it is ripe. Plants are deciduous, but the fall color is not nearly as spectacular as the spring bloom.

When, Where, and How to Plant
In the coldest zones, plant in spring after the soil is warmed. Plant in either spring or fall in all other zones. Fringe tree can grow in full sun, but it thrives in light or filtered shade. Tolerant of a wide range of soils, it is most adapted to moist, acidic soils that are well drained. Dry or rocky soils are not favorable. Add ample amounts of organic material to the planting area and the backfill.

Growing Tips
Established plants don't need extra fertilization. Fertilize young plants with a well-balanced formula once in the spring and again in the fall. Water to keep an even soil moisture. If rainfall is insufficient, water at least every ten days in summer, more often when it is exceptionally hot or dry. Apply a generous layer of mulch to maintain soil moisture and reduce watering frequency.

Regional Advice and Care
Prune in spring to remove dead or damaged wood and to keep the shape of the tree. Bloom is on the previous year's wood, so take care when pruning not to remove too much recent growth. Fringe tree is not susceptible to pests or disease, although it declines in highly alkaline soils.

Companion Planting and Design
Plant beneath or around large evergreen trees to create a woodland effect. Use generously along a shady border or as part of a hedge for its remarkable spring bloom. It is small enough to be a focal or accent tree near a patio or other small spaces.

Try These
Chinese fringe tree (*Chionanthus retusus*) is a similar tree, but the flowering clusters are even larger and showier. It is somewhat larger, growing to 25 feet with a naturally round form. Flowering around the same time, the flowers are a pure white as opposed to greenish white of fringe tree. The dark blue fruit ripens later, and fall foliage is more colorful. Chinese fringe tree prefers deep, acid soils, but is highly adaptable; however, like its American cousin, it does poorly in highly alkaline soils. This species is reliably hardy only through Zone 8.

Honey Mesquite

Prosopis glandulosa

Other Name Mesquite

Bloom Period and Seasonal Color
Spring to fall, pale yellow

Mature Height x Spread
25 to 30 ft. x 30 to 50 ft.

Botanical Pronunciation
proh-SOH-pus gland-you-LOH-sah

My grandparents in Austin had an enormous honey mesquite in their backyard. It was the center of outside activity, sheltering picnic tables, providing climbing opportunities, shading chairs and the long bedroom windows from the hot summer sun. Like most honey mesquite, it probably was not planted, and its huge stems rose and fell in odd, contorted ways. These trees are native over most of the state, and although we tend to think of them either as too common to care about or pests to remove, in historic times they were vital for lumber, fuel, and food. Honey mesquite is one of the best native trees for light, filtered shade under which almost anything will grow, and it has endurance to any level of care or neglect.

When, Where, and How to Plant
Plant in spring after all danger of frost is past and the soil is warm. Planting may continue through early summer. Choose a location in the full sun that will accommodate the ultimate size and width of the tree. Honey mesquite tolerates a wide range of soils but grows best in deep soils that are well drained.

Growing Tips
Honey mesquite does not require supplemental fertilization. During the first few years after planting, water once or twice a month in summer to establish a good root system. After that, trees grow fine on natural rainfall. Rely on natural rainfall in winter.

Regional Advice and Care
Honey mesquite can be difficult to prune well. Take out small branches that are crossing or are growing to the middle in summer. Never prune when temperatures are cold. Young plants are often multi-trunked, and it is best to select one or two leaders at that time and keep the rest pruned out.

Companion Planting and Design
Honey mesquite can grow very large, particularly in the southern half of the state, making it a significant statement in a garden. Many perennials and succulents do well under its shade, but take care not to plant other large trees closely. Use it to shade a western wall, windows, or the roof.

Try These
Velvet mesquite (*Prosopis velutina*) has dark, almost black, furrowed bark and gray-green leaves. It is semi-deciduous, and the leaves are not the brilliant green so characteristic of honey mesquite when they emerge. Screwbean mesquite (*P. pubescens*) is an intricately branched tree or large shrub with small leaflets and fragrant, bright golden flowers that are followed by the distinctive, coiled pods and is hardy to 0 degrees Fahrenheit. The pods of all mesquite are edible but are especially tasty in these three species. The South American Argentine mesquite (*P. alba*), Chilean mesquite (*P. chilensis*), black mesquite (*P. nigra*), and their countless hybrids are taller, up to 50 feet, and more upright than the North American species. Most are reliably hardy only in Zones 9 and 10.

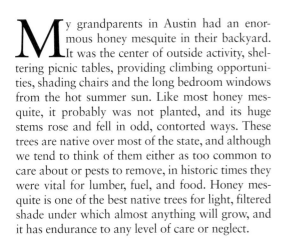

Jelly Palm

Butia capitata

Other Name Pindo palm

Bloom Period and Seasonal Color
Summer, yellow, reddish

Mature Height x Spread
10 to 20 ft. x 6 to 10 ft.

Botanical Pronunciation
bue-TEE-uh KAP-ih-tah-tuh

Zones 8 to 10

Jelly palm is a short, solitary, palm whose trunk is wider at the base giving it a vase shape. The stout trunk is covered with the hefty, gray leaf bases in regular rows. These leftovers from years of leaf pruning form an attractive feature of mature plants and are persistent for many years. The blue-green feather-shaped leaves rise up in a stiff arch from the crown and fall back down in a graceful curve toward the trunk and almost cover it. The flowering stalk is 3 feet long with yellow to reddish flowers and both male and female flowers on the stalk. The bright orange or yellow round fruit tastes delicious. Jellies and other condiments are commonly made from the fruit wherever jelly palm is grown.

When, Where, and How to Plant
Plant only when the soil is warm, from late spring through midsummer. Jelly palm grows best in full sun, but will grow in light shade. Jelly palm is tolerant of a wide range of soils except highly alkaline or poorly drained ones. Add good-quality compost or other organic matter before planting.

Growing Tips
Apply palm specific or organic fertilizer monthly during warm weather. Water established plants once a month in summer, more often if it is exceptionally hot or dry. Rely on rainfall in winter. Jelly palm grows well in a lawn, but should be watered deeply once a month in addition to the lawn watering.

Regional Advice and Care
Prune dead leaves and spent blooming stalks anytime. Never remove living leaves; it decreases the vigor of the plant. Leaf bases should be cut, not pulled off. Jelly palm is not susceptible to pests or disease but becomes chlorotic in highly alkaline soils when watered too shallowly where drainage is poor.

Companion Planting and Design
Jelly palm is an excellent specimen or focal plant in a small garden or courtyard. Combine it with other tropical plants for an exotic look around pools or patios, to fill a corner or barren spot, or to line drives or walkways.

Try These
The var. *odorata*, a short, compact plant with a bushy look, and var. *strictor*, a more upright, few-leaved plant, are rarely offered by name, but have been introduced to the trade from various sources and sold simply as jelly palm. This mixing has contributed to a noticeable and extensive variability in plants for sale. *Butia yatay* is similar but taller with a thicker trunk. These species hybridize readily when grown in close association, and some authors suggest that many of the plants offered as *B. capitata* are in fact hybrids. *xButiagrus* is a rare hybrid between jelly palm and Queen palm (*Syagrus romanzoffiana*) that is a handsome, tall, single-trunked plant with long, stiffened leaves. It resembles a coconut palm but is nearly as hardy as jelly palm.

Mexican Buckeye

Ungnadia speciosa

Bloom Period and Seasonal Color
Spring, pink, purple

Mature Height x Spread
12 to 30 ft. x 8 to 12 ft.

Botanical Pronunciation
ung-NAY-dee-ah spee-see-OH-sah

Zones 8 to 10

There was a wonderful Mexican buckeye that sprang up on its own behind the fence of my parents' house in Austin. Every spring, just before the leaves emerged, the rich, dark brown branches erupted in hundreds of dark, rosy pink flowers. It didn't last long, but it was a glorious sight. The leaves of this plant are large, shaped like a pointed hand and dark green. In the fall, they turn a pale yellow before they fall. The jet black seeds are held in rounded capsules that make excellent additions to dried arrangements. Mexican buckeye naturally occurs over limestone areas of Central Texas into far western Texas and New Mexico. The further west you go, the smaller the plants and the darker the bloom color.

When, Where, and How to Plant
Plant in fall or spring in warm zones. In cold zones, plant in spring while the plant is still dormant but as soon as the soil can be worked. Mexican buckeye grows well in full sun or light, filtered shade. Locations with morning sun and relief from reflected heat are ideal. Mexican buckeye requires excellent drainage but handles a wide range of soils, including dry or rocky ones.

Growing Tips
Apply slow-release or organic fertilizer annually in spring, especially to young plants growing in highly alkaline soils. Established plants do not need fertilization. Water established plants once or twice a month in summer, unless it is exceptionally hot or dry. In cooler zones, water even less often. Rely on natural rainfall in winter in all zones.

Regional Advice and Care
Prune in early spring while the plant is still dormant to remove damaged or dead wood. Mexican buckeye is naturally multitrunked but can be trained to a small tree by removing three or four of the lowest branches each year. Do not remove over a quarter of the plant in a single year. Mexican buckeye is not susceptible to pest or disease and is highly resistant to cotton root rot.

Companion Planting and Design
Blend with other shrubs in a mixed hedge or border planting. Locate it where the stunning spring flowering can be appreciated. Trained as a tree, it makes a good focal or specimen plant in a small garden, patio, or courtyard.

Try These
This is a monotypic genus, meaning this is its only species. The true buckeyes of the genus *Aesculus* are mainly eastern plants. These are generally large trees and would be useful in the north and eastern zones of Texas. The exception is the scarlet buckeye (*Aesculus pavia*) of Central Texas. Redbud (*Cercis canadensis*) also flowers in shades of pink before the leaves emerge. A number of stone fruit, including peaches, cherries, apples, and native plums (*Prunus* spp.), are also small trees with extravagant bloom before the leaves emerge.

Mexican Plum

Prunus mexicana

Bloom Period and Seasonal Color
Spring, white

Mature Height x Spread
15 to 35 ft. x 15 to 25 ft.

Botanical Pronunciation
PROO-nus mex-eh-KAY-nah

Zones 8 to 10

When I was a child, our neighbors had a small grove of wild plums that their son and I devoured each summer. They were not Mexican plums, but whenever I see this lovely tree I recall that place and his mother's spectacular plum cake. Mexican plum is a deciduous tree with a straight, smooth, trunk that in old age forms gleaming, blue-gray bark. The abundant fragrant, pure white flowers emerge before the leaves. This alone would make it a wonderful garden plant, but in midsummer to early fall the fruit turns yellow, then mauve, and finally purple, signaling that it is ripe. The thin, light green leaves have prominent veins that give them a quilted look and turn pale yellow to orange in fall.

When, Where, and How to Plant
Plant in either fall or spring, although spring is best in the coldest zones. Choose a site in full sun or light, filtered shade. Mexican plum grows in any soil that is well drained from sandy to clay, slightly acid to alkaline.

Growing Tips
Mexican plum does not require extra fertilizing. Summer watering frequency depends on temperature. When it is exceptionally hot or dry, water two or three times a month with a deep soak. Otherwise, rely on natural rainfall or a deep soak once a month. Natural rainfall is sufficient in the winter. Mulch around the root zone, taking care not to let the mulch touch the bark, to maintain soil moisture.

Regional Advice and Care
Prune in early spring before the leaves emerge to remove dead or damaged wood. Take care not to prune heavily so you do not compromise flowering and fruiting. This tree has excellent natural form and doesn't need regular pruning for shape. Mexican plum is not susceptible to pests or disease.

Companion Planting and Design
Plant as an understory tree beneath large, evergreen trees. Use it as a focal or accent plant in smaller gardens, around patios or seating areas, or within a courtyard.

Try These
American plum (*Prunus americana*) is similar. In fact, some authors consider Mexican plum a variety of it. This species does best in deep, moist soils. Chickasaw plum (*P. angustifolia*) is a thicket-forming shrub to small tree with reddish fruit in clusters near the branch tip. It is widely grown for its delicious fruit. Escarpment black cherry (*P. serotina*) is a medium-sized Hill Country native with long clusters of white flowers in spring. Cherry laurel (*P. caroliniana*) is an evergreen, small tree native to eastern Texas with white flowers followed by dark dry fruit that persist through the winter. Flowering plum (*P. cerasifera*) is a small, short-lived Asian species that does not make fruit but is grown for its intense spring bloom. Although fruit of almost all species is edible, leaves and seed contain various amounts of toxins and should never be eaten.

Parsley Hawthorn

Crataegus marshallii

Bloom Period and Seasonal Color
Spring, white

Mature Height x Spread
10 to 25 ft. x 10 to 15 ft.

Botanical Pronunciation
krah-TEE-gus mar-SHAL-ee-eye

Zones 8 to 9

The rose family has given a great deal to gardeners, not only an array of fruit (plums, apples, peaches, and cherries) but excellent ornamental shrubs as well. Parsley hawthorn is among the best, with all the features that make woody members of this family such great garden plants. Parsley hawthorn is a small tree with branches in regular layers resulting in a roughly pyramidal shape. The finely divided leaves resemble those of parsley, hence the common name. They turn a burnished red in the fall, making it a stunning shrub in all seasons. The pure white flowers are prolific in the spring. Bees adore it for its nectar and pollen. Flowers are followed by bright red berries that remain on the plant throughout the fall.

When, Where, and How to Plant
Plant in fall or spring after frost danger is past and the soil can be worked. Parsley hawthorn grows well in full sun or light, filtered shade. Although it adapts to a wide range of soils, it needs good drainage. It is especially well suited to sandy or loamy soils that are acidic.

Growing Tips
Fertilize young plants in spring, again two or three months later, and then in fall with a well-balanced fertilizer. Mature plants need to be fertilized only once in spring as the leaves emerge. Water to maintain even soil moisture and prevent plants from completely drying out. In the eastern third of the state, natural rainfall is often sufficient, particularly in winter. Renew a generous layer of mulch annually to maintain soil moisture and fertility.

Regional Advice and Care
Prune when dormant to remove dead or damaged limbs. Parsley hawthorn has excellent natural form and rarely needs pruning for shape. This species is somewhat susceptible to fungal disease like rust, but good air circulation and healthy plants are the best prevention. Plants become chlorotic in alkaline soils.

Companion Planting and Design
Use parsley hawthorn as part of a mixed border or hedge planting. It grows well in light shade and can be part of the understory of plants beneath large trees. The year-round interest and striking form make it a good choice for a focal or accent plant.

Try These
Texas hawthorn (*Crataegus texana*) is similar but has undivided leaves. This species is not commonly offered but is an excellent choice for coastal gardens. Mayhaw (*C. opaca*) grows in moist woodlands and needs a similar location in the garden. This species grows to 30 feet, blooms white or pink, and has large, delicious, edible fruit frequently made into jams or jellies. Gregg's hawthorn (*C. greggiana*) is native to the Hill Country with hairy, serrate-edge leaves and gray thorns. It is the species with the greatest tolerance for alkaline soils. Cockspur hawthorn (*C. crus-galli*) is a widespread species with big, widened thorns, glossy green leaves, and abundant white flowers.

Pecan

Carya illinoinensis

Bloom Period and Seasonal Color
Spring, green-white

Mature Height x Spread
60 to 125 ft. x 50 to 100 ft.

Botanical Pronunciation
CARE-ee-uh ill-eh-noy-ee-EN-sis

The pecan is the state tree of Texas and enjoys a long history with all residents, mainly for its tasty nuts. These nuts have been used since recorded history for food and trade and were often all that stood between survival and starvation. Pecan is a fast-growing but long-lived tree that naturally occurs along rivers and streams. Trees still growing at Mt. Vernon were a gift from Jefferson and planted by Washington in 1786. The long, compound leaves turn bright yellow in the fall in some individuals, whereas in others merely fade away. It is reputed to be the first to lose its leaves and the last to leaf out. Trees often alternate a year of abundant nut production with one of modest fruiting.

When, Where, and How to Plant
Plant container-grown plants in fall or spring. Plant bare-root trees during your zone's dormant season. Choose a site that will accommodate the height and crown spread of the tree and that is in full sun. Although trees can grow in partial shade, their size can make it difficult to find such a location. Pecans need deep, fertile soils with good drainage. Avoid rocky or shallow soils. No special preparation is necessary before planting.

Growing Tips
Use a well-balanced, nitrogen fertilizer that can be broadcast around the drip line of the tree. Check the package for application amounts, and feed half just before leaves emerge and the rest in May. In some areas, zinc foliar sprays are used, but check with local sources in your area. Water deeply and at regular intervals, weekly when trees are young and at least monthly as they age. Be sure to apply water evenly around the root zone, which is roughly equal to the drip line of the tree.

Regional Advice and Care
Prune dormant trees to remove dead wood and encourage a strong branching habit. Take out no more than a quarter of the mass of a tree in any given year. Healthy trees have few problems, although those in the eastern half of the state may be susceptible to pecan scab or downy spot. Webworms cause cosmetic damage. Trees often exude sap in late summer, which is annoying but not unhealthy.

Companion Planting and Design
This a big tree that is best used as an overall shade tree in gardens large enough to accommodate it.

Try These
Native pecan trees are widely offered and are reputed to have the best flavor. Their nuts are usually small and hard shelled. 'Western' is a soft shell variety. 'Choctaw' and 'Desirable' are old varieties with good-tasting fruit and are recommended for East Texas. Other varieties to consider are 'Cheyenne', 'Caddo', 'Kiowa', 'Sioux', and 'Wichita'. There is a wide variation in disease resistance, nut production, flavor, and size; check with local authorities for best varieties for your area.

Pine

Pinus spp.

Bloom Period and Seasonal Color
Evergreen

Mature Height x Spread
15 to 60 ft. x 25 to 50 ft.

Botanical Pronunciation PIE-nus

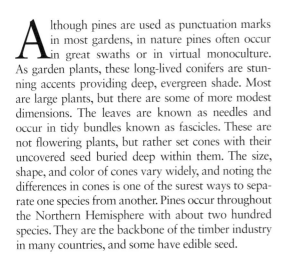

Although pines are used as punctuation marks in most gardens, in nature pines often occur in great swaths or in virtual monoculture. As garden plants, these long-lived conifers are stunning accents providing deep, evergreen shade. Most are large plants, but there are some of more modest dimensions. The leaves are known as needles and occur in tidy bundles known as fascicles. These are not flowering plants, but rather set cones with their uncovered seed buried deep within them. The size, shape, and color of cones vary widely, and noting the differences in cones is one of the surest ways to separate one species from another. Pines occur throughout the Northern Hemisphere with about two hundred species. They are the backbone of the timber industry in many countries, and some have edible seed.

When, Where, and How to Plant
Plant pines in fall or early in spring as soon as the soil can be worked. Avoid summer planting. Buy plants small; pines resent root disturbance, and small plants establish and grow to good size quickly. Choose a site that accommodates the full height and width of the mature tree and is in full sun. Pines have a wide tolerance to soil types, but check local sources for those that are best suited to your area. All pines require excellent drainage.

Growing Tips
Fertilize young pines once in spring. Mature plants do not need to be fed. Water deeply at long intervals for best results. Shallow or frequent watering results in shallow rooting, which can cause windthrow as the plants mature.

Regional Advice and Care
Prune in late spring, but not summer, to shape or remove dead or damaged limbs. Pines do not need regular pruning for shape; they have excellent natural form. Few pests or diseases affect healthy pines. Pines that are deeply stressed either by drought or cold will lose significant numbers of small limbs or needles.

Companion Planting and Design
Almost all pines are best used as a specimen or focal tree. Some have wide enough crowns to serve as shade trees. Taller species provide shade to western walls or windows, as well as the roof. Needle shed is common in summer, so plant there where that won't be a problem.

Try These
In Central and western Texas try pinyon pine (*P. edulis*), a gnarled, compact tree with edible seeds; Afghan pine (*P. eldarica*), a tall, fast-growing pine tolerant of high heat and alkaline soils but hardy to 5 degrees Fahrenheit; Aleppo pine (*P. halepensis*), hardy to 15 degrees Fahrenheit and with few, large, widely spaced large branches and billowing form, and stone pine (*P. pinea*), a symmetrical pyramid-shaped when young that matures into a straight-trunked tree with an umbrella-shaped crown. The seed are the pignoli, or pine nuts, of Italian cooking. In the east look for the native loblolly (*P. taeda*), yellow pine (*P. echinata*), or longleaf pine (*P. palustris*).

Prairie Flame Leaf Sumac

Rhus lanceolata

Bloom Period and Seasonal Color
Summer, white

Mature Height x Spread
10 to 15 ft. x 10 to 20 ft.

Botanical Pronunciation
RUSE LANCE-ee-oh-lah-tuh

Zones 8 to 10

Prairie flame leaf sumac is one of a number of species of *Rhus* that are small trees with brilliant fall foliage. In nature, prairie flame leaf sumac forms thickets that are greatly valued as the plant world's first responders to disruption and for erosion control. Many gardeners have found that when the plant is not routinely mowed or burned, this habit is greatly reduced. The white flowers of the female plants are in tall pyramids above the foliage. They are followed by bright red fruit that is persistent through the winter and, although tart, is delicious alone or in drinks. The shiny, deep green leaves turn glowing red to orange in the fall. This species has a long history of providing food, dyes, and tannage.

When, Where, and How to Plant
Plant in fall or spring as soon as the soil can be worked. Prairie flame leaf sumac grows well in full sun or light, filtered shade. It grows best in alkaline soils that are extremely well drained, but has shown tolerance of a wider range of soils as long as the drainage is excellent.

Growing Tips
Prairie flame leaf sumac does not need extra fertilization. Water long, deep soaks often enough so the soil does not dry out completely but is not consistently wet. Apply a generous layer of mulch annually to maintain even soil moisture and lessen watering frequency.

Regional Advice and Care
Prune infrequently and only to remove dead or damaged wood. Frequent pruning encourages the formation of root suckers. Prairie flame leaf sumac resists most pests and disease.

Companion Planting and Design
Plant generously near or around large trees to form a woodland garden. Mix with other shrubs to create a hedge or boundary planting. The spectacular fall display makes it ideal as a focal or accent planting.

Try These
Shining sumac (*Rhus copallinum*) is similar but grows to 35 feet and with a stronger tendency to form thickets. The shiny green leaves turn purplered in the fall, and on female plants, the white flowers are followed by dull red fruit. Generally, prairie flame leaf sumac grows west of a line followed by I-35, whereas this species grows east of that line. Staghorn sumac (*R. typhina*) has drooping leaves on long, crooked trunks with erratic but interesting branching. This species also forms thickets but has a softer, fern-like appearance. It is particularly well suited to fast-draining soils in cold areas. The fall leaves are brilliant reddish orange, and the bare, twisted twigs of winter not only provide strong winter interest but are the source of the common name. Elm-leaf sumac (*R. coriaria*) is widely known for its dried, powdered fruit known as sumac. It has a bright, lemon flavor and is used in salads and to flavor meat, as well as a component of the spice blend *za'atar*.

Rusty Blackhaw

Viburnum rufidulum

Bloom Period and Seasonal Color
Spring, white

Mature Height x Spread
10 to 18 ft. x 8 to 12 ft.

Botanical Pronunciation
vi-BUR-num rue-FID-you-lum

Zones 7 to 9

Although viburnums are a well-known group, rusty blackhaw remains more uncommon than it ought to be. This durable small tree or shrub has glossy, deep green leaves held on extended reddish petioles, which turn various shades of red or orange in the fall. The 4-inch flowering heads are packed with white flowers. These flowering heads are so prolific the plant seems to burst into illumination once in flower. The flowers are followed by dark blue, waxy fruit. Plants are not able to pollinate themselves, so it is necessary to have at least two around to get the fruit. Despite being one of the handsomest of all native viburnum, they often fail to bloom every year. But the wait is more than worth it.

When, Where, and How to Plant
Plant in fall or spring in the warmest areas. In colder areas, plant in spring once the soil can be worked. Rusty blackhaw grows well in full sun or light, filtered shade. This species is tolerant of a wide range of soils, but does particularly well in deep, fertile soils with excellent drainage.

Growing Tips
Fertilize once in spring just as leaves emerge using a balanced formula. Water young plants regularly to establish. Mature plants are extremely drought tolerant and need only monthly watering in the summer unless the weather is exceptionally hot or dry. Rely on natural rainfall in the winter in all zones.

Regional Advice and Care
Prune in spring after flowering is finished to remove dead or damaged wood. Plants bloom after the leaves emerge, so take care not to prune too early. Alternately, prune dead wood only in the fall. Rusty blackhaw sends up suckers from the roots, which can be removed anytime. Rusty blackhaw is not susceptible to pests or disease.

Companion Planting and Design
This is a fine choice to plant beneath larger trees to create a woodland garden. Use as part of a mixed border or hedge. When pruned to a small tree it makes a charming focal or specimen plant for a small garden, patio, or courtyard.

Try These
'Royal Guard' is compact and narrowly upright with leaves that turn burgundy to maroon. Blackhaw viburnum (*Viburnum prunifolium*) is similar and occurs from Texas northward to the Great Lakes. Where their ranges overlap, these species intergrade, but rusty blackhaw has larger, deeper green leaves and much showier flower clusters. Arrowwood (*V. dentatum*) grows in East Texas and has more open flowering heads and serrated leaves. Chinese snowball (*V. macrocephalum*) is semi-evergreen with remarkable, large globes of flowers. Flowers begin light green but finish pure white. Both sweet viburnum (*V. awabuki*) and sandaqua viburnum (*V. suspensum*) grow well in the shade in hot, humid areas. The extremely cold-hardy American cranberry bush (*V. trilobum*) has white flowers in an open head and bright red berries in the fall.

Shantung Maple

Acer truncatum

Bloom Period and Seasonal Color
Spring, insignificant

Mature Height x Spread
20 to 25 ft. x 15 to 20 ft.

Botanical Pronunciation
AY-sir trun-KAH-tum

Zones 7 to 8

For hundreds of years Asian gardeners have revered the elegant grace of maples. Shantung maple has found the same regard, particularly in northern gardens where it has been enjoyed for its drought and heat tolerance within those zones as well as its brilliant fall display. As is true for all maples, the greenish white flowers of spring are easily overlooked. But they are followed by the distinctive two-winged pod, called a samara, that I think resembles the wings of an insect and that turn red when mature. The leaves have five triangular lobes that are reddish purple at first but turn medium green. In the fall, this maple is resplendent with leaves in various shades of yellow and orange, often blended or lined with purple and red.

When, Where, and How to Plant
Plant in spring once all danger of frost is past and the soil can be worked. Choose a site in either full sun or light, filtered shade. Shantung maple prefers moist, acidic soils with good drainage, but will tolerate any moderately fertile, well-drained soil.

Growing Tips
Apply balanced fertilizer annually in spring. Water to maintain even soil moisture, as frequently as weekly if conditions are exceptionally hot or dry. Mulch the roots with 4 to 6 inches of organic mulch to maintain soil moisture and soil fertility. Take care not to let the mulch touch the bark of the tree.

Regional Advice and Care
Prune in spring to remove any damaged wood or shape the tree. Shantung maple has excellent natural form and does not need regular pruning as a rule. This species is not susceptible to pests or disease.

Companion Planting and Design
Shantung maple is a good choice to plant in groves amid larger trees to create a woodland garden effect. Its small stature makes it a good focal or accent plant for small gardens or patios. Pick a site where the glorious fall color can best be enjoyed.

Try These
Japanese maple (*Acer palmatum*) grows up to 30 feet tall and is widely grown for its intensely colored fall leaves. There are countless varieties and selections of this species chiefly for form, size, and fall color. Trident, or three-toothed, maple (*A. buergerianum*) is also an Asian species that grows to 30 feet and is recommended for the Gulf Coast. The Texas native southern sugar maple (*A. barbatum*) is similar in size to Shantung maple with red fall foliage and has shown good results in both Dallas and Houston. Other Texas natives include big-toothed maple (*A. grandidentatum*), growing to 15 feet with good heat and alkaline resistance and splendid fall color, chalk maple (*A. leucoderme*), growing to 25 feet with the highest heat and drought tolerance of any maple listed here, and red maple (*A. rubrum*), growing to 60 feet with brilliant red fall foliage.

Shumard Oak

Quercus shumardii

Bloom Period and Seasonal Color
Spring, insignificant

Mature Height x Spread
50 to 80 ft. x 40 to 80 ft.

Botanical Pronunciation
KWER-kus shoe-MAR-dee-eye

Zones 8 to 10

There is a splendid Shumard oak in our neighbor's yard. I like this oak as a borrowed tree because, although it is gorgeous, it is so densely branched that it creates a dark, deep shade beneath it. The massive, sturdy trunk becomes buttressed at the base with age, and most of the branches grow horizontally, giving the entire tree a pleasant pyramidal shape. The leaves are up to 7 inches long and are cut into deep lobes that end with a sharp tip or spine. They are deep green in the summer, but turn purple to rusty or fiery red in the fall often in batches over a long time. The 1-inch-long acorns are as wide and topped with a small, narrow cap.

When, Where, and How to Plant
Plant in fall or spring as early as the soil can be worked. Select a location that accommodates the height and the wide spreading crown in the full sun. Shumard oak is tolerant of a wide range of soils as long as the drainage is excellent. Avoid sites with poor drainage or where water ponds regularly.

Growing Tips
Established plants do not need supplemental fertilizer. Young plants can be fertilized with a well-balanced formulation once in spring. Water young plants two or three times a month in summer. Established trees grow well on natural rainfall. If it is exceptionally hot or dry, provide a deep soak once a month. Rely on rain in winter.

Regional Advice and Care
Prune in spring or early fall to remove dead or damaged wood. Avoid pruning in late spring or summer when oak wilt fungus is most active. Shumard oak is susceptible to oak wilt fungus where that disease is prevalent. Check with local sources for activity of the fungus or resistant species in your area.

Companion Planting and Design
Shumard oak needs ample room even in a large garden and may be the only shade tree in a modest-sized one. Its dense shade is useful to protect western walls or windows, as well the roof.

Try These
Texas red oak (*Quercus texana*) is similar but typically less massive. Buckley oak (*Q. buckleyi*) is also virtually identical. Plants are routinely offered with any of these three names. There is a mare's nest of taxonomic back and forth about the status of all these species, and opinion varies whether they are three distinct species or one extensive hybrid swarm with significant geographic variation. They are virtually indistinguishable, and it may not matter from a gardener's perspective. Lacey oak (*Q. laceyi*) is a popular replacement for Shumard oak in Central Texas because of its resistance to oak wilt. This is a striking plant with blue-green, long, barely lobed leaves. It grows to 30 feet, is less massive and more upright, and has a preference for dry, alkaline soils.

Southern Live Oak

Quercus virginiana

Bloom Period and Seasonal Color
Spring, insignificant

Mature Height x Spread
40 to 60 ft. x 40 to 60 ft.

Botanical Pronunciation
KWER-kus ver-jin-ee-AY-nah

Zones 8 to 10

I lived for a time in southern Louisiana, where it seemed that every property that could hold one had an ancient southern live oak gracefully draped with Spanish moss. These are truly long-lived majestic trees. Mature southern live oak trees tend to spread further than they grow tall, adding to their remarkable beauty and iconic form. The leathery, gray-green leaves are small and held in congested clusters on the tree. They are usually gray or lighter green on the underside. Considered evergreen because it holds its leaves through the winter, in fact the leaves fall in waves as the new leaves emerge. Acorns are small and black and brown and have a sharp tip. The small, smooth cup often remains on the tree after the acorns fall.

When, Where, and How to Plant
Plant in fall or spring as early as the soil can be worked in a site in full sun. Give them plenty of room to mature both horizontally and vertically. Southern live oak handles a wide range of soils, but it is best to avoid soils that are poorly drained, where ponding is occasional, or that have fast-draining deep sand.

Growing Tips
Established trees do not need fertilization. Fertilize young trees once in spring. Water young trees two or three times a month through the summer. Established trees need water only during times of extended drought when a deep, monthly soak is sufficient. Natural rainfall is all that is required in winter.

Regional Advice and Care
Prune in spring or early fall to remove dead, damaged, or errant limbs. Avoid pruning the late spring or summer when oak wilt fungus is most active. Southern live oak is somewhat susceptible to oak wilt. Check with local authorities for occurrence of this disease and replacement species for your area.

Companion Planting and Design
Consider this a specimen or focal tree, and give it ample room to grow, and especially spread, through its long life. Even young trees make wonderful shade trees and protect hot walls or windows well.

Try These
The Hill Country native escarpment live oak (*Quercus fusiformis*) was formerly considered a western variety of southern live oak, but is now considered a separate species. This species has slightly smaller leaves that are broadest toward the base. It is considerably more drought, heat, and alkaline tolerant than is southern live oak. Unfortunately, it is also much more susceptible to oak wilt fungus. Both of these species can grow from rhizomes (underground stems) and form thickets in favorable conditions. One of the most famous of these thickets occurs on the southern coast near Rockport in the Goose Island State Park. From East Texas to Houston, water oak (*Q. nigra*) is an excellent choice with small, deep green leaves that are barely lobed. Small, nearly round acorns are barely covered by the thin cap and often occur in pairs.

Southern Magnolia

Magnolia grandiflora

Bloom Period and Seasonal Color
Spring to summer, white

Mature Height x Spread
50 to 60 ft. x 30 to 60 ft.

Botanical Pronunciation
mag-NOH-lee-ah gran-deh-FLOR-ah

Zones 8 to 9

Southern magnolia is an icon of eastern Texas and the deep South both within the forests as well as the old gardens. Southern magnolia is a large tree with wide, shallow spreading roots that in old trees are often visible above the ground. Trees have a regular symmetry throughout their lives, and I always think they look like an aging countess that owns the room she just entered. The leaves are huge, dark green, often paler on the underside, and firm. They make excellent additions to dried arrangement. The flowers are equally oversized, pure white, and delightfully fragrant. They can be cut and used in arrangements but bruise easily, so handle with care. The fruit is a conical pod with bright red seed inside.

When, Where, and How to Plant

Plant in fall, particularly in the warm parts of its range, or in spring as soon as the soil can be worked. Choose a site that will accommodate the formidable height and spread of a mature tree. In addition, plant Southern magnolia away from buildings and other large trees. The spreading root system can cause heaving as the tree matures. Southern magnolia needs to grow in deep, acidic, moist soils and fails to thrive in soils or conditions that are otherwise.

Growing Tips

In its natural range, Southern magnolia does not need extra fertilization. Water young trees two or three times a month in summer if rainfall is scarce. Older trees have enormous, spreading root systems and are difficult to water sufficiently. It is best to grow this plant where it will receive 35 inches of rain a year or more and rely on natural rainfall.

Regional Advice and Care

Prune carefully in spring to remove branches that are growing too low or have become damaged. Southern magnolia is not susceptible to pests or disease.

Companion Planting and Design

This is one of the few trees that resents companions. It is best to use it as a specimen or focal plant in gardens that are large enough to accept its mature size.

Try These

'Little Gem' grows 12 to 15 feet tall with smaller leaves. Sweetbay (*Magnolia virginiana*) is a smaller tree up to 20 feet tall with delicate leaves and a slender form. The fragrant, creamy white flowers are followed by prominent cones of bright red seeds. Saucer magnolia (*M. xsoulangiana*) is a deciduous hybrid between two Asian species that grows to 25 feet tall with upright, bright pink flowers. Star magnolia (*M. stellata*) is a deciduous Japanese species with fragrant, narrow-petaled white flowers. The native cucumber tree (*M. acuminata*) is the source of the yellow blossom color of many new hybrids. The rarely offered native pyramid magnolia (*M. pyramidata*) has exquisite, open-petaled white flowers and grows to 20 feet tall. All of these grow best in the eastern third of Texas.

Sweet Acacia

Acacia farnesiana

Other Name Huisache

Bloom Period and Seasonal Color
Winter to spring, gold

Mature Height x Spread
15 to 25 ft. x 15 to 25 ft.

Botanical Pronunciation
ah-KAY-shuh far-nee-zee-AN-ah

Zones 8b to 10

Sweet acacia is an intricately branched, thorny tree with a spreading crown. It is often found in dense thickets growing more as a shrub than a tree. But it makes a handsome shade tree where there is room for it. Plants are deciduous to semi-deciduous depending on temperature. The tiny, fern-like, dark green leaves are congested along dark brown branches. The small golden puff ball flowers are so prolific that the tree appears to change from a deep green to gold overnight. When in full bloom, its sweet fragrance fills the garden and gives the tree its common name. In southern Europe sweet acacia is an important part of the perfume industry. The rounded woody pod is dark brown to black and tapered at both ends.

When, Where, and How to Plant
Plant in fall or spring. Select a location in full sun and where the ultimate height and spread of the tree can be accommodated. Although this species tolerates a wide range of soils, it does best in deep, well-drained, fertile soil. Adding a generous layer of compost or mulch to the backfill helps improve drainage.

Growing Tips
Apply slow-release or organic fertilizer annually in spring to young plants. Established plants do not need supplemental fertilization. Water young plants every seven to ten days during summer. Established plants need a deep, monthly soak, particularly when the weather is exceptionally hot or dry. Rely on natural rainfall in the winter.

Regional Advice and Care
Prune after flowering to remove dead wood, damaged limbs, or crossing branches. Sweet acacia has a strong multitrunked habit when young but can be trained to a single trunk by removing lower branches and suckers annually in the spring. Thin out the crown every two or three years if it becomes too dense to help prevent windthrow. Sweet acacia is occasionally infested with borers, but healthy trees usually recover quickly.

Companion Planting and Design
Use sweet acacia as a primary shade tree where there is room for it. Sweet acacia tolerates growing within a lawn, but as true for all trees, don't rely on the lawn watering alone. If left unpruned, sweet acacia makes an impenetrable hedge or boundary plant.

Try These
Sweet acacia is often sold as *Acacia smallii*, a name with no standing. There are forms of sweet acacia with greater cold tolerance that grow as more of a shrub than a tree, but these are considered just geographic variations. Blackbrush acacia (*A. rigidula*) has deep green, glossy leaves on stiff branches and whitish light gray bark. Flowers are pale yellow and in congested series of catkins with dark brown, flat pods. Twisted acacia (*A. schaffneri*) branches form a distinctive twisting pattern as it matures. The small compound leaves are held on reddish brown stems. The fragrant yellow, puffball flowers are followed by long, straight, flat pods.

Sweet gum

Liquidambar styraciflua

Bloom Period and Seasonal Color
Spring, insignificant

Mature Height x Spread
40 to 60 ft x 20 to 30 ft

Botanical Pronunciation
lick-wih-DAM-bar stye-rah-SIFF-loo-ah

Zones 7 to 9

I have never lived permanently where there is real fall color. But one year we spent a couple of months in East Texas and witnessed the unfolding of the seasonal brilliance of those forests. It was sweet gum that amazed me the most with its range of fall color in shades of yellow, red, red-orange, and burgundy often on the same tree. This large, deciduous tree is firmly at home in the mildly acidic, deep soils of the eastern section of the state. It has a straight trunk with a narrow, pyramidal crown that rounds out as it matures. The huge leaves are cut into five segments and look something like a star. The fruit is a woody, spiny sphere that is attractive in dried arrangements.

When, Where and How to Plant
Plant in fall or spring as soon as the soil can be worked. Pick a location that will accommodate the ultimate height and width of the tree and is in full sun. Sweet gum prefers to grow in deep, mildly acidic soils. It struggles in alkaline or dry soils, often becoming chlorotic under these conditions.

Growing Tips
Young plants may be fertilized up to three times a year beginning after the leaves have emerged in the spring. Apply a well-balanced, dry formulation around the entire drip line of the tree at two month intervals after that. Water young trees regularly and deeply, and avoid letting the soil dry out completely. Established trees have huge root systems and are difficult to water enough if they are not growing in a region that receives at least 35 inches of rain a year.

Regional Advice and Care
Prune while dormant to remove dead or damaged wood. Old trees are often too large to prune, but will shed dead limbs in high winds. Tent caterpillars and aphids are found on the trees but rarely cause significant damage. Sweet gum is resistant to most other pests and diseases.

Companion Planting and Design
This is a big tree that will provide excellent shade in a garden large enough to accommodate it. In larger gardens, it can be planted toward the border or within a mixed forest planting. Use it to shade the western side and roof of a building.

Try These
Sweet gum has a number of selections, chiefly developed in California, that are efforts to reduce the amount of fruit as well as for specific foliage color in the fall. Most of these are not as reliable in Texas gardens as those from native stock. They include 'Palo Alto' with bright red to red-orange fall foliage; 'Burgundy' with long persistent, red to purplish leaves; 'Festival' with yellow to pinkish leaf color; and 'Autumn Glow' with yellow to reddish foliage. Sweet gum is a good timber tree, particularly for furniture, and the gum was once used medicinally and as chewing gum.

Texas Ash

Fraxinus texensis

Bloom Period and Seasonal Color
Spring, insignificant

Mature Height x Spread
35 to 50 ft. x 25 to 35 ft.

Botanical Pronunciation
FRAX-en-us TEX-en-sis

Zones 8 to 10

Texas ash is a tall, deciduous tree found growing naturally in a wide swath through Central and southern Texas. The compound leaves have five rounded leaflets. In the fall the leaves turn a vivid red to red-orange, making it one of the few trees with striking fall foliage in South Texas. Although among the first trees to turn, it can be as late as Thanksgiving for the fall show to begin. Despite being a fast-growing tree, Texas ash is long-lived and has few of the problems that plague most other ash trees. The small, pale white flowers are held in clusters at the end of the stems. They are unremarkable except to some species of butterflies that feed avidly on their pollen and nectar.

When, Where, and How to Plant
Plant in fall for best results. If planting in spring, it is important to plant early so that roots establish well before summer. Consider the ultimate size and width when choosing a location, and avoid power lines or other overhead obstructions. Plant in full sun. Texas ash grows well in almost any soil, but needs good drainage and moderate fertility.

Growing Tips
Fertilize trees once in spring and again in fall. Use a balanced formulation and spread it around the drip line of the tree. Mature trees rarely need fertilizing. Water deeply at long intervals, monthly for established trees. Rely on natural rainfall in winter.

Regional Advice and Care
Prune while the tree is dormant to remove dead or damaged limbs or remove branches that are growing too low. Avoid removing more than a quarter of the tree in any year. Texas ash is not susceptible to pests or disease. Emerald ash borer has become a major, and lethal, pest of ash trees in the Midwest and East although so far has not been found in Texas.

Companion Planting and Design
This is a stunning choice for an accent or focal tree in a large yard. In smaller gardens, it may be all the shade needed. It is tall enough to shade western walls or windows or provide relief from intense heat on the roof.

Try These
White ash (*Fraxinus americana*) is a bigger tree with larger leaflets and a wide, rounded crown that is consistent into old age. Some authorities consider Texas ash to be variety of white ash. White ash grows best in deep, moist, fertile soils such as those of East Texas. Gregg's ash (*F. greggii*) is a shrub or small tree with small dark green leathery leaves and pale bark. It is well adapted to hot locales and dry rocky soils. Green ash (*F. pennsylvanica*) has been widely planted in most of the United States east of the Rockies; however, the spread of emerald ash borer as a major pest of this species has resulted in recommendations to avoid planting it.

Texas Ebony

Ebenopsis ebano

Bloom Period and Seasonal Color
Spring to fall, cream white

Mature Height x Spread
15 to 30 ft. x 15 to 20 ft.

Botanical Pronunciation
EBB-an-op-sis EE-bahn-oh

Zones 9 to 10

Texas ebony (syn. *Pithecellobium flexicaule*) naturally occurs in what is left of the tangled thorn forests of far south Texas and lining the southern Rio Grande Valley. It is evergreen with deep green leaves densely clustered on the twisted gray branches. I like its dense, complicated branching and use it both as a specimen tree and an impenetrable hedge. The thorny branches twist and change direction repeatedly, making it attractive to a wide range of birds for nesting within its thorny branches. The flowers are elongated, creamy white puffballs that are sweetly fragrant and spring up throughout the year. They are followed by long, curved, dark brown pods that are velvety when young. The sturdy pods both open and closed are persistent on the tree for months.

When, Where, and How to Plant
Plant in fall in warm or frost-free areas. Otherwise, plant in spring when all danger of frost is past and the soil is warm. Planting can continue through early summer. Choose a location in full sun for best form, although Texas ebony will grow well in light filtered shade. Texas ebony tolerates almost any soil conditions from deep, well-drained, fertile soil to rocky ones, even growing well in heavy clays.

Growing Tips
Apply slow-release or organic fertilizer to young plants annually in spring. Established plants do not need fertilizer. Established plants thrive on natural rainfall but when the weather is particularly hot or dry, water deeply once or twice a month. Natural rainfall is sufficient in winter.

Regional Advice and Care
Remove dead or damaged wood in the spring after all danger of frost is past or into the summer. The complicated, twisted branching pattern of Texas ebony makes pruning for shape difficult. To raise the crown, cut out a few side branches every summer until you have the desired height. Texas ebony is not susceptible to pests or disease.

Companion Planting and Design
Texas ebony makes a fine shade tree for a small yard, patio, or courtyard. Use it to protect a hot wall or window or around pools where reflected heat is intense. Left unpruned it can be planted singly or within a mixed group of other shrubs to form hedge or boundary planting. Used this way it makes an excellent windbreak.

Try These
Tenaza (*Havardia pallens*) is a closely related species native to far south Texas. It grows to 15 feet tall with a wide spreading habit and medium green leaves. The flowers are similar but are intensely and beautifully fragrant in most individuals. Tenaza is hardy in the warmest parts of Zone 9. Mexican ebony (*H. mexicana*) is a tall, open-canopied tree with gray-green leaves and pale gray bark. It is not often offered, but makes a good tree for high light shade. Its cultural requirements are the same as those for Texas ebony.

Texas Olive

Cordia boissieri

Other Name Mexican olive

Bloom Period and Seasonal Color
Summer to fall, white

Mature Height x Spread
15 to 25 ft. x 10 to 15 ft.

Botanical Pronunciation
KOR-dee-ah boy-zee-AIR-ee

Zones 9 to 10

I am a great fan of white flowering trees in the summer. I find them soothing when the heat is intense. One of my all-time favorites is Texas olive. I first saw it long ago at the South Texas home of a high school friend. Her mother was an avid gardener, and she had planted a hedge of these plants to protect her yard from the wind. They were immense and in full flower every time I saw them. In southern Texas this large evergreen is widely grown for its deep green leaves that form the backdrop for its pure white flowers with a delicate yellow throat. The fruit has a superficial resemblance to olives, but is not edible except to birds and deer.

When, Where, and How to Plant
Plant in spring once all danger of frost is past and the soil is warmed. Planting can continue through early summer. Texas olive grows in a wide range of soils but needs excellent drainage. Avoid heavy clays or areas where water collects or ponds.

Growing Tips
Texas olive does not need supplemental fertilization. Water deeply at long intervals. Established plants are significantly drought tolerant and need monthly watering in the summer only when it is exceptionally hot or dry. Rely on natural rainfall in the winter.

Regional Advice and Care
Texas olive has excellent natural form and rarely needs pruning for shape. Prune any frost damage or dead wood in spring once all danger of frost is past. Grown as far north as Austin and San Antonio,

Texas ebony survives all but the most severe freezes and is root hardy to 20 degress Fahrenheit.

Companion Planting and Design
Use Texas olive as an accent or focal tree in a small yard, near a patio, or around a pool. Leave it unpruned as part of a mixed hedge or boundary planting. Its great drought and heat tolerance means it can be used at the back of a large garden or anywhere that does not receive routine maintenance.

Try These
Cordia is a tropical genus, and Texas olive is one of the most northern of its species. Other woody cordia are more frost tender and are successfully grown only in far south Texas or in sheltered positions along the coast. Geiger tree (*Cordia sebestina*) is a tree of similar stature to Texas olive. Geiger tree has brilliant, orange-red flowers throughout the summer. Yellow cordia (*C. lutea*) is more of a shrub, with light green leaves and large clusters of bright yellow flowers. Little-leaf cordia (*C. parviflora*) is a moderate-sized, intricately branched shrub with tiny crimped gray leaves. The flowers appear pure white in small clusters throughout summer. This is an extremely xeric species that grows without extra irrigation everywhere but the deserts. Even there it only needs intermittent watering during summer. It is hardy at least to San Antonio.

Texas Palmetto

Sabal mexicana

Bloom Period and Seasonal Color
Spring, white

Mature Height x Spread
20 to 50 ft. x 10 to 20 ft.

Botanical Pronunciation
SAY-ball mex-eh-KAY-nah

Zones 8 to 10

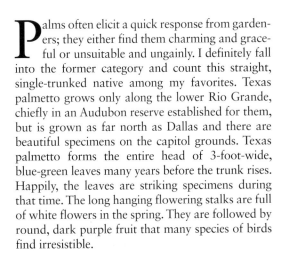

Palms often elicit a quick response from gardeners; they either find them charming and graceful or unsuitable and ungainly. I definitely fall into the former category and count this straight, single-trunked native among my favorites. Texas palmetto grows only along the lower Rio Grande, chiefly in an Audubon reserve established for them, but is grown as far north as Dallas and there are beautiful specimens on the capitol grounds. Texas palmetto forms the entire head of 3-foot-wide, blue-green leaves many years before the trunk rises. Happily, the leaves are striking specimens during that time. The long hanging flowering stalks are full of white flowers in the spring. They are followed by round, dark purple fruit that many species of birds find irresistible.

When, Where, and How to Plant

Plant in late spring and through the summer. Texas palmetto fails quickly when planted in cool soils. Texas palmetto transplants readily when it is young (with two or three leaves) or after it has begun to show a trunk. Otherwise, it is difficult to transplant successfully. Choose a site in full sun or light filtered shade with plenty of space for development of the leaves and ample vertical room. Texas palmetto grows well in any well-drained soil.

Growing Tips

Fertilize young plants annually in late spring using any designated palm fertilizer. Mature plants rarely need extra fertilization. Water every two or three weeks in summer until a plant is fully mature. By that time, it can grow easily on natural rainfall, particularly in the eastern part of the state. Rely on natural rainfall in winter everywhere.

Regional Advice and Care

Prune flowering or fruiting stalks anytime. Prune only *completely* dead leaves and leave a short stub. Never strip off the leaves. More aggressive pruning causes a serious loss of vigor.

Companion Planting and Design

Use as an accent or focal plant when the palm is young. Plant mature trees in groves or to line drives or boundaries. Texas palmetto is good choice around pools or in groups to shade hot walls or windows. Dead leaves last a long time and make good roof material for ramadas or seating areas.

Try These

Cabbage palm (*Sabal palmetto*) grows to 30 feet tall and is widely grown throughout the deep South. It tolerates wetter soil conditions than does Texas palmetto. Sonoran palmetto (*S. uresana*) has blue-gray leaves and grows to the same size as Texas palmetto. This palm is an outstanding choice for dry areas and is hardy to about 20 degrees Fahrenheit. Dwarf palmetto (*S. minor*) is a stemless palm growing to 10 feet found throughout the eastern half of the state in wet or swampy areas. This species grows well in either shade or sun, is hardy through Zone 7b, and prefers evenly moist soils.

Texas Persimmon

Diospyros texana

Bloom Period and Seasonal Color
Spring, white

Mature Height x Spread
10 to 20 ft. x 10 to 15 ft.

Botanical Pronunciation
dye-OSS-per-us tex-AN-ah

Zones 7b to 10

Texas persimmon is an elegant, semi-deciduous tree that is frequently multi-trunked, which is how I think it looks best. It grows naturally in the Hill Country and South Texas brush, where it stands out for its dense green foliage and stunning pale trunks. The bark is light gray and in most individuals peels away to reveal a white or pinkish layer reminiscent of the bark on crape myrtle. The urn-shaped white flowers are clustered along the stem with male and female flowers on separate plants. Both are so small as to be insignificant. Female flowers are followed by 1-inch round black fruit that is sweet when ripe. Fruit ripens from late July through early fall and is rapidly eaten by birds and other animals.

When, Where, and How to Plant
Plant in fall or spring in warm zones. In colder areas, plant in spring after frost danger is past and the soil can be worked. Locate in the full sun, although in desert zones it does well in light, filtered shade. Texas persimmon grows best in shallow, alkaline soils but is remarkably tolerant of a wider range of soils with excellent drainage. Avoid heavy clays or sites that are poorly drained or retain water.

Growing Tips
Texas persimmon does not need supplemental fertilization. Water established plants deeply but infrequently. If a summer is particularly hot or dry, water twice monthly, but monthly watering, or natural rainfall, is usually sufficient. Rely on natural rainfall in winter everywhere.

Regional Advice and Care
Prune in spring just as the leaves emerge to remove dead or damaged limbs. Texas persimmon flowers on the wood formed the previous season, so prune carefully to avoid losing flowers and fruit. Take special care not to use string pruners or other cutting tools near the thin bark. Texas persimmon is not susceptible to pests or disease.

Companion Planting and Design
Use as a striking focal or accent tree, particularly in small gardens, patios, or courtyards. Blend with other large shrubs in a mixed hedge or planting or as part of a native garden.

Try These
Common persimmon (*Diospyros virginiana*) grows as a shrub or to a tall tree depending on conditions. It has a graceful spreading crown with yellow flowers that are hidden by the foliage and ripens sweet, edible, orange fruit in the fall as the leaves turn red-purple. Japanese persimmon (*D. kaki*) is the most commonly grown fruiting species, with large, flattened, orange fruit. There are numerous cultivars and selections, and all are highly adaptable but grow best in deep, rich soils that are well drained. Some of the best varieties for fresh eating are 'Saijo', 'Giombo', and 'Hachiya', as well the somewhat sweeter 'Fuyu' and 'Jiro'.

Texas Pistache

Pistacia mexicana

Bloom Period and Seasonal Color
Spring to summer, white

Mature Height x Spread
12 to 20 ft. x 6 to 10 ft.

Botanical Pronunciation
pis-TAH-shee-ah mex-i-KAN-ah

Zones 8b to 10

I first saw Texas pistache on a tour of Peckerwood Gardens near Hempstead. While I was familiar with a number of other pistache trees, this one impressed me. Now I live where it grows easily, but find that unfortunately it is not more widely used. Texas pistache is a small tree with a generally rounded form owing to its strong multitrunked habit. The glossy, dark green leaves are a striking red color in the spring as they emerge. Plants are deciduous or semi-evergreen depending on temperature. The flowers are white but not particularly showy, but the prominent, red fruit on the female plants is highly ornamental. It is held in upright clusters at the ends of the stems, and, although not palatable to us, birds love it.

When, Where, and How to Plant
Plant in fall or spring. Select a site in full sun, but Texas pistache also grows in light, filtered shade. Give it enough room for its ultimate width. Texas pistache grows naturally in highly alkaline, rocky soils that can be dry for extended periods of time. It will tolerate other soils except those that are highly acidic or poorly drained.

Growing Tips
Supplemental fertilizer is not necessary for established trees. Young trees may be fertilized once in spring, just as leaves emerge. Water established trees every three or four weeks in summer if rainfall is scarce. Rely on natural rainfall in winter.

Regional Advice and Care
Some experts recommend cutting the plant back by half early in the spring for two or three years to increase the number of stems. When growing it as a small tree, take the opposite approach and remove a few of the many stems each year until you have the number desired. Texas pistache is not susceptible to pests or disease.

Companion Planting and Design
When grown as a small tree, Texas pistache is an excellent focal or accent plant in a small garden, patio, or courtyard. The fruit attracts a lot of birds, so plant it where these visitors can be enjoyed. As either a tree or shrub, incorporate it into a mixed hedge or boundary planting.

Try These
Chinese pistache (*Pistacia chinensis*) is a deciduous tree with fiery red fall foliage. This species is hardy through Zone 7 but requires deep soils and regular, deep irrigation and is listed as invasive in some areas of Texas. Mastic (*P. lentiscus*) has a similar habit to Texas pistache but is a denser plant. It tolerates great heat and drought. Pistachio (*P. vera*) has an edible nut and grows best in deep soils with regular, deep irrigation but is enormously heat tolerant. Large commercial stands are still found in southern Arizona and New Mexico. Mount Atlas pistache (*P. atlantica*) is a large, semi-evergreen to deciduous tree with excellent drought tolerance once established but is hardy only to Zone 9b.

Western Soapberry

Sapindus saponaria var. *drummondii*

Bloom Period and Seasonal Color
Spring, white

Mature Height x Spread
10 to 50 ft. x 10 to 30 ft.

Botanical Pronunciation
sah-PIN-dus sap-o-NAR-ee-ah druh-MUN-dee-eye

Western soapberry is a single-trunked tree with branches along its entire length. When young, it often looks more like a tall shrub than a tree but in time forms a rounded crown. The large, compound leaves turn a glorious lemon yellow or gold in the fall. The flowers are small, creamy white, and occur in clusters up to 10 inches long and 6 inches wide. They are followed by equally attractive yellow to gold berries that are poisonous to humans but feasted upon by birds. Fruit holds for a long time, often until the next season. The fruit is also the source of saponin, a compound that allows it to be used to make soap. The pliable wood splits easily and is widely used in basket-making.

When, Where, and How to Plant
Plant fall or spring after the soil has warmed and is easily worked. Choose a location in full sun, although western soapberry will grow in light filtered shade. This species tolerates almost any kind of soil or drainage.

Growing Tips
Western soapberry does not need supplemental fertilization. Water young plants two or three times a month for the first two or three summers. After that, decrease watering to once a month, less if there is ample rain. In most areas, natural rainfall is sufficient for established plants. Rely on natural rainfall alone in winter in all zones.

Regional Advice and Care
Prune dead or damaged limbs or errant growth early just as leaves emerge. Young plants frequently produce root suckers that can be retained to form a large, almost colonial, shrub or removed in spring to create a single-trunked tree. This tendency slows and usually stops as the plants mature. Remove flowering or fruiting stalks anytime.

Companion Planting and Design
Use western soapberry in a mixed hedge or boundary planting. Its ease of culture makes it suitable for areas that receive minimal care. Incorporate it into a woodland garden for its brilliant fall display.

Try These
Black hickory (*Carya texana*) grows to 40 feet tall and also has compound leaves that turn yellow or gold in the fall. This is a solitary tree of similar height, but more spread, than western soapberry and grows well in either rich, deep soils or rocky, shallow ones. Smoke tree (*Cotinus obovatus*) grows to 30 feet tall with blue-green leaves that turn a resplendent orange or red in the fall. Its large flowering heads hold countless tiny flowers that float and sway in the breeze, giving the illusion of smoke, hence the common name. This is a drought-tolerant, disease-resistant species of the Hill Country that resents being overwatered or overfertilized. Another small tree with bright yellow fall foliage is wafer ash (*Ptelea trifoliata*). Wafer ash is a smaller tree with intricate branching and a rounded crown. The spring flowers are fragrant with attractive pods throughout the summer.

Windmill Palm

Trachycarpus fortunei

Bloom Period and Seasonal Color
Summer, cream-white

Mature Height x Spread
10 to 40 ft. x 10 to 15 ft.

Botanical Pronunciation
tray-key-CAR-pus FOR-tune-eye

Zones 7b to 10

Windmill palm comes from the mountains of Asia and has been cultivated in both warm and cold zones for decades. Windmill palm has a solitary trunk that is densely covered with persistent, tough leaf bases inside of which is a dense mat of dark brown fiber, giving the plant a shaggy look. The short deep green fan-shaped leaves are rounded and widely spaced with long, thin petioles. The movement of this open head in a breeze looks like a windmill to some, hence its common name. Plants have male and female flowers on separate plants. In both, the stalk is nearly smothered by a large woody boat-shaped bract before they emerge. Female flowers produce the glossy blue fruit. Plants grow slowly but are long-lived and cold tolerant.

When, Where, and How to Plant
Plant in late spring or summer when soils are completely warmed. In hot areas choose a location in either light filtered shade or morning sun. In cooler areas, grow in full sun. Windmill palm grows best in well-drained, fertile soils. Amend the soil generously with compost or other organic material prior to planting.

Growing Tips
Apply slow-release or organic fertilizer annually in the spring. Use a product specially formulated for palms. In hot summer areas, water established plants every week or two during the summer. In cooler zones, watering once a month is sufficient. In all zones, reduce watering to once every month or two in the winter, or rely on natural rainfall.

Regional Advice and Care
Prune dead leaves or spent blooming stalks anytime. Do not prune living leaves unless they present a danger or are damaged and leave a short stub attached to the stem. Windmill palm is not susceptible to pests or disease and does not get chlorotic in alkaline soils.

Companion Planting and Design
Windmill palm makes a superb specimen or accent plant in small gardens or courtyards. Use it to provide contrast to large perennial plantings or as part of a large mixed hedge or boundary planting. The spare form and firm, deep green leaves of this species make it particularly effective in formal or Asian-style gardens. Plant in groups to create a dramatic effect around pools, seating areas, or patios. Windmill palm grows well in large containers or planters.

Try These
Needle palm (*Rhapidophyllum hystrix*), native to Florida and adjacent states, is reported to be hardy to minus 5 degrees Fahrenheit once established but also withstands hot summers. This palm forms a large ball of a plant with broad, fan-shaped leaves. Mediterranean fan palm (*Chamaerops humilis*) is a fan-leaved palm native to Europe that forms numerous multiple trunks and is hardy through most of Zone 8. Mature, unpruned plants are a great sphere, but stems can be removed to retain just a few, which forms a stunning multitrunked specimen plant. Leaves are deep green, rarely silver, and rounded on long thorned petioles.

VINES

Vines are the explorers in a garden, seeking out any congenial place to catch a ride to the sun, wandering high up a tree or out over the roof of a shed. This audacious growth is what makes them useful and attractive in gardens. They cover their supports or even a wall quickly; they bloom fast and usually for a long time. Despite taking up so little space, vines provide a vivid, long-lasting show.

Many vines have tendrils, those tiny extensions that twirl around a stem, leaf, or branch that give the plant a steppingstone approach to growing. Vines of this type will attach to almost anything, including other plants. It is often necessary, particularly when they are young, to direct their growth to whatever support has been provided.

Other vines simply fling out long, slim branches that hang over the branches of trees or shrubs, letting the host's branches hold it up. This type of vine sometimes needs to be attached to its support when first planted to direct its growth.

Vines are delicate and wispy like Texas clematis, offering a gentle complement to a larger planting when placed on a trellis or a pole. Or they are robust like crossvine, full of leaves and flowers, covering anything that gets in their way, practically shouting their way through the other plants in the garden. Some vines like bougainvillea are really shrubs that have long enough stems to train up a trellis or a wall. We treat them all as if they were vines, but if they were left to their own devices they would just crawl and wander from a woody center.

Bougainvillea

Ivy & Virginia creeper

Vines Serve Many Purposes

Vines are endlessly useful in a garden. Trained up a trellis or other support, they easily create living walls or roofs for open-sided patios or ramadas, protecting them from hot sun or drying winds.

Using a plant instead of cinder block, wood, or metal to roof or cover the side of a patio has many advantages. The sheer mass of the plant deflects the full blast of the sun's rays from the surface of the patio and its inhabitants. The leaves absorb some of the heat as well. In addition, each leaf is transpiring all day long, releasing minute amounts of water vapor that help lower the air temperature. In the end, these uses are just a bonus package, because the real reason we love to plant vines is their propensity to bloom with vivid flowers over a long season.

Vines also can be planted to create a sense of density and surprise in the garden. When planted so that they use a tree as their trellis, it becomes a pleasant shock to see a hackberry suddenly appear to bloom when an intertwined coral vine springs out its extravagant pink flowers. In small gardens, where a vine can get out of control fast, they may be planted to great effect on a solitary pole or dead tree trunk. With only minimal pruning and training, the vine can be encouraged to remain entirely vertical. The effect is dramatic and exciting, adding both height and interest to a limited space. Using a vine this way can also help clear up the decision about what to do with an ugly stump that is too difficult to remove.

Vines are just as useful on the ground as they are in the air. Many are well suited to use as groundcovers. Virginia creeper is a particularly intriguing choice to use in this way.

Whatever we ask of them, vines are ready to perform. They hide ugly views and perk up mundane fences, especially the ubiquitous chain-link fence. They are the masters of quick color and soothing shade. Arbors covered with a vine become a focal point in the garden, and walls taken over by a traveling coral vine or lush bougainvillea become an intriguing destination rather than a solid barricade.

Bougainvillea

Bougainvillea hybrids

Bloom Period and Seasonal Color
Fall to summer, magenta, pink, red, white, orange, salmon

Mature Length 15 to 30 ft.

Botanical Pronunciation boo-gan-VIL-lee-uh

Zones 9 to 10

ougainvillea is a shrubby vine with thin, light green leaves that mask sharp, woody thorns. Most garden forms are hybrids between *Bougainvillea spectabilis* and *B. glabra*. Bougainvillea withstands extremes of heat and is considerably more drought tolerant than it is typically grown. Bougainvillea does not have tendrils and therefore needs a sturdy trellis, arbor, or wall to support it. In warm winter areas, bougainvillea blooms year-round, but the color is most intense in the late winter and early spring. In colder areas, where it is a splendid container plant, bougainvillea is winter deciduous and flowers in the summer. The small, white, tubular flower is surrounded by large, showy, vividly colored bracts. These papery bracts are why the bloom lasts for such a long time.

When, Where, and How to Plant
Plant in spring after all danger of frost is past. In frost-free areas, fall planting is also possible. Choose a location in full sun, even one with intense, reflected heat. Bougainvillea is tolerant of a wide range of soils but does require excellent drainage. Water thoroughly after planting. Be patient; it can take months for bougainvillea to settle in and resume growth after planting.

Growing Tips
Apply slow-release or organic fertilizer to plants in the spring and fall for the first two to three years. Established plants rarely need supplemental fertilizer. More frequent fertilization grows leaves at the expense of bloom as well as burns the leaves. Water established plants every ten days to two weeks in the summer and never more than once a month in winter.

Regional Advice and Care
Prune in spring after frost danger is past and new leaves emerge to remove dead or damaged stems. Lightly prune in the summer to control growth or train the plant. Bougainvillea is not susceptible to pests or disease, although leaf cutters and flea beetles may mar the leaves in spring.

Companion Planting and Design
Bougainvillea is a dramatic specimen or accent plant when grown as a free-standing shrub or as a thick cover for a wall, trellis, or arbor. It is arresting when grown along a hillside or cascading from a large planter. Bougainvillea is a colorful choice near patios or pools for its long season of color and tolerance for intense, reflected heat. Bougainvillea grows well in containers as long as it is large enough to support the plant.

Try These
There are numerous varieties in almost every imaginable color. One of the most resilient and widely grown is 'Barbara Karst', which has long-lasting, deep magenta bracts. 'San Diego Red' (also sold as 'Scarlet O' Hara' or 'San Diego') is a vivid red with purple undertones. There are white cultivars, but they tend to revert to a pinkish tone over time. Dwarf forms, and the striking 'Torchglow', which crams its bloom into tall spires, are also worthwhile garden plants.

Carolina Jessamine

Gelsemium sempervirens

Other Name Carolina jasmine

Bloom Period and Seasonal Color
Late winter to early spring, yellow

Mature Length 20 ft.

Botanical Pronunciation
jel-SEM-ee-um sem-per-VYE-renz

Carolina jessamine is a large, fast-growing woody vine native to the eastern part of the state and on to Virginia and Florida. The glossy, deep green leaves are evergreen, although they often have a dusky purple or yellow tinge in the winter. Carolina jessamine is root hardy throughout the state, but will lose its leaves and stems in a severe or prolonged freeze. The fragrant flowers are held in small clusters at the tips of the branches and are bright yellow. The bloom is extremely profuse, particularly in the spring. In warm winter areas, it often begins to bloom early in the winter and will continue through spring. The flowers, leaves, and roots are poisonous if eaten, so do not plant near livestock or grazing animals.

When, Where, and How to Plant
Plant in spring. Choose a location in full sun for best flowering. Plants in semi-shade tend to run to the sun and easily become overwhelming. Carolina jessamine grows in any well-drained soil but favors those that are slightly acidic to neutral. Provide a trellis or other support at the time of planting and add compost or other organic amendments to get it off to a faster start.

Growing Tips
Carolina jessamine rarely needs supplemental fertilizer unless the soil is very poor. In that case, provide well-balanced or organic fertilizer once in the spring. Water regularly, up to weekly, during establishment. After that water enough to maintain even soil moisture, particularly when the weather is hot.

Regional Advice and Care
Carolina jessamine grows fastest right after its spring bloom. Time pruning for a month or so after that to help ensure that regrowth is not overwhelming. Lightly prune anytime it is warm to remove damaged or dead stems, shape, or reduce size. Do not burn prunings or add prunings to a compost pile; Carolina jessamine is poisonous. It has few pests or disease problems.

Companion Planting and Design
Use Carolina jessamine to hide an unsightly fence, block a view, or otherwise enclose an area of the garden. This species is renowned for its size and growth rate, and it rises to the top of a large tree if given the opportunity. It makes a great backdrop to large, colorful perennial beds, and its classic use is along the supports of a porch or surrounding a pergola. Because of its dangerous leaves, putting it far to the back where children or pets rarely encounter it can be helpful.

Try These
'Pride of Augusta' has double flowers with a ruffled edge to the petals. 'Pale Yellow' has light, buttery flowers. Winter jasmine (*Jasminum nudiflorum*) is a winter-flowering plant with long, green, arching stems. Growing more as a fountain-shaped shrub than a vine, this true jasmine has smaller flowers that are not fragrant. Japanese jasmine (*J. mesnyi*) has bright yellow double flowers and also grows as a large bush.

Confederate Jasmine

Trachelospermum jasminoides

Other Name Star jasmine

Bloom Period and Seasonal Color
Spring to summer, white

Mature Length 12 to 40 ft.

Botanical Pronunciation
tray-kell-lo-SPER-mum jazz-min-OY-dees

Zones 8 to 10

Neither Confederate nor a jasmine, this lovely evergreen vine has been a part of American and European gardens for centuries. Originally from China, Confederate jasmine has sharp-tipped, glossy, deep green leaves that are held on a tangle of wiry stems. The small, pinwheel-shaped, pure white flowers are intensely fragrant and have a long flowering season. This vine has tenacious aerial roots that allow it to climb almost any surface. Although grown in parts of Zone 8, including Dallas, in the colder parts of the zone it will freeze to the ground. It can be used as an annual there because its fast growth permits a significant flowering season. Even where it grows well, a heavy mulch on the roots carries it through any severe winter weather.

When, Where, and How to Plant
Plant in spring in full sun or filtered shade. Plants attach with aerial roots, so it is necessary to provide a structure or sturdy trellis immediately. Confederate jasmine grows in any well-drained soil, but those that are well amended and fertile are best. Add generous amounts of good-quality compost or other organic matter to the bed. Work it in well before planting. Provide a 4- to 6-inch layer of mulch to keep the soil evenly moist.

Growing Tips
It is rarely necessary to fertilize established Confederate jasmine. For first-year plants apply a well-balanced or dry granular organic fertilizer once in spring and directly after bloom. Water Confederate jasmine regularly through its first summer, weekly if the weather is exceptionally hot or dry. After that, plants have good drought tolerance, and watering can be reduced to two or three times a month depending on temperature. Natural rainfall is usually sufficient in winter.

Regional Advice and Care
Prune in spring when the first flush of new growth appears to remove damaged or dead wood, reduce the overall size, or shape the plant. Lightly prune through early summer to maintain shape and size. Confederate jasmine is not susceptible to most pests and disease.

Companion Planting and Design
Planting this vine to grow up a tree—as is often done—is tricky because the vine can become so large and heavy that it makes the tree susceptible to falling or windthrow. Use along a fence, against a blank wall like a garage, or on a sturdy trellis. Confederate jasmine can also be grown as a groundcover. Because it roots freely where stems meet the ground, it is excellent for erosion control on steep banks. The seductive, sweet aroma carries far, so that even plants on the garden's periphery will perfume an entire area.

Try These
'Variegatum' is a variegated form whose leaves are marked with cream, but it is less vigorous than the type. 'Madison', which is also offered as *T. mandaianum*, is a similar plant but has yellow flowers, and it is reported to survive to 0 degrees Fahrenheit.

Coral Vine

Antigonon leptopus

Other Name Queen's wreath

Bloom Period and Seasonal Color
Summer to fall, pink, red, white

Mature Length 20 to 40 ft.

Botanical Pronunciation
an-TIG-oh-non lep-TOE-puhs

Zones 8 to 10

It seems that anywhere you garden there is a vine that defines the look and feel of the area. In the southern half of the state, it is coral vine. Its long wands grow quickly, and the wide, raspy, heart-shaped leaves are dense enough to provide welcome shade. In mild winters, coral vine merely loses a few leaves, but in a severe cold snap it dies to the ground. Recovery is quick, but a thick layer of mulch helps protect the roots. Bountiful clusters of small deep pink to pastel pink or white flowers smother the vine throughout the summer until frost forestalls the bloom. This charming Mexican vine is well behaved in most of the state, but has become a pest species in southern Florida.

When, Where, and How to Plant
Plant in spring once all danger of frost is past and the soil is warm. Planting can continue into early summer. Coral vine grows well in light shade, but has the best bloom in full sun. Coral vine tolerates almost any fast-draining soil whether highly enriched and fertile or rocky. Add a generous layer of compost or mulch to the backfill when planting. Mulch the plant heavily and water in well. To keep the plant where you want it, provide a trellis or arbor to support the vine at the time of planting.

Growing Tips
Apply slow-release or organic fertilizer annually in spring, especially when plants are young. Mulch plants heavily to prevent the soil from drying out too quickly and to protect the roots in winter. Although coral vine survives on minimal water, it flowers best if watered every week or two

in summer, particularly during dry spells. Rely on natural rainfall when temperatures moderate and throughout the winter.

Regional Advice and Care
Prune in the spring just as the leaves emerge to remove winter-damaged stems, direct growth, or reduce its size. Lightly prune in the summer to maintain shape and train the plant. Coral vine is not susceptible to pests or disease.

Companion Planting and Design
Coral vine makes a stunning summer and fall display on a trellis or arbor that shelters a seating area. It can take almost any amount of heat, even reflected heat, and helps cool southern or western windows and walls. It is an admirable choice to smother an unsightly fence. When left on its own it will clamber up any nearby tree. Use as a specimen or focal plant in a small courtyard or patio.

Try These
'Baja Red' is a selection found in Baja, Mexico, that has dark coral red flowers. A white-flowering form, sometimes sold as 'Album', is not as common. The clear white contrasts particularly well against darker shrubbery or brightens a spot in light shade. Plant all three colors together, letting the resulting mix of colors create an arresting display.

Crossvine

Bignonia capreolata

Bloom Period and Seasonal Color
Spring, orange, yellow, or red

Mature Length 15 to 30 ft.

Botanical Pronunciation
big-NOH-nee-ah kap-ree-oh-LAH-tah

Zones 8 to 10

The vigorous crossvine is native to East Texas and along the coast to Victoria. It grows by tendrils, some of which end in a claw. These small projections allow it to cling to almost any surface, making it a good choice for a wooden fence or going up a wall. The large, tubular flowers are typically orange to orange-red with various amount of yellow in the interior. They are prolific on the vine, making a vivid and arresting display when in full bloom. In the southern parts of its range it is evergreen, but further north the leaves are deciduous and turn reddish purple. Some people are allergic to the pollen and others may have a reaction to the sap; use gloves if necessary.

When, Where, and How to Plant
Plant in spring after all danger of frost is past and the soil is warm. Crossvine grows in either sun or shade, although the bloom is more extravagant in full sun. The ideal situation is shade on the base and full sun for the top. Mulch the roots heavily when planting and provide support for the stems.

Growing Tips
Fertilize in the spring with a well-balanced, slow-release fertilizer, or provide a well-balanced, dry organic fertilizer. Water established plants once or twice a month in summer. This plant grows best with deep soaks at long intervals, rather than continuous shallow watering.

Regional Advice and Care
Prune in early spring to remove any damaged stems, redirect growth, or reduce the size. It can be cut by half to control its size. Crossvine has no serious pests and is not susceptible to disease.

Companion Planting and Design
This vine is so commanding in bloom, it is common to use singly as an accent or focal plant. Plant it to hide an unsightly fence or provide a colorful backdrop for a mixed perennial bed. The nearly evergreen leaves make it a good choice to cover an arbor, ramada, or other seating area.

Try These
'Tangerine Beauty' was selected by Greg Grant from a yard in San Antonio, and it has deep orange flowers with a prominent yellow interior. 'Helen Fredel' was located in the yard of a woman by this name. This crossvine selection has dark orange flowers with minimal interior yellow. 'Atrosanguinea' is a deep brick red throughout. The similar trumpet creeper (*Campsis radicans*) is native to the eastern half of Texas. The glossy, dark green leaves of this deciduous species turn red in fall. The large trumpet-shaped flowers are orange to reddish orange. Trumpet creeper sends out aerial rootlets as well as freely rooting from stems that fall on the ground. This makes it hard to manage and allows it to run outside cultivation. 'Crimson Trumpet' is pure red, 'Flava' is entirely yellow, and 'Madame Galen' is a French introduction reputed to be less aggressive.

Passion Vine

Passiflora incarnata

Bloom Period and Seasonal Color
Summer, purple, pale lavender, pink lavender, blue

Mature Length 12 to 20 ft.

Botanical Pronunciation
pass-eh-FLOR-ah in-kar-NAH-tah

Zones 7 to 9

Passion vine is a sprawling vine native to the eastern half of Texas. The leaves are split into three lobes, and the plants are entirely deciduous in the winter. The flowers are oddly gorgeous, with the petals and sepals split into thin, hair-like segments that curl and frill. The floral parts are prominent and colorful in the center. It receives its common name from someone's idea that the various floral parts represented aspects of the passion of Christ. The large, yellowish fruit is edible, making a sweet pop in the mouth. This pop is the source of the other common name, maypop. Gulf fritillary butterfly's larvae feed on the leaves, which is not a problem for older plants, but young ones might need some protection.

When, Where, and How to Plant
Plant in spring when soils are warm and all danger of frost is past. This vine grows and blooms best in full sun. Amend the soil with ample amounts of good-quality compost or other organic matter, turning it into the backfill as well. Provide a trellis or support for the tendrils to attach as the plant grows.

Growing Tips
Fertilize in spring as leaves emerge with a well-balanced or organic fertilizer. Passion vine also does well with slow-release formulations. Water regularly to keep the soil evenly moist and mulch heavily during hot or dry weather.

Regional Advice and Care
Prune lightly in summer to direct growth. This vine is deciduous, and the previous year's growth can be cut to the ground as soon as leaves fall. Butterfly larvae can cause extensive damage to the leaves of new or small plants. Cover to protect or remove caterpillars by hand until the plant is large enough to recover.

Companion Planting and Design
The delicate leaves and extraordinary bloom make passion vine a fine choice for a focal or accent planting. Set it in a large pot or along the side of seating area where the flowers can be enjoyed regularly. Plant generously or mix with other vines along a fence to create a colorful backdrop.

Try These
Yellow passion vine (*Passiflora lutea*) is native to the rich, moist forests of East Texas and farther east. The light yellow flowers are 1 inch across. *P. foetida* is native to western and far southern Texas into southern Arizona. The small flowers are blue to lavender, and the foliage has a strong aroma. It grows best with intense heat and highly alkaline soil. Blue passion vine (*P. caerulea*) is sky blue, but there are numerous selections, including white. This well-known ornamental also has countless hybrid forms. It is hardy to Zone 8. Red passion vine (*P. coccinea*) has large, scarlet flowers and large leaves. It grows best in areas with moderate to frost-free winters. Otherwise, culture is the same as for all passion vines.

Texas Clematis

Clematis texensis

Bloom Period and Seasonal Color
Spring to summer, red, rose-pink, maroon

Mature Height 6 to 10 ft.

Botanical Pronunciation
KLEM-ah-tus tex-EN-siss

Zones 8 to 10

Clematis is a large and popular genus of flowering vines. The lesser known native Texas clematis is also an outstanding garden plant throughout the state. Texas clematis is a great favorite of mine, with its delicate, sparsely leaved stems that twine up its support in the early spring. The down-turned flower has firm, almost leathery, petals that are inflated like a bell but end in a wide flare. Flowers tend to arise in waves through the summer, extending the bloom for many weeks, even months, in good conditions. Each flower lasts a long time, which helps account for this long blooming cycle. In late summer, the plant begins to fade and ultimately becomes deciduous. This is a slower-growing vine than are some, but it becomes larger each year.

When, Where, and How to Plant
Plant in spring once all danger of frost is past and the soil is warm. Amend the bed or hole with ample amounts of compost or other organic matter. Mix the amendments in well into the hole and the backfill. Set the plant slightly higher than the soil line and then mulch the root area.

Growing Tips
Apply a well-balanced or slow-release fertilizer in spring once the leaves have emerged. In fertile soils, Texas clematis needs no further fertilization. Water every ten days to two weeks while the plant is growing, more frequently if the weather is exceptionally hot or dry. Natural rainfall is sufficient when deciduous.

Regional Advice and Care
Texas clematis grows slowly, so pruning is rarely needed for the first few years. Prune lightly in spring to remove dead or damaged stems and to shape. Plants bloom on new growth, so do not remove any more than is necessary. Texas clematis is not susceptible to pests or disease.

Companion Planting and Design
Texas clematis makes a showy backdrop for smaller perennials, and their denser foliage helps hide its bare lower stems. Texas clematis takes a great deal of heat, even reflected heat, making it useful on a hot wall or around a pool.

Try These
British horticulturists have used this species since the late nineteenth century to create a number of stunning hybrids. Among the most widely available are 'Duchess of Albany', with open, upright, acutely tipped, two-toned pink flowers; 'Etoile Rose', with down-turned, deep rose flowers; and 'Princess of Wales', with upright, deep rose-red flowers. The closely related purple clematis (*Clematis pitcheri*) has the same down-turned flower style, but its flowers are larger and a deep, royal purple. The well-known garden clematis *Clematis xjackmanii* thrives in the eastern and northern parts of the state in more acidic, moist, and fertile soils. It is much more difficult in the southern or western parts of the state. The roadside native old man's beard, (*C. drummondii*), is extremely heat and drought tolerant but is rarely considered ornamental.

Texas Wisteria

Wisteria frutescens

Bloom Period and Seasonal Color
Spring, blue, lilac, white

Mature Length 30 ft.

Botanical Pronunciation
wiss-TEER-ee-ah froo-THE-senz

Texas wisteria, also known as American wisteria, is a woody, deciduous vine that is native through eastern and southeastern Texas as well as large parts of the eastern United States. This is a strong woody vine whose flowers are held in long, cascading heads. Each blue, purple, or lavender pea-like flower has a rich, sweet fragrance. Flowering begins early but after the leaves emerge. The exquisite flowers are followed by long, hanging pods that feel like velvet and remain on the plant through the summer. This is a sturdy plant that requires firm support to look its best. Unlike the extremely aggressive Chinese wisteria (*Wisteria sinensis*), Texas wisteria does not invade native streams and woods or displace native species, but still provides a luxurious spring bloom.

When, Where, and How to Plant
Plant in spring when the soil is warm and all danger of frost is past. Texas wisteria prefers to grow in a slightly acidic, moist, well-drained soil. There is no need to provide additional amendments if this is your garden soil, but adding some compost or other organic material helps if the soil is poorly drained. Choose the spot with care; this plant resents being transplanted and often fails when relocated once it is established in the ground.

Growing Tips
Apply superphosphate or organic fertilizer high in phosphorus in early spring to stimulate good flowering, depending on the requirements of your soil. Otherwise Texas wisteria needs no supplemental fertilization. Water to maintain moderate soil moisture, as often as weekly when the weather is particularly hot or dry. Do not let the plants dry out completely. A thick layer of mulch, 4 to 6 inches, helps maintain the moist, humus-rich soil conditions this species favors.

Regional Advice and Care
Prune Texas wisteria carefully. Lightly tip prune in early spring to shape and clean up winter damage. Once flowering is complete prune out the flowering heads. Aggressive pruning, particularly early in the season, stimulates too much foliage growth at the expense of flowering. Wisteria hosts a number of leaf-chewing insects, but their damage is rarely more than cosmetic. Remove by hand if there are just a few, or use appropriate controls following package directions completely.

Companion Planting and Design
Texas wisteria is a splendid choice to cover an arbor or pergola, use on a sturdy post, or anchor one side of a seating area. Because it is deciduous, it provides deep shade and luscious bloom and fragrance during the hot summer, but it allows in the warming winter sun. Use against a wall or along an unsightly fence to serve as a background for perennial or mixed plantings.

Try These
'Blue Moon' grows to 15 feet with blue flowers that occasionally repeat bloom once or twice in summer. 'Dam B' has a paler flower, and is a popular cultivar, particularly in Texas. 'Nivea' has pure white flowers.

Virginia Creeper

Parthenocissus quinquefolia

Bloom Period and Seasonal Color
Spring, insignificant

Mature Length 20 to 40 ft.

Botanical Pronunciation
par-theh-noh-SISS-us kwin-kwih-FOLE-ee-ah

Native to the eastern half of Texas and throughout the eastern United States, Virginia creeper is a vigorous vine with outstanding fall foliage. The leaves are divided into five leaflets and in some selections are up to 6 inches long. The leaves are among the first to color in the fall in brilliant shades of red, purple, maroon, or mauve. Plants grow from aerial rootlets that cling to almost any surface. Although the greenish flowers are tiny, prominent clusters of blue fruit follow. This fruit is favored by a number of species of birds but is harmful to people. The leaves and stems may cause skin irritation in sensitive individuals. It is best to handle plants carefully or with gloves if you are not sure.

When, Where, and How to Plant

Plant in spring in full sun for best growth and abundant leaf production. Virginia creeper grows well in any well-drained soil, even alkaline and sandy soils. Amend the soil with good-quality compost or other well-composted organic matter. Situate the plant with a sturdy trellis or arbor, or plant against a wall to support its growth.

Growing Tips

Virginia creeper rarely needs supplemental fertilization, but if desired, apply a well-balanced or dry organic fertilize once in spring. Water to maintain even soil moisture, and it is best never to let the soil dry out completely. In dry soils, provide a 4- to 6-inch layer of mulch to keep the soil moist and cool. Mulch the roots heavily in the winter as well.

Regional Advice and Care

Prune in spring as the leaves begin to emerge or lightly prune in the summer to shape or direct growth. Remove fruit anytime after it forms or leave it for birds to enjoy. This plant is poisonous; it's best not to compost the prunings but rather dispose of them in the trash.

Companion Planting and Design

Use Virginia creeper to hide an unsightly fence or block a view. It is a beautiful complement to a tall wall or along the side of a building. The autumnal color is so dramatic and vivid; be sure to place it where this can best be enjoyed. It can also be used as an effective groundcover or erosion control when left to grow along the ground.

Try These

'Monham' Star Showers™ has foliage that is splashed with cream to white. 'Hacienda Creeper' is a selection from an unnamed species that resembles Virginia creeper but has smaller, glossy green leaves that likewise turn red in the fall. Leaves are persistent until new growth pushes them out in the spring. Although it is root hardy to Zone 7, this vine is evergreen in milder climates. Boston ivy (*Parthenocissus tricuspidata*) is widely grown, particularly in older gardens, as a groundcover or a vine. Use it with care; it is an invasive plant in most of the United States.

Yellow Butterfly Vine

Callaeum macroptera

Bloom Period and Seasonal Color
Spring to summer, yellow

Mature Length 10 to 15 ft.

Botanical Pronunciation
kah-LAY-ee-um ma-CROP-ter-ah

Zones 8 to 10

Yellow butterfly vine is an elegant plant with dense foliage and both attractive flowers and fruit. The dark green leaves form a striking backdrop for the bright yellow flowers that are so prolific they nearly smother the foliage when in full bloom. The petals of each blossom are narrowed at the base and then flare at the end like a paddle. The resulting fruit is equally distinctive. It is a large, papery, four-sided pod, each edge of which extends outward to form a ruffled wing, hence the common name. The pod begins bright chartreuse but as the seed matures fades to pale tan and is widely used in dried arrangements. Yellow butterfly vine is immune to heat, but in cold winters, it may be briefly deciduous.

When, Where, and How to Plant
Plant in spring when all danger of frost is past and the soil is warm. Yellow butterfly vine tolerates afternoon shade in hot areas, but full sun is best in all zones for the best bloom. Yellow butterfly vine is tolerant of a wide range of soils, including highly alkaline ones as long as there is excellent drainage. Amend the hole with a generous amount of compost or other organic matter when planting. Mulch the roots after planting and throughout the life of the plant to keep the soil from completely drying out.

Growing Tips
Apply slow-release or organic fertilizer to young plants once in spring. Established plants do not require supplemental fertilizer, but an annual application in spring makes the plant grow faster. Water established plants two or three times a month in summer, more often when it is exceptionally hot or dry. Water monthly in winter.

Regional Advice and Care
Prune in the spring to remove winter damage and dead stems or to shape. Cut to within 2 feet of the ground if the vine has become too large. Lightly prune after flowering to shape. Plants often lose leaves in the hottest part of the summer but recover when temperatures moderate. Maintain regular watering but do not fertilize during this time. Yellow butterfly vine is not susceptible to pests or disease.

Companion Planting and Design
Provide a trellis, arbor, fence, or other support for yellow butterfly vine. It is dense enough to hide an unsightly fence, mask an unsightly view, or provide a background for colorful spring-flowering perennials. Interplant with summer-flowering vines, such as coral vine, to provide year-round color and interest. Yellow butterfly vine also grows well in a large container.

Try These
The closely related, but less widely available, lilac butterfly vine (*Mascagnia lilacina*) has flowers with the same pinwheel shape in shades of lavender or deep purple. This is a delicate vine with widely spaced leaves on thin stems, making it excellent in containers or blended with other vines to hide the sparse foliage.

TIPS AND STRATEGIES FOR A LOW-WATER USE GARDEN IN TEXAS

As Texas' population continues to grow, local water providers are faced with greater demand without increasing supplies. This results in both higher rates and greater water use restrictions. Coupled with a pattern of short and long droughts, it is important to design and maintain gardens that conserve water.

To help reduce water use in the garden, consider the following tips and strategies. Many of the plants in this book are appropriate for low-water use gardens.

1. Use low-water use plants. This is the single best strategy for lowering the water use in your garden. While local native plants are the obvious choice, there is a wide array of plants in all regions that are equally well adapted. Check that plants are suitable for your soil type and rainfall regime.

2. Group plants by their water needs. Gather plants with the highest water needs into raised beds, or small areas. Beds with plants that have mixed water needs result in some being overwatered, while others are not getting enough.

3. Eliminate or reduce lawn. Lawns are one of the single highest users of water in the garden. Retain only lawn that is actively used, replacing the rest with perennials, ornamental grasses, shrub borders, groundcovers, or hard surfaces like rock or gravel.

4. Amend the soil. Adding compost or other organic products to sandy or rocky soil increases the soils ability to hold water. More water in the soil is more water for plant's roots. Adding the same type of amendments to clay soils opens the spaces between the particles and allows roots to better absorb soil moisture.

5. Use mulch. Apply mulch generously to all plants, regardless of their type. By covering the surface, mulch slows down the evaporation from the soil. It also cools the soil, which slows down evaporation as well. Organic mulches add nutrients and increase soil's texture and fertility over time. Inorganic mulch has the same effect on evaporation, but the surface is hot. Use plants that are well-suited to such increased heat with this mulch.

6. Use efficient irrigation methods and practices. Water is best applied directly to the roots of plants. Check drip irrigation emitters often for clogging, flush the entire system annually to remove salts, repair leaks as soon as they appear.

Replace soaker hoses every three to four years to prevent clogging by salt buildup.

Build a small berm around the perimeter of tree or shrub, or even an entire bed. Fill it up, let it soak in, and repeat if necessary until the entire root zone is wetted.

Sprinkler systems waste as much as half their water through evaporation. Run a sprinkler in the dark, ideally right before dawn, and check for leaks regularly.

Water any lawn without using sprays or sprinklers and soak the ground down 6 inches. Water again when soil is moist 3 inches down, usually once a week.

Timers assure that the appropriate amount of water is being sent to the plants.

7. Harvest rainwater. Capturing, directing, or saving water can be as simple as a bucket under the eaves or as elaborate as a cistern system. The point is to use as much rainwater as possible and prevent runoff. Use gutters and direct their outfall to a large bed or tree. Gently contour the entire garden so that no water leaves the site. Create small ponding areas if possible. Dig a slight trench along driveways or sidewalks to direct runoff to planting beds.

8. Consider exposure. Use only plants that well suited to full sun in such locations. Plants that are best grown in shade use considerably more water in full sun.

Wind, especially consistent wind, dries plants out quickly. Use large evergreens or fences along the border of the garden to reduce wind effects. Place plants on the lee side of large evergreen shrubs or walls to reduce wind effects.

LAWN REPLACEMENT

Lawns, particularly those that are not used consistently or that take up most of the garden, are enormous consumers of water. Bermudagrass generally takes the equivalent of 42 inches of rain annually to stay green and lush despite the fact that it is winter dormant. Some areas of the state can expect that much or more rain in a year, but most regions fall far short, especially in the summer when the grass is growing.

In this time of serious drought and with ever-increasing restrictions on outdoor water use, it only makes sense to think carefully about how much lawn to maintain or whether to have any at all. Gardeners in all regions of the state have a bountiful supply of perennials, shrubs, bulbs, and other plants to use instead of lawns. Creating a more diverse, colorful, and lively garden that won't break the water budget is entirely within reach. By taking the plunge to reduce or eliminate your lawn, you open up your garden not only to more birds and butterflies, but also create a more interesting and exciting place.

The ancient gardens of the Middle East and North Africa, where water has never been abundant, offer exquisite examples of spectacular gardens with no lawns. They are based on the use of courtyards often with a fountain surrounded by planting beds, and make abundant use of enclosed patios and sheltered seating areas. Gardens like this also make a significant color addition to the garden with stone, mosaic, brick, or tile.

Removing the Lawn

Taking out all or a part of a lawn isn't difficult, but it can be time consuming. Some grasses can be removed by pulling or digging them out. St. Augustine can be effectively removed this way, as can zoysia. It is often easier and more effective to pull or till out the grass in the late winter or early spring when it is more or less dormant, or at least not actively growing.

Bermudagrass in all its forms is quite different. It is nearly impossible to remove entirely from a large area without the use of herbicides. In a small bed or where it shows up only irregularly, bermudagrass can be removed by hand if it's combined with good timing.

Hand removal of bermudagrass is most effective in the winter while it is dormant. Using a shovel, sharpshooter, or turning fork get under the root zone and turn the soil. Remove all the roots, shoots, and plants that you find or see. You will never get them all, but you can make enormous headway with this technique.

Taking out bermudagrass by simply pulling it up is rarely effective because even the smallest root piece will take hold and make a new plant as soon as water is available. Breaking off the roots just seems to invigorate them for new growth. Much the same is true of St. Augustine, but it is easier to find the entire plant and remove it than it is for bermudagrass.

If you want to remove bermudagrass with herbicides, the ones that work the best are products with the active ingredient glyposate. These products are sold under a number of trade names; check the label to be sure this is the active ingredient. This chemical is systemic, meaning it must enter the vascular system of the plant to work effectively. Therefore, it must be used when the grass is actively growing.

Begin the removal process after bermudagrass has broken dormancy in the spring and started active growth. Water the entire area well to encourage the grass to grow quickly and steadily. Do not mow the lawn, just let it grow.

Once the grass is growing well, apply the product. Follow the label directions for application rates closely. Choose a calm day to prevent unwanted drift of the herbicide to other plants. Protect plants that are too close to the spray with cardboard, plastic sheets, or wood.

It takes about a week to notice the first results and up to two weeks to know how much of the lawn is dead. Do not mow or remove any of the grass yet. When applied uniformly and according to label directions up to 95 percent of the lawn is dead after the first application. Make another application two weeks after the first on any grass that appears to be growing or alive. A week or so after the second application, remove all the dead grass and rake the area to clean it up. Glyphosate is rated to be persistent in the soil for about 72 hours so there is minimal danger of it affecting any plant that was not directly sprayed.

Continue to water the area to encourage any remaining living bermudagrass to show up. There are always a few stragglers left. Keep a spray bottle handy with the herbicide and spray as sprouts appear to eradicate it completely. The roots are deep and can arise months later. Seed can drift in from a great distance. It helps to be vigilant during the first summer.

You can begin to plant a month after the final application. You can use precisely this same technique to remove any kind of lawn grass. Just be sure that the grass is actively growing.

What to Put in Place of a Lawn

For many gardeners the most difficult part of lawn replacement is not the removal, it is deciding what to do with the space that used to be lawn. There are a number of strategies, or design ideas, to help solve this problem. They can be used together if you have a large area or taken up one at a time. The ideas below are merely a start. Don't be afraid to try whatever suits your own taste, your garden style, and your climate. In the end, whatever you decide will probably astound you by how much livelier, interesting and, colorful the area has become.

Expanded beds. If you have existing beds, either within the lawn area or on its edges, consider increasing their size by extending them further into the new area. Such extended beds are most visually pleasing if they retain the same shape or curve of the original. This is also a good time to consider adding beds of perennials or even mixed shrub and perennial beds if there is room. In a large area such beds can become like a centerpiece of the garden. If it is a front lawn that has been eliminated or reduced, consider creating a slight mound. This will have the effect of making the plants seem taller than their natural growth to afford more privacy.

Increase the number or size of paths. If the existing paths were too narrow or did not get you to precisely the places you need to go, this is a great time to expand their width or redirect them.

Consider widening a path at some point to allow space for a birdbath, a piece of art, or a striking plant. This is a particularly effective technique if the old lawn stretched out from a patio or other seating area. Gravel, stone, or brick paths, in colors that blend well into the garden, provide the unity that can hold the entire garden together. In addition, these are useful parts of the garden that now take no water to maintain.

Add a seating area. Patios, seating areas, and ramadas are also excellent ways to use former lawn space. Such additions create a base or frame that encourages new or expanded beds to surround them thereby taking up even more former lawn area. In a small garden, the entire former lawn can be replaced in this way. In a larger garden, seating areas can be established throughout the garden, or as an extension of an existing porch.

Plant groundcovers. Using plants that are either planted closely together or that spread over the ground is an easy way to replace all or part of a former lawn. The choices depend on your taste and your garden's style. For a confined or limited area, consider a handsome ornamental grass or, where appropriate, Texas beargrass. These bunching plants take little water or care and quickly fill in the space. Within the area that runs from the street to the sidewalk, short grasses, well adapted bulbs, or low growing, low-water use perennials turn a strip of plain grass into a colorful small garden that uses much less water.

Where foot traffic is more intense, consider cut out paving stones that can be filled in with low-water use grasses such as Habiturf™ or buffalo grass. In some areas low growing thymes or dichondra can also fill in these pavers. One of the easiest groundcovers to create is to plant a vine on the ground. Many perennial vines form long extensions that over time cover a lot of ground. Almost any vine will work for this use.

Crowding plants together closely creates a functional groundcover even if the plants do not have long runners. Good choices would be plants that form tight rosettes like daylilies or monkey grasses or semi-trailing perennials like plains zinnia, trailing lantana, or shrimp plant. Look for plants that are well suited to your area and don't be afraid to plant generously.

Incorporate low-water-use grasses. For those areas that are kept in lawn it could help your water bill considerably to replace it with one of the low-water-use grasses for lawns. This includes most forms of buffalo grass in areas where it does well. The blend called Habiturf™ is most effective in the southern half of the state. Both of these lawn choices grow with considerably less water than typical lawn grasses and are most attractive when they are mowed infrequently. While they don't allow for playing croquet quite as well, they certainly provide that sweep of green for those who can't live without it.

You have options to a lawn—and may just like it better!

Even a small patio can help eliminate the need to maintain a lawn.

COPING WITH DEER

Deer are a major garden pest in many parts of Texas. They cause serious and long-lasting damage by not only eating plants but using them to bed down and rub off antlers. Deer are not just a rural problem, either. Many cities find that they have immense deer populations within their boundaries. This pest is a vexing and difficult pest to manage. There are few strategies that help, but all of them require vigilance by the gardener and are subject to the tastes of the particular deer population.

Never Feed Deer

This should be obvious, but it is often the case that deer populations, particularly in cities, are initially encouraged into an area by artificial feeding. Once there, and when feeding continues, these deer herds become large and lose their fear of human activity.

Exclusion

This is the only strategy that can be called truly successful. It is both expensive and often not attractive in an urban garden, but it does work. Deer can jump up to 8 feet, so any straight, vertical fence must be at least that tall. A 6-foot fence will work if it is slanted at a 45 degree angle. Two parallel 4-foot fences spaced 5 feet apart is also successful.

Deer avoid jumping into areas that they cannot see, so a standard wood or masonry fence can work well. So-called deer fencing is generally heavy- duty plastic or wire mesh that is 7 feet tall and strung on metal posts. It works well in large areas or where a solid barrier fence is not desirable.

You can also enclose a new bed or individual plant. Deer sample much more than eat, and keeping them from trying out a recent planting helps in some cases. Any enclosure still must be as sturdy and tall as those described above.

Dogs

Dogs are sometimes useful in discouraging deer. However, the dog must always be on patrol and have the size and disposition to intimidate deer.

Repellants

Repellants work, when they do, by exuding a smell, taste, or touch that deer don't like or by startling them. A wide variety of home or commercial products have been recommended over time including bars of soap, mothballs, bloodmeal, coyote scat, human hair, rotten eggs, or fabric softener strips. Pepper sprays made of very hot peppers like

Habañero combined with dishwashing liquid can be sprayed on plantings on a weekly basis or after rains to deter deer. Electric wires, monofilament strands and flashing lights or sounds with a trip wire mechanisms have been used to startle deer causing them to run away. Many repellants work for a while but lose effectiveness over time as deer become accustomed to them.

Plant Barriers

Plants can be used to create visual barriers in much the same way as a block wall. Certain plants can create a so-called "smell barrier" by surrounding an area with plants deer find particularly distasteful, such as rosemary, Mexican oregano, and most species of *Salvia*. Plants like large, or vigorously pupping, agaves or prickly pear cactus can also create significant physical barriers to deer. Finally, filling the garden with plants that deer are known not to prefer helps establish your garden a less desirable feeding ground.

But be aware that deer can and will eat almost anything if they are hungry enough. They are also drawn to water, particularly during extended dry spells. And a deer in rut is an animal that has lost its mind and will go and eat anywhere at all.

Deer like to bed down for the night in protected areas, particularly if they have fawns. Keeping plants pruned high, or surrounding low-growing shrubs with undesirable plants, can help.

Keeping deer out of the garden can be a major chore in many areas of Texas.

INVASIVE PLANTS
IN TEXAS

Plants are designated as naturalized when they jump out of cultivation and establish and reproduce on their own. Some plants, however, take this step but then leap to being designated invasive, or pest species, when they crowd out or seriously diminish native populations in a given area.

Turning from a beloved garden plant to a reviled invasive pest can happen quickly or it can take decades to show up. Many of the plants that are now known to be invasive have been in cultivation for a long time. Clearly something changed and it is not always clear what that was. The result is the same; invasive plants that begin to take over native plant communities, creating ecological havoc and becoming so extensive so quickly they are hard to eradicate.

Whether or not a plant is an invasive pest is usually a matter of where it lives. A plant that is a horrific pest in one part of the country or one area of the state may be entirely benign in another climate or area. Therefore, to understand or assess whether a plant is invasive, it is best to use sources that are as local as possible. Even then, it is advisable to read the information completely, and remember that in a place as big as Texas things can be quite different in El Paso than they are in Houston.

Some of the most widely recognized and significant pest species in the state are noted below in this list from the Texas Department of Agriculture. Details are found on their website at www.texasagriculture.gov. In addition, a number of public and private organizations work to identify invasive species through the Invasive Plant Atlas of the United States (IPAUS). To find out more, particularly for your local area, check the website www.texasinvasives.org.

To prevent the further spread of invasive species, know what they are and what they look like. Do not buy them, but find desirable or similar substitutes, particularly ones that are native to your area. If you find that you have an invasive species that is too large to remove try these tactics to keep it under control: 1) cut off seeds before they mature, 2) watch for free seedlings and pull them out quickly, and 3) watch for spreading stems or roots and pull them up regularly.

Plants Listed as Noxious and Invasive by the Texas Department of Agriculture

(partial list)

Balloonvine (*Cardiospermum halicacabum*)
Brazilian peppertree (*Schinus terebinthifolius*)
Giant reed (*Arundo donax*)
Itchgrass (*Rottboellia cochinchinensis*)
Paperbark (*Melaleuca quinquenervia*)
Purple loosestrife (*Lythrum salicaria*)
Rooted water hyacinth (*Eichhornia azurea*)
Salvinia (*Salvinia* spp.)
Serrated tussock (*Nassella trichotoma*)
Torpedograss (*Panicum repens*)

Invasive Plants That Are Illegal to Sell in Texas

(Complete list from the Texas Agriculture Department's Noxious and Invasive List)

Chinese tallow tree (*Triadica sebifera*)
Kudzu (*Pueraria montana* var. *lobata*)
Saltcedar (*Tamarix* spp.)
Tropical soda apple (*Solanum viarum*)

Serious Pest Species as Listed by IPAUS

(partial list)

Chinese pistache (*Pistacia chinensis*)
Chinese wisteria (*Wisteria sinensis*)
Common periwinkle (*Vinca minor*)
English ivy (*Hedera helix*)
Heavenly bamboo (*Nandina domestica*)
Mimosa (*Albizia julibrissin*)
Pampas grass (*Cortaderia selloana*)
Scarlet firethorn (*Pyracantha coccinea*)

PLANTS FOR NATIVE GARDENS

Genus	epithet	variety	common name	type
Gaillardia	pulchella		Indian blanket	annual
Coreopsis	tinctoria		Plains coreopsis	annual
Lupinus	subcarnosa		bluebonnet	annual
Portulaca	oleracea		purslane	annual
Helianthus	annuus		sunflower	annual
Lupinus	texensis		Texas bluebonnet	annual
Coreopsis	grandiflora		tickseed	annual
Crinum	americanum		crinum	bulb
Cooperia	drummondii		rain lily	bulb
Iris	fulva		Louisiana irs	bulb
Hymenocallis	galvestonensis		spider lily	bulb
Hymenocallis	lirosme		spider lily	bulb
Hymenocallis	caroliniana		spider lily	bulb
Hymenocallis	latiolia		spider lily	bulb
Yucca	rostrata		beaked yucca	desert perennial
Opuntia	engelmannii		desert prickly pear	desert perennial
Opuntia	phaecantha		desert prickly pear	desert perennial
Dasylirion	wheeleri		desert spoon	desert perennial
Dasylirion	leiophyllum		green sotol	desert perennial
Yucca	pallida		pale-leaved yucca	desert perennial
Yucca	glauca		Plains yucca	desert perennial
Opuntia	santa-rita		purple prickly pear	desert perennial
Manfreda	virginica		rattlesnake master	desert perennial
Hesperaloe	parviflora		red hesperaloe	desert perennial
Agave	lechuguilla		shindagger	desert perennial
Manfreda	sileri		Siler's tuberose	desert perennial
Dasylirion	texanum		sotol	desert perennial
Yucca	treculeana		Spanish dagger	desert perennial
Manfreda	maculosa		spice lily	desert perennial
Nolina	texana		Texas bear grass	desert perennial
Yucca	thompsoniana		Thompson's yucca	desert perennial
Yucca	rupicola		twisted leaf yucca	desert perennial
Bouteloua	dactyloides		buffalograss	grass
Muhlenbergia	capillaris		Gulf muhly	grass
Muhlenbergia	rigens		deer grass	grass
Chasmanthium	latifolium		inland sea oats	grass
Muhlenbergia	lindheimeri		Lindheimer's muhly	grass
Uniola	paniculata		sea oats	grass
Muhlenbergia	reverchonii		seep buhly	grass
Salvia	greggii		autumn sage	perennials
Melampodium	leucanthum		blackfoot daisy	perennials
Tetraneuris	acaulis		Angelita daisy	perennials
Oenothera	drummondii		beach evening primrose	perennials
Conoclinium	coelestinum		blue mistflower	perennials
Pteridium	aquilinum		bracken fern	perennials
Asclepias	tuberosa		butterfly milkweed	perennials
Berlandiera	lyrata		chocolate flower	perennials
Polystichum	acrostichoides		Christmas fern	perennials
Hibiscus	moscheutos		common rose mallow	perennials
Phlox	pilosa		downy phlox	perennials
Oenothera	speciosa		evening primrose	perennials
Anisicanthus	quadrifidus	wrightii	flame anisicanthus	perennials
Tetraneuris	scaposa		four-nerve daisy	perennials

Genus	epithet	variety	common name	type
Gaura	lindheimeri		gaura	perennials
Aquilegia	chrysantha		golden columbine	perennials
Glandularia	gooddingii		Goodding's verbena	perennials
Berlandiera	texana		green eyes	perennials
Hibiscus	martianus		heartleaf hibiscus	perennials
Penstemon	trifolius		Hill Country penstemon	perennials
Melampodium	cinereum		hoary blackfoot	perennials
Poliomintha	incana		hoary rosemary mint	perennials
Phlox	divaricata		Louisiana phlox	perennials
Adiantum	capillis-veneris		maidenhair	perennials
Salvia	farinacea		mealy blue sage	perennials
Ratibida	columnifera		Mexican hat	perennials
Conoclinium	greggii		mistflower	perennials
Salvia	regla		mountain sage	perennials
Anisacanthus	linearis		narrow-leaf anisacanthus	perennials
Echinacea	angustifolia		narrow-leaf coneflower	perennials
Echinacea	pallida		pale coneflower	perennials
Anisacanthus	puberulus		pink anisacanthus	perennials
Zinnia	grandiflora		Plains zinnia	perennials
Callirhoe	digitata		poppy mallow	perennials
Glandularia	bipinnatifida		Prairie verbena	perennials
Echinacea	purpurea		purple coneflower	perennials
Penstemon	baccharifolius		rock penstemon	perennials
Hibiscus	coccineus		scarlet rose mallow	perennials
Ruellia	malocasperma		softseed ruellia	perennials
Calylophus	berlandieri		square-bud primrose	perennials
Calylophus	hartwegii		sundrops	perennials
Asclepias	incarnata		swamp milkweed	perennials
Pavonia	lasiopetala		Texas rock rose	perennials
Malvaviscus	arboreus	drummondii	Turk's cap	perennials
Artemisia	ludoviciana		Western mugwort	perennials
Zinnia	acerosa		white zinnia	perennials
Penstemon	cobaea		wild foxglove	perennials
Callirhoe	involucrata		winecup	perennials
Thelypteris	kunthii		wood fern	perennials
Achillea	millefolium		yarrow	perennials
Oenothera	macrocarpa		yellow evening primrose	perennials
Wedelia	texana		zexmenia	perennials
Callicarpa	americana		American beautyberry	shrubs
Bauhinia	lunarioides		Anacacho orchid tree	shrubs
Berberis	trifoliolata		agarita	shrubs
Fallugia	paradoxa		Apache plume	shrubs
Leucophyllum	minus		Big Bend cenizo	shrubs
Acacia	greggii		catclaw acacia	shrubs
Leucophyllum	frutescens		cenizo	shrubs
Celtis	ehrenbergiana		desert hackberry	shrubs
Tecoma	stans		esperanza	shrubs
Rhus	virens		evergreen sumac	shrubs
Rhus	aromatica		fragrant sumac	shrubs
Acacia	berlandieri		guajillo	shrubs
Hibicus	moscheutos		hardy hibiscus	shrubs
Caesalpinia	mexicana		Mexican bird of paradise	shrubs
Galphimia	angustifolia		narrow leaf goldshower	shrubs
Vauquelinia	corymbosa		narrow leaf rosewood	shrubs
Ilex	decidua		possumhaw	shrubs
Acacia	angustissima		prairie acacia	shrubs

Genus	epithet	variety	common name	type
Aesculus	pavia		scarlet buckeye	shrubs
Leucophyllum	candidum		silverleaf cenizo	shrubs
Rhus	trilobata		skunkbush sumac	shrubs
Rhus	glabra		smooth sumac	shrubs
Rhododendron	viscosum		swamp azalea	shrubs
Rhododendron	oblongifolium		Texas azalea	shrubs
Eysenhardtia	texana		Texas kidneywood	shrubs
Lantana	urticoides		Texas lantana	shrubs
Sophora	secundiflora		Texas mountain laurel	shrubs
Morella	cerifera		wax myrtle	shrubs
Rhododendron	canescens		wild azalea	shrubs
Aloysia	wrightii		Wright's bee bush	shrubs
Ilex	vomitoria		yaupon	shrubs
Sophora	tomentosa		yellow sophora	shrubs
Ehretia	anacua		anacua	trees
Taxodium	distichum		bald cypress	trees
Ulmus	americana		Amercan elm	trees
Viburnum	dentatum		arrowwood	trees
Acer	grandidentatum		big-toothed maple	trees
Prunus	serotina		black cherry	trees
Carya	texana		black hickory	trees
Acacia	rigidula		blackbrush acacia	trees
Viburnum	pruinifolium		blackhaw viburnum	trees
Quercus	buckleyi		Buckley oak	trees
Quercus	macrocarpa		bur oak	trees
Prunus	caroliniana		Carolina laurel cherry	trees
Ulmus	crassifolia		cedar elm	trees
Acer	leucoderme		chalk maple	trees
Prunus	caroliniana		cherry laurel	trees
Prunus	angustifolia		Chickasaw plum	trees
Quercus	muehlenbergii		chinkapin oak	trees
Crataegus	crus-galli		cockspur hawthorn	trees
Magnolia	acuminata		cucumber tree	trees
Chilopsis	linearis		desert willow	trees
Diospyros	virginiana		eastern persimmon	trees
Diospyros	virginiana		Eastern persimmon	trees
Juniperus	virginiana		Eastern red cedar	trees
Cercis	canadensis		Eastern redbud	trees
Quercus	fusiformis		escarpment live oak	trees
Quercus	fusiformis		escarpment live oak	trees
Sophora	affinis		Eve's necklace	trees
Cornus	florida		flowering dogwood	trees
Chionanthus	virginicus		fringe tree	trees
Fraxinus	pennsylvanica		green ash	trees
Fraxinus	pennsylvanica		green ash	trees
Fraxinus	greggii		Gregg's ash	trees
Crataegus	greggiiana		Gregg's hawthorn	trees
Crataegus	greggia		Gregg's hawthorn	trees
Prosopis	glandulosa		honey mesquite	trees
Quercus	laceyi		Lacey oak	trees
Pinus	taeda		loblolly pine	trees
Pinus	taeda		loblolly pine	trees
Pinus	palustris		longleaf pine	trees
Pinus	palustris		longleaf pine	trees
Crataegus	opaca		mayhaw	trees
Ungnadia	speciosa		Mexican buckeye	trees

Genus	epithet	variety	common name	type
Quercus	polycarpa		Mexican oak	trees
Prunus	mexicana		Mexican plum	trees
Juniperus	ashei		mountain cedar	trees
Quercus	lyrata		overcup oak	trees
Crataegus	marshallii		parsley hawthorn	trees
Carya	illinoiensis		pecan	trees
Pinus	edulis		pinyon pine	trees
Quercus	stellata		post oak	trees
Rhus	lanceolata		Prairie flame leaf sumac	trees
Magnolia	pyramidata		pyramid magnolia	trees
Acer	rubrum		red maple	trees
Cornus	drummondii		Rough leafed dogwood	trees
Viburnum	rufidulum		rusty blackhaw	trees
Rhus	copallinum		shining sumac	trees
Quercus	shumardii		Shumard oak	trees
Cotinus	obovatus		smoke tree	trees
Quercus	virginiana		Southern live oak	trees
Magnolia	grandiflora		Southern magnolia	trees
Acer	barbatum		Southern sugar maple	trees
Quercus	michauxii		swamp chestnut oak	trees
Acacia	farnesiana		sweet acacia	trees
Liquidambar	styraciflua		sweet gum	trees
Magnolia	virginiana		sweetbay	trees
Havardia	pallens		tenaza	trees
Fraxinus	texensis		Texas ash	trees
Ebenopsis	ebano		Texas ebony	trees
Crataegus	texana		Texas hawthorn	trees
Cordia	boissieri		Texas olive	trees
Sabal	mexicana		Texas palmetto	trees
Diospyros	texana		Texas persimmon	trees
Pistacia	mexicana (texana)		Texas pistachio	trees
Quercus	texana		Texas red oak	trees
Acacia	schaffneri		twisted acacia	trees
Halesia	diptera		two-winged silverbell	trees
Ptelia	trifoliata		wafer ash	trees
Quercus	nigra		water oak	trees
Nyssa	aquatica		water tupelo	trees
Sapindus	saponaria	drummondii	Western soapberry	trees
Fraxinus	americana		white ash	trees
Quercus	alba		white oak	trees
Quercus	phellos		willow oak	trees
Ulmus	alata		winged elm	trees
Pinus	echinata		yellow pine	trees
Gelsemium	sempervirens		Carolina jessamine	vine
Bignonia	capreolata		crossvine	vine
Clematis	drummondii		old man's beard	vine
Passiflora	incarnata		passion vine	vine
Passiflora	foetida		passion vine	vine
Clematis	pitcheri		purple clematis	vine
Campsis	radicans		red honeysuckle	vine
Clematis	texensis		Texas clematis	vine
Wisteria	frutescens		Texas wisteria	vine
Parthenocissus	quinquefolia		Virginia creeper	vine
Passiflora	lutea		yellow passion vine	vine
Gomphrena	hageeana	Strawberry Fields	gomphrena	vine

PUBLIC GARDENS TO VISIT IN TEXAS

This listing is a sample of some of the many public gardens, large and small, that are found throughout the state. For a complete listing of all gardens, including specialty or interesting nurseries, look to *The Texas Garden Resource Book: A Guide to Garden Resources Across the State* by Nan Booth Simpson and Patricia Scott McHargue.

Amarillo Botanical Garden
1400 Streit Drive
Amarillo, Texas 79106
806-352-6513
www.amarillobotanicalgardens.org

Centennial Museum and Chihuahuan Desert Gardens
University of Texas at El Paso
500 West University
El Paso, Texas 79902
915-747-5565
www.museum.utep.edu

Clark Garden Botanical Park
567 Maddux Road
Weatherford, Texas 76088
940-682-4856
www.clarkgardens.com

Corpus Christi Botanical Gardens & Nature Center
8545 South Staples Street
Corpus Christi, Texas 78413
361-852-2100
www.stxbot.org

Dallas Arboretum and Botanical Society
8525 Garland Road
Dallas, Texas 75218
214-515-6500
www.dallasarboretum.org

Fort Worth Botanic Garden and Japanese Garden
3220 Botanic Garden Boulevard
Fort Worth, Texas 76107
817-871-7686
www.fwbg.org

Lady Bird Johnson Wildflower Center
4801 LaCrosse Avenue
Austin, Texas 78739
512-232-0100
www.wildflower.org

Mast Arboretum at Stephen F. Austin State University
2900 Raquet Street
Nacogdoches, Texas 75962
936-468-1832
www.sfagardens.sfasu.edu

Mercer Arboretum and Botanic Gardens
22306 Aldine Westfield Road
Humble, Texas 77338
281-443-8731
www.hcp4.net/mercer

San Antonio Botanical Gardens
555 Funston Place
San Antonio, Texas 78209
210-207-3250
www.sabot.org

Shangri La Botanical Gardens and Nature Center
2111 West Park Avenue
Orange, Texas 77630
409-670-9113
http://starkculturalvenues.org/shangrilagardens

Tyler Municipal Rose Garden
420 South Rose Park Drive
Tyler, Texas 75702
903-597-3130
www.texasrosefestival.com

Zilker Botanical Gardens
2220 Barton Springs Road
Austin, Texas 78746
512-477-8672
www.zilkergarden.org

REFERENCES

Calhoun, Scott. *The Gardener's Guide to Cactus: The 100 Best Paddles, Barrels, Columns, and Globes*. Timber Press: Portland, 2012.

Editors, *Southern Living Magazine*. *The Southern Living Gardening Book*. *Southern Living Magazine*: Birmingham, Alabama, 2004.

Editors, *Sunset* Magazine. *The New Sunset Western Garden Book*. Sunset Publishing Corp: Menlo Park, California, 2012.

Garrett, Howard. *Texas Trees*. Taylor Trade Publishing an imprint of the Rowman and Littlefield Publishing Group: Lanham, Maryland, 2002.

Garrett, Howard. *Plants for Houston and the Gulf Coast*. University of Texas Press: Austin, 2008.

Garrett, John Howard. *Plants of the Metroplex*. University of Texas Press: Austin, 1998.

Gill, Dan, and Dale Groom. *Month-by-Month Gardening in Texas*. Cool Springs Press: Nashville, 2000.

Irish, Mary, and Gary Irish. *Agaves, Yuccas and Related Plants*. Timber Press: Portland, Oregon, 2000.

Irish, Mary. *Perennials for the Southwest*. Timber Press: Portland, Oregon, 2006.

Irish, Mary. *Trees and Shrubs for the Southwest*. Timber Press: Portland, Oregon, 2008.

Lady Bird Johnson Wildflower Center. Austin. Native Plant Database. Available from: www.wildflower.org/plants/

Ogden, Scott. *Garden Bulbs for the South*. Second Edition. Timber Press: Portland, Oregon, 2007.

Ogden, Scott. *Gardening Success with Difficult Soils: Limestone, Alkaline Clay, and Caliche*. Taylor Publishing Company: Dallas, 1992.

Ryan, Julie. *Perennial Gardens for Texas*. University of Texas Press: Austin, 1998.

Wasowski, Sally. *Native Texas Plants: Landscaping Region by Region*. Texas Monthly Press: Austin, 1988.

Welch, William C., and Greg Grant. *Heirloom Gardening in the South: Yesterday's Plants for Today's Gardens*. Texas A&M University Press: College Station, 2011.

GLOSSARY

Alkaline soil: soil with a pH greater than 7.5. It often has limestone in it.

All-purpose fertilizer: powdered, liquid, or granular fertilizer with a balanced proportion of the three key nutrients—nitrogen (N), phosphorus (P), and potassium (K). It is suitable for maintenance nutrition for most plants.

Annual: a plant that lives its entire life in one season. It is genetically determined to germinate, grow, flower, set seed, and die the same year.

Bare root: describes plants that have been packaged without any soil around their roots. Roses are commonly sold this way. Often young shrubs and trees purchased through the mail arrive with this way.

Beneficial insects: insects or their larvae that prey on pest organisms and their eggs. They may be flying insects, such as ladybugs, parasitic wasps, praying mantids, and soldier bugs, or soil dwellers such as predatory nematodes, spiders, and ants.

Berm: a narrow, raised ring of soil around a tree. It is used to hold water that will be directed to the root zone.

Bract: a modified leaf on a plant stem near its flower, resembling a petal. Often it is more colorful and visible than the actual flower, as in dogwood or bougainvillea.

Bud union: the place where of a plant was grafted onto another (the rootstock). It is commonly found on roses and fruit trees.

Canopy: the overhead branching area of a tree, usually referring to its extent including foliage.

Cold hardiness: the ability of a plant to survive the winter cold in a particular area with little or no damage.

Composite: a flower that is actually composed of many tiny flowers. This is the typical flowering style of the sunflower family. Typically, they are flat clusters of tiny, tight florets, sometimes surrounded by wider-petaled florets. They often are highly attractive to bees and beneficial insects.

Compost: organic matter that has undergone progressive decomposition by microbial and macrobial activity until it is reduced to a spongy, fluffy texture. Added to soil of any type, it improves the soil's ability to hold air and water and to drain well.

Corm: a modified underground stem that is a swollen, energy-storing structure analogous to a bulb, at the base of the plants as in crocus and gladiolus.

Crown: In palms it describes the entire set of leaves. In trees it describes the entire above ground growth that supports the leaves. In many other plants it describes the location near the base of the leaves that is at, or just beneath, the surface of the soil the roots meet the stem, as in agave or aloe.

Cultivar: a CULTIvated VARiety. It is a form of a plant, usually naturally or spontaneously occurring, that has been identified as special or superior and is purposely selected for propagation and production.

Deadhead: a pruning technique that removes faded flower heads from plants to improve their appearances, abort seed production, and stimulate further flowering.

Deciduous plants: unlike evergreens, such plants, most often trees or shrubs, lose their leaves in the fall.

Desiccation: drying out of foliage tissues, usually due to drought or wind.

Division: the practice of splitting apart plants to create several smaller, rooted segments. The practice is useful for controlling the plant's size and for acquiring more plants; it is also essential to the health and continued flowering of certain ones.

Dormancy: the period, usually the winter, when plants temporarily cease active growth and rest. Dormant is the verb form, as used in this sentence: Some plants, like spring-blooming bulbs, go dormant in the summer.

Drought tolerant: indicating a plant that grows with minimal supplemental water once it is established. Also indicates plants that can survive for extended periods on regular or low natural rainfall.

Established: the point at which a newly planted tree, shrub, or flower begins to produce new growth, either foliage or stems. This is an indication that the roots have recovered from transplant shock and have begun to grow and spread.

Evergreen: perennial plants that do not lose their foliage annually with the onset of winter. Needled or broadleaf foliage will persist and continues to function on a plant through one or more winters, aging and dropping unobtrusively in cycles of three or four years or more.

Foliar: of or about foliage—usually refers to the practice of spraying foliage, as in fertilizing or treating with insecticide; leaf tissues absorb liquid directly for fast results, and the soil is not affected.

Floret: a tiny flower, usually one of many forming a cluster that comprises a single blossom, as in sunflowers.

Germinate: to sprout. Germination is a fertile seed's first stage of development.

Graft (union): the point on the stem of a woody plant where a stem from another plant is inserted so that it will join with it. Roses and fruit trees are commonly grafted. (Also termed bud union.)

Hardscape: the permanent, structural, nonplant part of a landscape, such as walls, sheds, pools, patios, arbors, and walkways.

Herbaceous: plants having fleshy or soft stems; the opposite of woody.

Hybrid: a plant that is the result of intentional or natural cross-pollination between two or more plants of the same species or genus.

Low water demand: describes plants that tolerate dry soil for varying periods of time. Often, they have succulent, hairy, or silvery-gray foliage and tuberous roots or taproots.

Mulch: a layer of material over bare soil to protect it from erosion and compaction by rain, and to discourage weeds. It may be inorganic (gravel, fabric) or organic (wood chips, bark, pine needles, chopped leaves).

Naturalize: (a) to plant seeds, bulbs, or plants in a random, informal pattern as they would appear in their natural habitats; (b) to adapt to and spread throughout an area outside their natural range (a tendency of some nonnative plants).

Nectar: the sweet fluid produced by glands on flowers that attract pollinators such as hummingbirds and honeybees, for whom it is a source of energy.

Organic material, organic matter: any material or debris that is derived from plants. It is carbon-based material capable of undergoing decomposition and decay.

Peat moss: organic matter from peat sedges (United States) or sphagnum mosses (Canada), often used to improve soil texture. The acidity of sphagnum peat moss makes it ideal for boosting or maintaining soil acidity while also improving its drainage.

Perennial: a flowering plant that lives over two or more seasons. Many die back with frost, but their roots survive the winter and generate new shoots in the spring.

pH: a measurement of the relative acidity (low pH) or alkalinity (high pH) of soil or water based on a scale of 1 to 14, 7 being neutral. Individual plants require soil to be within a certain range so that nutrients can dissolve in moisture and be available to them.

Pinch: to remove tender stems and/or leaves by pressing them between thumb and forefinger. This pruning technique encourages branching, compactness, and flowering in plants, or it removes aphids clustered at growing tips.

Pollen: yellow, powdery grains that are the plant's male sex cells. It is transferred to the female plant parts by means of wind or animal pollinators to fertilize them and create seeds.

Raceme: the arrangement of flowers along an elongated, unbranched axis. Each flower is attached with a small stem.

Rhizome: a swollen energy-storing stem structure, similar to a bulb, that lies horizontally in the soil, with roots emerging from its lower surface and growth shoots from a growing point at or near its tip, as in bearded iris.

Rootbound (or potbound): the condition of a plant that has been confined in a container too long, its roots having been forced to wrap around themselves and even swell out of the container. Successful transplanting or repotting requires untangling and trimming away of some of the matted roots.

Root flare: the transition at the base of a tree trunk where the bark tissue begins to differentiate and roots begin to form just before entering the soil. This area should not be covered with soil when planting a tree.

Rosette: formation of flowers or leaves around a central axis, as in the flowers of roses and the leaves of agaves.

Self-seeding: the tendency of some plants whose seed germinate readily where they fall around the yard. It creates many seedlings the following season that may or may not be welcome.

Semi-evergreen: tending to be evergreen in a mild climate but deciduous in a rigorous one.

Shearing: the pruning technique whereby plant stems and branches are cut uniformly with long-bladed pruning shears (hedge shears) or powered hedge trimmers. It is used when creating and maintaining hedges and topiary.

Slow-release fertilizer: fertilizer that is water insoluble and therefore releases its nutrients gradually as a function of soil temperature, moisture, and related microbial activity. Typically granular, it may be organic or synthetic.

Succulent: a plant with specialized tissue to hold water in either leaves, stems or flowers.

Sucker: a new, often vigorous, shoot from either the roots, grafted plants from the rootstock, or occasionally from the branch. Many plants produce suckers to form large plantings or colonies. Some plants produce suckers, either from the root or the branch s as a result of pruning or wounding.

Tuber: a swollen, root that is an underground storage structure, analogous to a bulb. It generates roots below and stems above ground (example: potato).

Variegated: having various colors or color patterns. The term usually refers to plant foliage that is streaked, edged, blotched, or mottled with a contrasting color—often green with yellow, cream, or white.

Wings: (a) the corky tissue that forms edges along the twigs of some woody plants such as winged elm; (b) the flat, dried extension of tissue on some seeds, such as maple, that catch the wind and help them disseminate.

INDEX

PHOTO CREDITS

MEET MARY IRISH

Mary Irish is garden writer, lecturer, and educator. She lived and worked in Arizona for 25 years, but she is a native Texan who returned home in 2012 and currently works at the San Antonio Botanical Garden managing the plant sales program. She and her husband Gary live in Castroville, Texas, a historic town in the South Texas plains.

She is the author, with Gary Irish, of *Agaves, Yuccas and Related Plants* published by Timber Press, 2000; *Gardening in the Desert* published by the University of Arizona Press, 2000; *Arizona Gardener's Guide* published by Cool Springs Press, 2003; and *Month-by-Month Gardening in the Desert Southwest* published by Cool Springs Press, also in 2003 with a revised edition entitled *Gardening in the Deserts of Arizona* in 2008; *Perennials for the Southwest*, published by Timber Press, 2006; and *Trees and Shrubs for the Southwest*, published by Timber Press in 2008; and *A Place All Our Own*, published by the University of Arizona Press, 2012.

She is a frequent contributor to national and regional publications including *American Gardener* and *NMPro*. In addition, Irish has worked as a consultant on projects for the Sunnylands Visitor Center in Rancho Mirage, California, Myriad Botanical Garden in Oklahoma City, downtown plantings for the City of Scottsdale and the Xeriscape Demonstration Garden in Glendale, Arizona, as well as for numerous homeowner associations and private gardens.

Irish is a very popular teacher who teaches classes regularly on the use and cultivation of agaves and succulents, woody plants, and low water use perennials. Her plant interests range widely with agaves and their relatives, bulbs, and drought hardy perennials at the top of the list.

She served as the Director of Public Horticulture at the Desert Botanical Garden in Phoenix for 11 years ending in 1999. She has served on the Board of the Arizona Nursery Association for 10 years, Native Seeds/SEARCH for 3 years, and Boyce Thompson Arboretum for 9 years, 6 as the Chair. Mary Irish has a B.A. from the University of Texas at Austin and M.S. in Geography from Texas A&M University.